A WORLD TRANSFORMED

Also by James Walvin:

Slavery in Small Things: Slavery and Modern Cultural Habits

Different Times: Growing Up in Post-War England

Crossings: Africa, the Americas and the Atlantic Slave Trade

The Zong: A Massacre, the Law and the End of Slavery

The Trader, The Owner, The Slave:
Parallel Lives in the Age of Slavery

Atlas of Slavery

Black Ivory: Slavery in the British Empire

Questioning Slavery

An African's Life:
The Life and Times of Olaudah Equiano, 1745–1797

Making the Black Atlantic: Britain and the African Diaspora

How Sugar Corrupted the World: From Slavery to Obesity

Freedom: The Overthrow of the Slave Empires

A WORLD TRANSFORMED

SLAVERY IN THE AMERICAS AND THE ORIGINS OF GLOBAL POWER

James Walvin

UNIVERSITY OF CALIFORNIA PRESS

University of California Press
Oakland, California
www.ucpress.edu

First published in Great Britain in 2022 by Robinson
An imprint of Little, Brown Book Group
www.littlebrown.co.uk

Typeset in Adobe Garamond Pro by Hewer Text UK Ltd., Edinburgh
Maps by Stephen Dew

Cataloging-in-Publication Data is on file at the Library of Congress.
ISBN 978-0-520-38624-2 (cloth : alk. paper)
ISBN 978-0-520-38625-9 (ebook)

Manufactured in the United States of America

31 30 29 28 27 26 25 24 23 22
10 9 8 7 6 5 4 3 2 1

For Jenny Walvin

Contents

Part Four: Managing Slavery

Part Five: Demanding Freedom

Part Six: A World Transformed

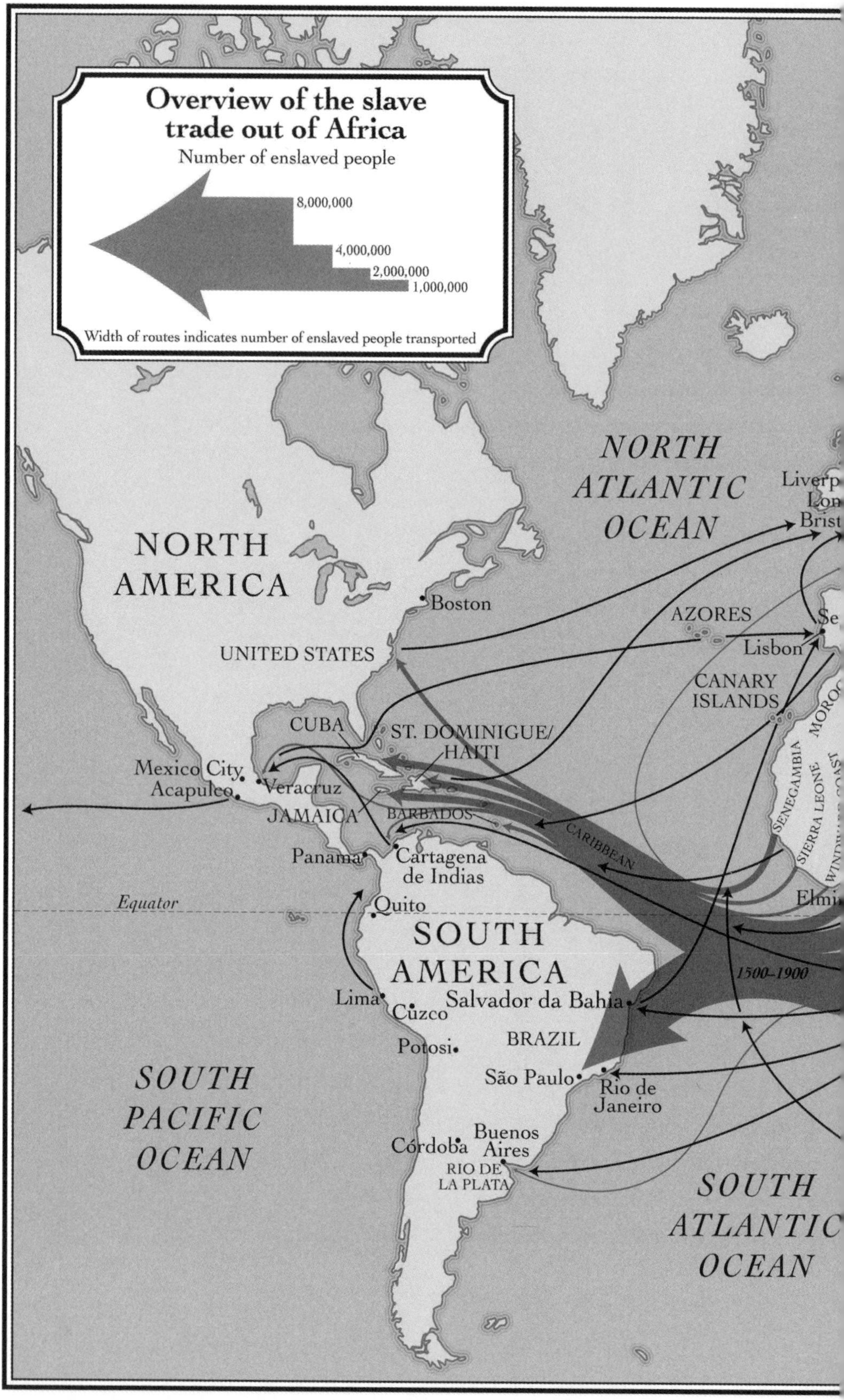

Overview of the slave trade out of Africa
Number of enslaved people
8,000,000
4,000,000
2,000,000
1,000,000
Width of routes indicates number of enslaved people transported
NORTH AMERICA
NORTH ATLANTIC OCEAN
Boston
UNITED STATES
AZORES
Lisbon
CANARY ISLANDS
CUBA
ST. DOMINIGUE/ HAITI
Mexico City
Veracruz
Acapulco
JAMAICA
BARBADOS
CARIBBEAN
Panama
Cartagena de Indias
Equator
Quito
SOUTH AMERICA
1500–1900
Lima
Cuzco
Salvador da Bahia
BRAZIL
Potosi
São Paulo
Rio de Janeiro
SOUTH PACIFIC OCEAN
Córdoba
Buenos Aires
RIO DE LA PLATA
SOUTH ATLANTIC OCEAN
SENEGAMBIA
SIERRA LEONE

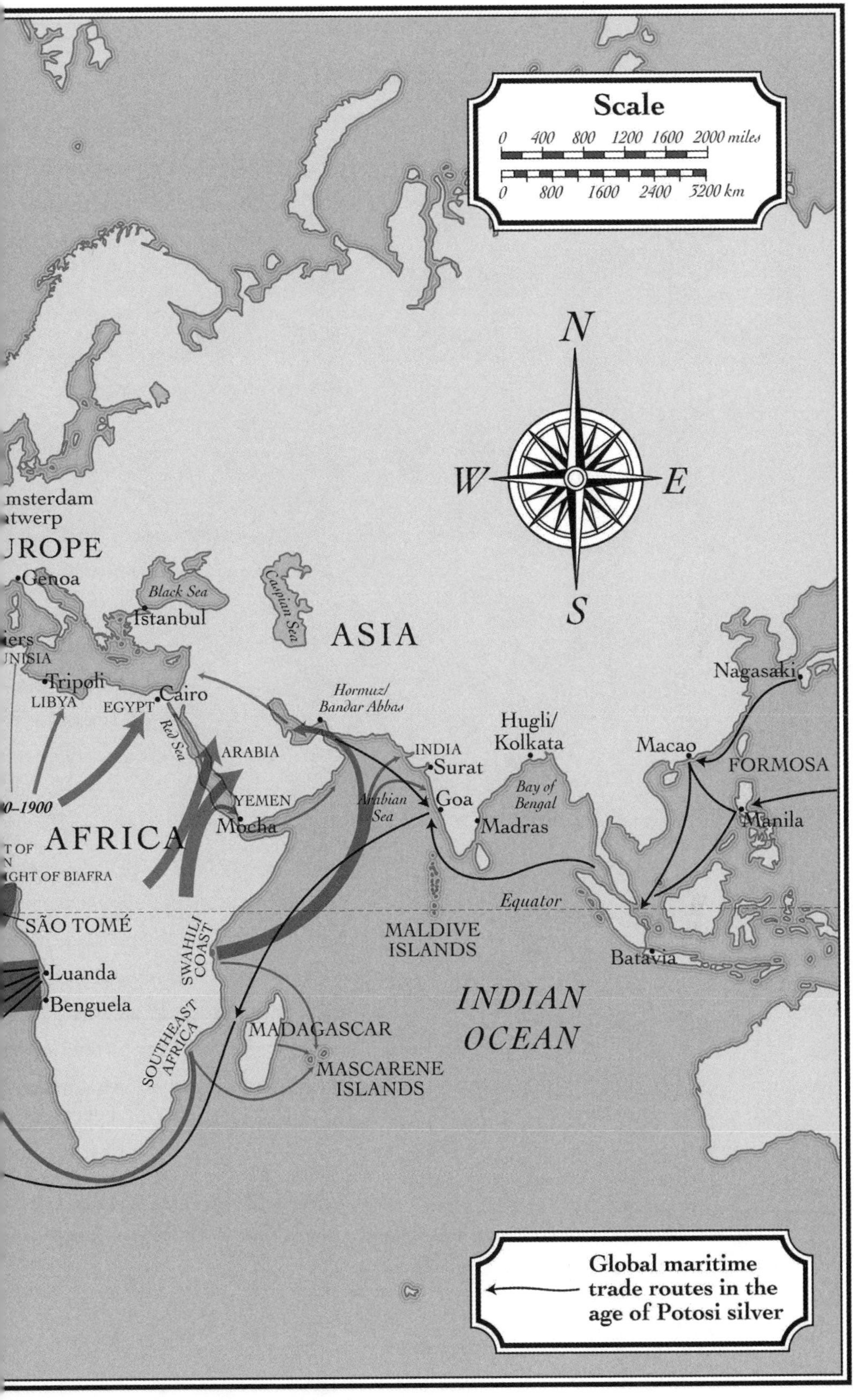

Scale
0 400 800 1200 1600 2000 miles
0 800 1600 2400 3200 km
N
W
E
S
Genoa
Black Sea
Caspian Sea
Istanbul
ASIA
Tripoli
LIBYA
EGYPT
Cairo
Red Sea
ARABIA
YEMEN
Mocha
AFRICA
Hormuz/
Bandar Abbas
INDIA
Surat
Goa
Arabian Sea
Hugli/
Kolkata
Bay of Bengal
Madras
Nagasaki
Macao
FORMOSA
Manila
Equator
SÃO TOMÉ
Luanda
Benguela
SWAHILI COAST
SOUTHEAST AFRICA
MADAGASCAR
MASCARENE ISLANDS
MALDIVE ISLANDS
INDIAN OCEAN
Batavia
Global maritime trade routes in the age of Potosi silver

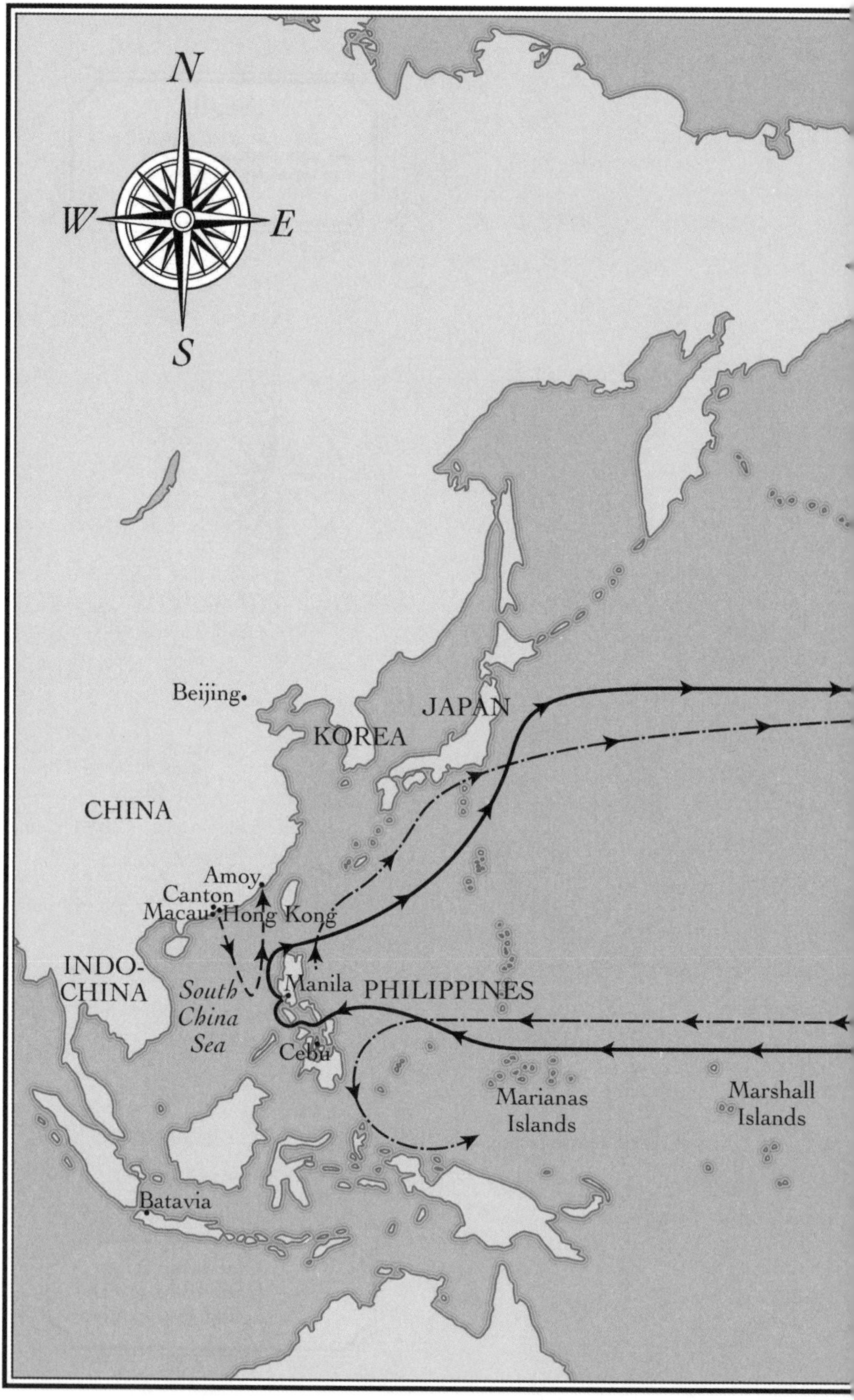
N
W
E
S
Beijing
JAPAN
KOREA
CHINA
Amoy
Canton
Macau
Hong Kong
INDO-
CHINA
South
China
Sea
Manila
PHILIPPINES
Cebu
Marianas
Islands
Marshall
Islands
Batavia

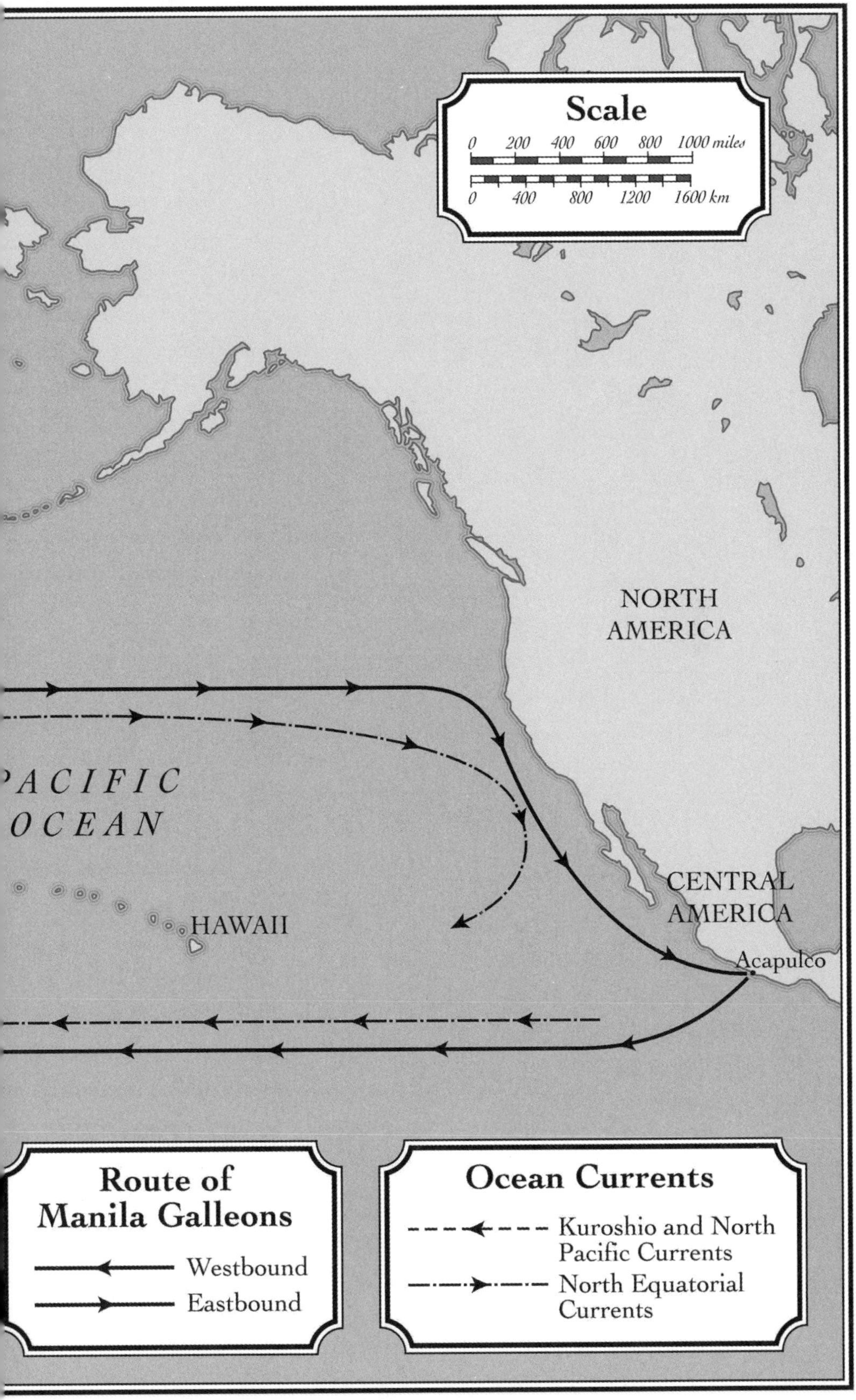
Scale
0 200 400 600 800 1000 miles
0 400 800 1200 1600 km
NORTH
AMERICA
PACIFIC
OCEAN
CENTRAL
AMERICA
HAWAII
Acapulco
Route of
Manila Galleons
Westbound
Eastbound
Ocean Currents
Kuroshio and North
Pacific Currents
North Equatorial
Currents

Introduction

FOR THE BEST part of four centuries, enslaved Africans were an inescapable and ubiquitous presence in the Atlantic world. The millions of Africans, loaded onto the Atlantic slave ships (and the legions who did not even survive to reach Africa's Atlantic coast) were the human cogs in a vast machine which transformed the face of the Americas, enhanced the well-being of the Western world, and created cultural habits we are familiar with today. This colossal enforced movement of humanity had consequences which reverberate down to the present day. For decades, scholars have argued about slavery and today there is a widespread acceptance that, from the late seventeenth century onwards, slavery was fundamental to the way the West emerged. Less well-known, however, is the fact that slavery exerted an influence far beyond the Western world. In its mature, complex forms (which varied greatly across the Americas) enslaved African labour created tentacles of economic activity which crept into distant corners of the world not normally associated with slavery. The networks spawned by slavery stretched from the edges of European entanglement with the native peoples of the Americas, to remote islands in the Indian Ocean, and onwards even to the economies of China and Japan. The slave economies came to exercise a powerful, at times irresistible, gravitational pull which drew to itself the products and markets of widely scattered societies. We can catch a sense of this by simply looking at the varied items carried as cargoes of outbound ships from Europe and the Americas heading to Africa. It is obvious too in the details kept in ledgers of American plantations, not to mention the vast quantities of slave-grown commodities – from tobacco to sugar – consumed by people in all corners of the world. By the time slavery was finally outlawed in Brazil in 1888, the world had become addicted to commodities which owed their origins to enslaved Africans.

For centuries, slavery in the Americas depended on the Atlantic slave ships for a continuing supply of enslaved labour. As the Atlantic trade grew in volume and importance, it became increasingly complex. Yet it was, from start to finish, a trading system that was brutal in the extreme. Though it delivered more than eleven million Africans to the Americas, it also killed huge numbers, damaged many more, and left all its survivors with traumatic memories of the oceanic crossing. It remains one of the strange contradictions of slavery that a system which involved violation and oppression on an extraordinary scale, was an essential aspect of a highly complex and sophisticated form of global trade, finance and record-keeping. As Atlantic slavery evolved, it generated a stunning volume of paperwork – and that paperwork enables us to reconstruct histories of slavery. Here lies one of the many great ironies of slavery: the very system which silenced the voices of the enslaved, which treated them as mere items of trade, also described and documented each and every aspect of their lives, their sufferings and their dying. The end result is that we know more about the enslaved than we do about almost any of their free labouring contemporaries, for the simple reason that an enslaved person was treated, from start to finish, as a thing: an object, a chattel. And as an object he or she entered the commercial documentation. The enslaved were registered, described and accounted for, from their first encounter with Atlantic slave traders, to the moment they died – at sea or on land. We know about their physical conditions, appearances, ailments, peculiarities, their abilities and personal characteristics, we know about their relationships and their children, their working lives and their dying days. All this is recorded in ways rarely documented for free labouring people of the same eras.

I began my own investigation into slavery in 1967, poring over the lives of an enslaved group of sugar workers in Jamaica. Their lives were entered in huge plantation ledgers, kept at the time on the estate itself. The first, most obvious and revealing fact – which leapt off the crumbling pages – was that the enslaved were listed and tallied just as the beasts of the field and were listed on opposite pages in the ledgers. They were mere items to be recorded alongside other possessions of the plantation owners (who by then were living in England). Many of those slaves had been born in Jamaica, but most were African, acquired by barter and trade, thousands of miles away, and all had been shipped to Jamaica on a slave ship.* The Africans living on Worthy Park in the1780s were but one small sample

* The terminology used for writing about slavery has changed quite rapidly in recent years. The word 'slave' suggests that the status of the enslaved is defined solely by their enslavement. I have tried to use the word sparingly and opt for alternative words. There are places, however, where the alternatives create literary clumsiness and I use the word for clarity and when it seems more useful.

of millions of others cast ashore in the Americas by an international fleet of slave ships. Today, the slave ship is a familiar image, used time and again to represent slavery itself. Those ships, counted in their many thousands, did more than transport Africans. They also carried huge cargoes of manufactured goods (from Europe, Asia and the Americas) to Africa, and returned to their home ports from the Americas freighted with slave-grown produce. Slave ships were supported by an armada of other merchant ships ferrying goods around the Atlantic's shipping lanes. But the slave ship was the prime engine of the entire system.

Here was a massive commerce in humanity and goods with ramifications in all corners of the globe. It was a business which attracted all of Europe's major maritime nations, and eventually, merchants and investors from Brazil and North America. It scattered Africans and their offspring to all corners of the world and, by the late eighteenth century, they could be found on the precarious frontiers of the Americas to the early settlements of Australia. They had, against their wishes, become global citizens.

***

On 5 July 1803, Captain Meriwether Lewis set off alone on what was to become an epic overland journey from Washington D.C. to the Pacific coast. Instructed by President Jefferson to form an expedition, Lewis gathered men and equipment as he moved westward. At Louisville he was joined by an old friend and military comrade, William Clark, who brought along a gang of seven men to accompany them, collecting more military and civilian personnel as they travelled on. By the time they set off along the Missouri River in May 1804, the expedition had grown to more than forty men, nosing into unfamiliar Indian territory, negotiating with native people who had little or no experience of outsiders. One man in particular attracted great curiosity among the Indians. Clark's personal servant – York – was a giant of a man. He was also a black slave. As the expedition progressed, they encountered Indians who had never before seen a black human being, and York become an object of bemused wonder. The Indians marvelled at the white man's weaponry, compass, magnets and quadrant – but they were astonished by York. In the words of a French trader who was dealing with the Arikara Indians on the Missouri River, the Indians were stunned by the sight of 'a large, fine man, black as a bear, who spoke and acted as one.'*

York proved much more than a curiosity as the expedition's hazardous journey progressed: he became indispensable. Possessed of great physical strength and endurance, York was to be even more important as an arbiter and mediator between the expedition and some of the native peoples they encountered. There were moments when the expedition faced annihilation by suspicious Indians but they were saved by the Indians' fear of York's imaginary magical powers: he was quite unlike any other person they knew.

For all that, York was a slave, just one among a vast army of enslaved people scattered across the Americas. At the time the Arikara Indians first looked in amazement at York there were almost 900,000 living in the young American Republic, the great majority located in the region between Delaware and Georgia (the impact of cotton was soon to change that by

* Robert B. Betts, *In Search of York: The slave who went to the Pacific with Lewis and Clark*, Boulder, Colorado, 1985, pp.57–58.

shifting the population south.*) In the first years of the new century, here was a man with African parents helping his master and companions to survive and to complete their mission while leaving native Indians dumbfounded.

York was born around 1771. (Frederick Douglass later wrote, 'I never met with a slave who could tell me how old he was.') His parents were Africans owned by William Clark's father. York's father was known as Old York (possibly after the York River in Virginia where Africans were landed to work in the local tobacco fields): his enslaved mother was named Rose.† York grew up enjoying the boyhood companionship of his master's son – William Clark – who was of a similar age. Eventually York became Clark's personal servant, accompanying him on his business travels between Virginia and Kentucky. Theirs was a distinctive bond which developed between master and man, sharing the close human intimacy of life and work together, travelling extensively on horseback and along the mighty river systems of the Ohio and Mississippi. At one point William became acquainted with President Jefferson, introduced by his old army friend, Meriwether Lewis – Jefferson's private secretary.‡

In July 1803, Clark joined the expedition to explore an overland route to the Pacific. The expedition needed men who were physically tough, accustomed to the rigours of life in the wilds and capable of enduring extreme, testing conditions. York fitted the bill perfectly. Thus it was that an African-American slave found himself heading west, servant to the man he had

* M. R. Haines and R. H. Steckel, eds., *A Population History of North America*, Cambridge, 2000, Table 10.2, pp.438–439.

† Robert B. Betts, *In Search of York*, pp.84–87.

‡ Robert B. Betts, *In Search of York*, p.107.

known since childhood, but who was now joint leader of an expedition that would transform the history of the USA. Whatever expectations the two men held of York, they were more than amply confirmed.

York's presence on the very edges of exploration in the North American wilderness ought not to surprise us, because by then the Atlantic slave ships had scattered millions of Africans and their children not merely to the eastern shores of the Americas but clean round the world. By the late eighteenth century Africans were being shipped across the Atlantic in greater numbers than ever, and they could be found wherever European adventure, trade and imperial expansion took hold. Africans and their offspring were everywhere.

***

For centuries, great swathes of European settlements in the Americas were maintained by a massive oceanic trade in humanity. But the slave ships taking enslaved Africans to the Americas formed only one aspect of an even larger maritime commerce which sustained economic and social life on both sides of the Atlantic – and far beyond. There were hundreds of ports and anchorages, some of them little more than a quayside – some major urban centres – but all part of the crossroads for people, animals and goods from around the world. Slave ships came from all points of the seafaring Atlantic (almost half of them from ports in the Americas) and their crews were equally international. Though all oceanic trade was harsh and dangerous, slave ships offered the most vile form of maritime work, combining the dangers of deep-water sailing with the inescapable threat posed by cargoes of angry Africans – the whole stinking brew laced with disease and death. Not surprisingly, the slave ships had persistent problems recruiting men for the worst leg of the journey – heading west across the Atlantic packed with Africans. Only the desperate, the drunk or the indebted stepped forward. John Newton, a Liverpool slave captain, thought his men 'the refuse and dregs of the Nation.'

Sailors joined British ships from throughout the British Isles, and from the far reaches of British dominion and trade. There were lascars from India, Swedes and Sicilians, alongside Africans and freed slaves from the Americas. It may seem odd at first glance to find Africans working on slave ships but they were essential. Disease on the African coast often depleted the ship's complement at the very time when all hands were required to control and manage growing numbers of Africans incarcerated below decks, and Africans were recruited to work on the difficult and dangerous transatlantic crossing. The men on ocean-going ships formed an international and cosmopolitan society. For some, the sea offered freedom: disguised as a sailor, an enslaved man might escape. Most famously, Frederick Douglass donned sailor's clothing to sail north to freedom in the USA in 1838. But for more than twelve million Africans, the ocean was a hellish introduction to a life of bondage.

Today, perhaps the most famous of former slaves who found a career at sea was Olaudah Equiano. Best known for his memoir (*Narrative*) with its account of his remarkable life as a slave and a freeman, Equiano's seafaring career provides a vivid insight into the international experiences of seaborne slaves. He served on no fewer than eighteen ships, both mercantile and Royal Navy, on voyages which took him from the eastern Mediterranean to North and Central America, and to a string of Caribbean islands. Most unusual of all, however, Equiano was almost certainly the first African we know of to sail to the Arctic. That perilous expedition in 1773 was dominated by hair-raising dangers and experiences; of arctic animals and sea life, of pack ice, icebergs and intense cold – with plenty of narrow escapes from disaster – before returning to Deptford, 'a voyage which had proved the impracticability of finding a passage that way to India.'*

Equiano was a very well-travelled man, but he was only one example of the Africans to be found on quaysides, in port cities throughout the Atlantic world, and at sea on the shipping lanes that laced the world's commercial systems. African faces could be seen in all corners of the globe – from the desolate waste of the Arctic to the treacherous American borderlands which separated invading Europeans (and their accompanying slaves) and native American people.

Equiano died in 1797, his late years marked by a short-lived public fame (and modest prosperity) thanks to his self-published memoir, and his tireless advocacy for abolition of the slave trade. Not the first African to denounce slavery to an English-reading public, Equiano was certainly the best known (though his name quickly faded from public view after his death). Much less successful – but now remembered for very different reasons – was Billie Blue. Born in 1767 of African parentage in Jamaica, New York, by 1796 Billie Blue lived in Deptford, London – part of that city's small black community and working as a chocolate-maker and dockside labourer. That year Billie was convicted at Maidstone of stealing sugar and

* Olaudah Equiano, *The Interesting Narrative and Other Writings*, Vincent Carretta, ed., London 1995 edn, p.177.

sentenced to seven years' transportation. After four years in convict hulks, he was transported to Australia in 1801 – and there he prospered. He married Elizabeth Williams, a female convict, and they had six children, living in the Rocks area of Sydney. Billie worked hard and by 1811 he was appointed a harbour watchman and constable, ferrying people around Sydney harbour. But his prosperous times ended when he was again convicted of theft. There followed various scrapes with the law, and Billie Blue slid into eccentric old age – dubbing himself 'commodore', he took to wearing a bizarre naval uniform, greeting arriving ships as if an appointed official. He also developed the habit of haranguing people in the streets and was periodically brought to court for various small offences. He died in 1834. His reputation has evolved in recent years as an eccentric early settler and one of the founders of Australia's small African community.*

An exact contemporary of Billie Blue was a woman who, in sharp contrast to Billie Blue, was to enjoy modern global fame (though in a much fictionalised form) via a major movie – *Belle* (2013). She was born in Jamaica in 1761 to an enslaved African mother: her father, Sir John Lindsay, was a Royal Navy officer stationed in the Caribbean. He returned to England with the child, entrusting her upbringing to relatives, Lord and Lady Mansfield, at their home, Kenwood House, north of London. The child was baptised Dido Elizabeth Belle in 1765 and raised and educated alongside a niece of a similar age at Kenwood. As she grew, Belle was given various tasks around the house and became part of the family's fashionable social life, mixing with

* Margaret Park, Blue, William (Billy) (c. 1767–1834), *Australian Dictionary of Biography*.

guests after dinner and in the garden. Lord Mansfield, perhaps most famous as Lord Chief Justice for his various rulings on slavery, died in 1793, bequeathing an annuity and a lump sum to Belle. He also asserted:

I confirm to Dido Elizabeth Belle her freedom.

He was clearly aware that, despite his legal rulings, the freedom of black people in England remained uncertain.

In December 1793 Belle married a Frenchman, John Davinier, in the fashionable church of St George's, Hanover Square. They had three sons, but Belle died in 1804 aged forty-three. Her husband later remarried and returned to France. Belle's last known descendant died in South Africa in 1975. Her London grave, in St George's Fields, disappeared in the 1970s, torn up in the redevelopment of roads in London's Bayswater.

She had vanished, joining millions of Africans and their offspring all consigned to unknown burial sites on both sides of the Atlantic. She survives, however, as a contemporary beauty, in the portrait (once thought to be by Zoffany) which hangs in the Mansfield family seat at Scone in Scotland.*

York, Equiano, Billie Blue and Dido Elizabeth Belle: here was a small group of people of African parentage – who may seem, at first glance, to have little else in common. York helped to forge a path across North America to the Pacific. Equiano created a respectable life for himself from what few opportunities came his way. Billie Blue ended his days on the far side of

* James Walvin, *Slavery in Small Things*, Oxford, 2017, pp.155–158; Paula Byrne, *Belle: The True Story of Dido Belle*, London 2014.

the globe, part of a distinctive black presence among the very first outside settlers in Australia. Dido Elizabeth Belle, born to an enslaved African mother, became a striking figure in the fashionable high society in England. These four people offer some important clues to a process that was, in their lifetimes, utterly transforming the human face of the world at large. They were four individual cases of a vast and seemingly endless tide of Africans forcibly removed from their myriad homelands and scattered ashore in distant (and to them totally unknown) places. And all for the benefit of alien people who bought and sold them as if they were mere beasts of the field. It was a slave system which had its origins in the relationship between two major European powers – Spain and Portugal – and was at the heart of their tortuous competition to lay claim to great stretches of the wider world.

Part One

THE TRADE

1

The Scattering of People

In March 1400, Maria de Luna, the devout Queen of Aragon, notable for her piety and her acceptance (unusual at the time) of Jews and Muslims, sent a very special gift to Carlos III, the King of Navarre: an enslaved African child named Sofia. She was dressed in a beautiful red cloak (at the time, red was thought to be the most beautiful of colours) made from the finest of Venetian silk. Sofia was to hold a special place in the king's court and was paraded alongside an array of other eye-catching sights: tiny people, peacocks, elaborately dressed troubadours and musicians – all of them intended to proclaim their monarch's lavish wealth and elevated status.

Sofia was not unique; indeed by then, small numbers of Africans were to be found scattered across Europe's royal households and courts. African musicians played at the courts of the Queens of Portugal and Austria and Henry VIII later had a Black trumpeter, John Blanke – who appeared in court documents and illustrations in 1509 and 1511. He too wore elaborate clothing – and a brown and yellow turban. Like Sofia before him, John Blanke was dressed in red – for the coronation of Henry VIII. Later the monarch gave him a gown of velvet cloth and a bonnet and hat as a wedding gift.* The lavishly dressed African musicians in royal courts testify to an eye-catching African presence in European royal circles. They naturally enjoyed a privileged life, far beyond the dreams of most other servants: their special treatment, roles and dress a reflection of their owners' high status. Yet for all that, they were slaves.

Many of the Africans who appear in such rarefied positions are likely to have arrived in Europe via the trans-Saharan caravan routes to North Africa. We know that Africans had then been taken onwards from North Africa, to Sicily, to Spain and Portugal and, later, to the wealthy homes of merchants in Italian city states. They were, however, rare and costly, but by the mid-fifteenth century that began to change with the arrival in Europe of growing numbers of enslaved Africans, ferried along the expanding sea routes between Europe and West Africa. The dazzling sight of a silk-clad Sofia in 1400 stands in stark contrast to the misery of the first enslaved Africans to arrive in Portugal a mere forty-four years later. Gomes Eannes de Zurara described the landing of 235 Africans, arriving by sea from West Africa at Lagos Bay in southern Portugal in 1444. Some of them:

> kept their heads low, and their faces bathed in tears . . . Other stood groaning very dolorously looking up to the height of heaven, fixing their eyes upon it, crying out loudly . . . others struck their faces with the palms of their

* Nuria Silleras-Fernandez, 'Black Slaves in the Court of a Fourteenth-Century Aragones Queen,' *Medieval Encounters*, 13, 2000, pp.545–565; See illustrations in Miranda Kaufman, *Black Tudors*, London, 2017; David Olusoga, *Black and British: A Forgotten History*, London, 2016, pp.59–60.

> hands, throwing themselves at full length upon the ground, while others made lamentations in the manner of a dirge after the custom of their country.*

The slave traders promptly separated them: 'fathers from sons, husbands from wives, brothers from brothers.'

This distressing account could stand as a signpost to the trade that was to endure for the next four centuries. Consider the account by a British doctor on entering a slave ship, just arrived in Brazil from Africa in 1843 – exactly four centuries after the first arrivals in Portugal. He was confronted by 362 Africans packed into the vessel:

> With disease, want, and misery stamped upon them with such painful intensity as utterly beggars all powers of description.†

Two eye-witness accounts, four centuries apart, yet describing identical miseries. Who, looking at those Africans in Lagos Bay in 1444, could possibly have imagined that here was the start of a maritime commerce that would become the largest enforced movement of humanity in recorded history? It was a trade that transformed the human face of the Americas, inflicted incalculable damage across swathes of Africa – and yet brought astonishing prosperity to the Western world.

***

* Hugh Thomas, *The Slave Trade: The History of the Atlantic Slave Trade, 1440–1870,* London, 1997, p.21.

† Robert Edgar Conrad, *Children of God's Fire: A Documentary History of Black Slavery in Brazil,* University Park, Pennsylvania, 1994 edn, p.43.

The numbers of people involved never fail to shock modern readers, and the historical sweep of their story is far-reaching. From the first days of Europe's early expansion to make maritime contact with the wider world (Vikings notwithstanding) through to the age of steam-powered oceanic travel in the nineteenth century, millions of Africans were scattered across the world. The driving force behind this phenomenon was the European (later the American) ambition to profit from distant markets and economies, and to find suitable labour to exploit the new-found lands of the Americas. It was to be Africa's fate (and long-term wound) to be the unwilling supplier of that labour. What followed was an unprecedented scattering of African people on an unique scale and with unprecedented consequences.

There was, of course, nothing new in slavery and slave trading. Both had been essential to any number of ancient civilisations and had been commonplace throughout Europe and the Mediterranean. When Columbus sailed westward in 1492, slavery was widespread in the Mediterranean, and was most notable in the vast lands of the Ottoman empire stretching from Basra to the Crimea and to Egypt. Slavery went unquestioned across North Africa: in Egypt, Tripoli, Tunisia, Algiers and Morocco. Barbary pirates raided mainland Europe for slaves. Between 1500 and 1580, for example, more than a quarter of a million white slaves were seized by Barbary pirates (at a time when fifty thousand Africans had been transported to the Americas). In the following century, an estimated 850,000 white slaves fell victims to the same pirates. Even later, between 1680 and 1800, as many as 175,000 were enslaved by Barbary pirates. Slavery was not, however, a monopoly of Muslim societies. A number of Christian societies in the Mediterranean

– Spain, Portugal and Venice – accepted slavery in their midst. Much further afield, sub-Saharan Africa had its own myriad slaving systems, the best known being the trans-Saharan caravan routes which for centuries had moved tens of thousands of Africans into a life of bondage in and around the Mediterranean. But everywhere we look, slaves tended to form only a relatively small proportion of local populations.*

Slave societies were generally serviced and kept alive by enforced migrations of slaves: slave trading was an umbilical cord which sustained slave systems everywhere. Societies absorbed enslaved people from distant places, using them to maintain their military forces, to work their land or ships, to toil at tasks others would not, or could not, even attempt – or to service the sexual pleasures of elites. Long-distance trafficking of slaves was essential for slave societies in the Old World long before it became a vital feature of the New. What happened in the Americas, however, shifted the story to an entirely different level.

A few simple facts stand out. Over the entire history of the Atlantic slave trade, the slave ships embarked twelve and a half million Africans. Indeed, before 1820 African arrivals in the Americas greatly outnumbered European settlers by three to one. European arrivals barely kept pace. In the three centuries to 1800, two and one third million white people crossed the Atlantic, but in the same period, eight and a half million Africans landed – against their will. Of course, Africans were scattered unevenly across the Americas and were concentrated

* David Richardson, 'Involuntary Migrations in the Early Modern World, 1500–1899', in D. Eltis, et al., *The Cambridge World History of Slavery*, Vol. 3, Cambridge, 2011, Ch.22.

mainly in tropical and semi-tropical regions where their labour was most needed in agriculture. In the process, two major catastrophes ensued. The sharp decline (in places the total collapse) of the native populations of the Americas – most striking in the Caribbean – paved the way for massive arrivals of Africans. Parts of the Americas, most strikingly Brazil and the Caribbean, were in effect Africanised. However, there were regions, notably in North America, where there were relatively few Africans, and where Europeans formed the bedrock of local society. Nonetheless it is important to remember that the *African* was the crucial pioneer settler in huge areas of the Americas. Without them, the Americas could never have been settled, still less developed and prospered, as it was.

In time, major settlements in the Americas came to need Africans, and the Atlantic slave traders needed African merchants to provide the enslaved labour destined for the slave ships. Apart from early piratical raids for African slaves, European traders were swift to develop personal and commercial relations with African traders and governing elites to acquire enslaved Africans. The numbers involved – more than six and a half million in the eighteenth century alone – could never have been achieved without the existence of a well-oiled trading system along an immense coastal stretch, which linked Africa to the slave ships. What drove so many Africans towards the slave ships were the fluctuating patterns of political and civil life *within* Africa. But those patterns, in their turn, were intimately linked to the demand created by events in the Americas. All this – internal African political and social forces, outside traders arriving by sea in search of slaves, and the labour demands of American markets – came to form a web of economic and human interdependency which shaped slavery in the Americas.

But why Africans? Why ship so many people, thousands of miles across a dangerous ocean? Why not use the indigenous peoples of the Americas? Why not use local Indians? In fact, from his first landfall, Columbus's encounter with Indians in Hispaniola prompted dreams of an unlimited supply of enslaved Indian labour, ideal for Spanish exploitation. In the event, the arrival of Columbus – and those who followed him – spelled disaster for the Indians. Ultimately it also proved disastrous for millions of Africans.

2

Spanish Origins

THE DEVELOPMENT OF European maritime and commercial links to West Africa and beyond – to India and Asia – was pioneered by Portugal. But the role of Spain (technically Castile until 1512) in the origins of slavery in the Atlantic has generally been overlooked. The belief that Spain's imperial ambitions were limited to the Americas and the Pacific has caused its interest both in Africa itself, and in enslaved Africans, to be overlooked. Columbus returned from his first voyage to the Americas promising Isabella and Ferdinand potential colonies brimming with 'many mines of metal' and a large population to labour at whatever the conquerors demanded:

> I believe we could take many of the males every year and an infinite number of women . . . May you also believe that one of them would be worth more than three black slaves from Guinea in strength and ingenuity.

Columbus clearly had ideas of turning the Caribbean into the kind of place he had seen on an earlier voyage to Africa (where the first fort at Mina – now Elmina – provided a base for the enslavement of local people). A year later, in February 1495, Columbus shipped 550 Taino Indians from Hispaniola to slave markets in Spain. Two hundred died en route and one half of the survivors were weak and sick on arrival in Europe. It was a terrible prelude to what was to unfold in the Atlantic in coming centuries.*

For all of Columbus's tempting promises, Spain was unsure where the best prospects lay: west in the Americas, or south – in Africa. Spain had dubious historical claims to 'Guinea' and to the trade in gold and enslaved Africans which stretched from Morocco to Arabia. Despite these claims, Spain's rulers remained undecided: should they look for major oceanic trade and conquest to the Americas – or to Africa? We now know of course that they opted for the Americas – and with devastating results. A mere fifty years after Columbus's first landfall, Spain had wiped out the people of the Caribbean, had destroyed the two most powerful empires in the Americas, the Aztec and the Inca, and claimed sovereignty over a vast stretch of the hemisphere – from California to Florida, south to Chile and the River Plate, along with important islands in the Caribbean. Plus their even more far-flung successes in the Philippines. The riches of this enormous empire soon poured back to the Iberian Peninsula, and in the process, Africa receded in Spanish ambitions. However, what Spain had *already* pioneered on the coast of Africa had created a human and commercial blueprint that was to help transform utterly the wider Atlantic world.

* For full details see Andres Resendez, *The Other Slavery: The Uncovered Story of Indian Enslavement in America,* New York, 2017, Ch.1, and B. W. Higman, *A Concise History of The Caribbean*, Cambridge, 2011, Ch.3.

The key to the neglected story of Spain and Africa lay in that small collection of Atlantic islands lying almost 1,000 km from Spain, but only 161 km off the African coast – the Canaries. The local population of Guanches people had remained untouched by the outside world until 1325 when a group of Genoese merchants arrived, to trade and settle. They were soon followed by Spanish, Portuguese and Italian expeditions. In 1344, Spain claimed the islands, establishing a foothold there and hoping to gain access to the fabled 'river of gold' in nearby Africa. They were supported by Rome, keen to convert the indigenous people. But the Papal Bull issued by Pope Benedict VII in 1403 classified the native people as infidel heretics, thus rendering them liable to enslavement. Thereafter, Spain's presence in the Canaries was totally changed.*

The Papacy had, however, created a major confusion: were the Guanches of the Canaries to be converted, by newly arrived priests, or were they to be enslaved because they were pagans? In the event, they fell victim to increasing numbers of slave traders who raided the islands with growing frequency. Though Papal policy, in 1344, had specified that baptism of the Guanches and of Africans who had been brought to the islands, *protected* them from enslavement, the *practice* of enslavement increased. Spain also invaded and conquered Las Palmas and Tenerife and local people keen to resist Spanish conquest were similarly designated as rebels, captured and enslaved.

Spain had in effect conquered the Canaries using the traditional justification of the medieval Crusades, declaring local

* Emily Burquist Soule, 'From Africa to the Ocean Sea: Atlantic Slavery in the origins of the Spanish Empire', *Atlantic Studies*, vol. 15, No. 1, 2018, p.21.

people to be infidels, who were then liable for enslavement. Shipped to Spain, or used for the development of the islands themselves, the slaves of the Canaries provided Spain with an invaluable apprenticeship in establishing a system of enslavement and slave trading. Though relatively small-scale and far removed from the massive Atlantic slave industry that followed, the enslavement of the people of the Canaries proved to be a 'stepping stone' into the world of Atlantic slavery.

The source of early interest in the Atlantic islands was gold, because both Spain and Portugal believed that African gold supplies lay somewhere in the Maghreb – a region to which Spain laid claim via the ancient Roman and Islamic links between North Africa and Spain. The Canaries now provided Spain with a base for expeditions to find that gold (they may even have ventured south along the sub-Saharan African coastline). But *the* crucial oceanic progress south was made by the Portuguese in a series of voyages which reached Madeira in 1419, the Azores in 1439 and Cape Verde in 1456. As they sailed ever further south, the Portuguese traded enslaved Moorish people for Africans, and it soon became apparent that African slaves offered new and promising commercial bounty. By 1450, a trade in enslaved Africans had become Portugal's most profitable commerce with Africa.*

Papal Bulls of 1452, which authorised Portugal's enslavement of Africans (as 'pagans') were altogether more severe than the Bulls supporting Spain in the Canaries. Portugal's request for Papal support for its activities in Africa was also designed to keep Spain *out* of the region. Here lay the origins of the belief that Spain was apparently uninterested in Africa – yet Spain

* Emily Burquist Soule, 'From Africa to the Ocean Sea', p.25.

had made repeated, though unsuccessful, efforts to establish control of, or gain access to, the lucrative trade crossing the Sahara. Spain had also tried to develop trade and dominion on the African Atlantic coast. Repeated royal claims of interest in Africa (and a number of voyages) are clear indications of Spain's ambitions towards sub-Saharan Africa. But its African ambitions were thwarted, and they failed to develop safe trading and military links. Once its American empire began to flourish and to lure Spain's main trading and military efforts to the far side of the Atlantic, Spain's direct involvement in Africa was quickly overshadowed – and even forgotten. At much the same time, and as Spain looked west, Portugal's expeditions on the African coast had exposed plentiful supplies of enslaved Africans and many were shipped for sale in Portugal or to the islands of São Tomé and Principe, where they formed the labour gangs of a new and thriving sugar plantations industry.

The story thereafter becomes much more familiar. Portugal consolidated its presence on the African coast by building elaborate defences and forts, designed initially to protect gold and personnel from the dangers posed by Africans but, more especially, from other Europeans. All of Europe's major maritime powers were keen to follow suit, with a rapid proliferation of defensive and trading posts dotting that stretch of the African coast (the Gold Coast). Those forts and trading posts became the conduit for the flow of gold from the interior Ashanti gold fields. They also became the depots for enslaved Africans destined for the slave ships and thence to the Americas.

Spain did not readily abandon its ambitions in Africa. A series of expeditions, clashes with Portugal, and dynastic conflicts culminated in war between the two nations. That war, ended by the Treaty of Alcáçovas in 1479, confirmed Portugal's sphere of influence in sub-Saharan Africa (or at least the coastal regions) and effectively cut Spain off from the main supply of enslaved Africans. Unable to develop its own Atlantic slave trade, Spain henceforth had to acquire Africans via other nations, and other agreements.

The Treaty of Alcáçovas was drafted *before* the 'discovery' of the Americas, and its clauses left both Spain and Portugal claiming total rights to the Americas. The Papacy acted as arbiter, issuing new Bulls (1493) dividing the Atlantic world between the two Iberian powers. In 1494 Spain, Portugal and the Papacy signed the Treaty of Todesillas, confirming a revised division of the Atlantic world. Reality on the ground, and at sea, gave a different shape to future events.

By now, Portugal had a thriving commercial interest both in African slaves and gold, but its adventurous fleets looked far beyond West Africa They sailed south, round the Cape and thence into the tempting commercial and strategic waters and locations of the Indian Ocean and beyond. African gold, and enslaved Africans were critical factors in enabling Portugal to look eastward to the riches of India and China – and even to Japan. The result, by the early sixteenth century, was that Lisbon became a global entrepôt: a city awash with commodities, people and animals from Africa and Asia. Prosperous homes boasted artefacts from Africa, Ceylon, India and China: African spoons, Chinese porcelain, Ceylonese carvings, and the streets of Lisbon were populated by more Africans (mostly enslaved) than anywhere outside Africa.

Though Spain found itself excluded – boxed out – of Africa, the Americas was a dazzling new world, replete (or so Columbus told his royal backers) with boundless potential. The gold, spices, timbers – and local Indian slaves – which Columbus talked of after his landings in Hispaniola promised bounty beyond the dreams of Spanish avarice. Spain had already benefitted greatly from the slave trade to and from the Canaries and now seemed poised to develop a new slave trade in Amerindians to Spain.* But the fate of those enslaved people was terrible in the extreme – and it also sealed the fate of future generations of Africans.

Within a single generation of Europeans arriving in Hispaniola, a catastrophe had overwhelmed the native people. By 1515, there were only ten thousand left on the island. Much the same was disastrously true for the people of the other Caribbean islands. They died quickly, horribly and in huge numbers, succumbing to violence, overwork and then to diseases. By 1542, when Bartolomé de Las Casas (an early settler in Hispaniola in 1502, but later a senior cleric and defender of the Indians) wrote his account of the destruction of Indian life, a tidal wave of suffering and devastation had swept across the islands, leaving a desolate human vacuum. It also left a labouring void for the new Spanish settlers who had hoped to use local labour for the various tasks in the new settlements. There is a shocking irony which forms a prelude to this story. The suffering and the genocide of the Taino peoples of the Caribbean led inexorably to the sufferings of millions of Africans who found themselves dragooned in growing numbers onto the Atlantic slave ships, thence to the misery of labour on American plantations (or to the mines in Hispaniola).

Among the first to report on these disasters was Las Casas, now a Dominican Friar, the first Bishop of Chiapas and 'Protector of the Indians':

* Emily Burquist Soule, 'From Africa to the Ocean Sea', p. 30.

> I myself who am writing this and saw it and know most about it can hardly believe that such was possible.*

Las Casas was describing the cataclysmic death rates which were directly related to the excessive work regimes imposed by Spanish settlers. It was also clear that they urgently needed a new source of labour. Las Casas, back in Spain in 1517, persuaded Charles V to grant a licence permitting African slaves to be shipped direct from Africa to the Caribbean. The trade was subcontracted to merchants from Genoa who agreed to transport four thousand Africans to Hispaniola. In fact Africans had *already* been transported to Hispaniola. In 1505, King Ferdinand had sent one hundred slaves direct to the island to work in the mines: fifty more followed in 1510. In 1519 a licence had allowed a merchant to establish a trading depot on Cape Verde specifically for exporting slaves to the Caribbean and by 1550 there were fears that the growing numbers of Africans might even lead to slave revolt. Though it is difficult to calculate accurately the numbers shipped from Cape Verde, these early voyages clearly transported more Africans to Spanish America than historians have previously reckoned. By the mid-sixteenth century, in the words of Toby Green, it was 'a process which would not be reversed'. Moreover, the merchants involved were keen to *increase* the flow of Africans across the Atlantic.

We now know that enslaved Africans had been shipped across the Atlantic from the early days of Spanish settlement and that the Portuguese had developed their own slave trade *between* various African coastal regions, in addition to shipping Africans back to Portugal. Spain too had developed its own

* Quoted in Andres Resendez, *The Other Slavery*, p.39.

system of African slaving, to and from the Atlantic islands, and it was *this* trade – the commercial experience and brute practice of trading in African humanity – which formed the springboard for *the* critical transformation in this entire story: the carefully planned enforced migration of vast numbers of Africans westward across the Atlantic. Although the later Atlantic crossings were on a totally different scale, *the system* had been firmly grounded in the experiences, commercial optimism and the brutal manhandling of the much smaller trade in Africans pioneered in the eastern Atlantic.*

***

The labour force which Columbus thought he had discovered among native Indians in the Caribbean had, within a half century, been Africanised. By 1560 Las Casas reckoned that thirty thousand Africans had been imported into Hispaniola over the past forty-two years. He calculated one hundred thousand had been landed in the Indies as a whole. By the end of the sixteenth century, something like two thousand Africans a year were landing in Hispaniola, though many were transhipped onwards, to other parts of Spanish America. This pattern was to become a central feature of the Spanish empire thereafter; Africans arriving in one place, but destined for enslaved labour in more distant locations.

This trade in Africans became a complex, industrial system which ensnared millions of people. It was transformed, initially,

* Toby Green, *The Rise of the Trans-Atlantic Slave Trade in West Africa,* 2012, Ch.6, and *A Fistful of Shells: West Africa from the Rise of the Slave Trade to the Age of Revolution,* London, 2019, pp.143–148.

by the introduction into the tropical Americas of sugar cultivation. Spanish settlers in the Caribbean, but especially Portuguese settlers in Brazil, soon realised that plans for sugar plantations could never come to commercial fruition without regular and reliable supplies of labour. And in both the Caribbean and Brazil, native labour simply vanished (it died, fell sick or fled) leaving settlers with the one human resource they had perfected on the far side of the Atlantic: enslaved Africans. This nexus – African slaves in newly conquered lands – had already been tested and proved to be enormously viable in the Iberian Peninsula and on the Atlantic islands. It now came into its own in the Americas.

Within a century of Columbus's first landfall, African slaves had become part of the warp and weft of Spanish life in the Americas. Africans, enslaved and free, had been familiar in Iberian life long before the European expansion into the Americas: they were used extensively, for instance, in the punitive work of land reclamation in the Algarve. Not surprisingly, Africans accompanied Europeans in their early probes into the Americas. In fact Africans were a striking feature of all of Spain's major settlements, conquests and conflicts across the Americas. Wherever Spain fought, conquered and settled, there too we find Africans. Africans had become an inescapable human feature of the changing face of the Americas.

3

Spain and the Other Slavery

SPAIN'S EARLY INTEREST in the Americas was in the Caribbean islands. According to Las Casas, the islands were a 'beehive of people' and, he claimed, 'were densely populated with natives called Indians.' Sixty years later, the local Taino population – described by Columbus as 'affectionate and without malice' – had effectively ceased to exist.* Theirs was a savage fate and the depopulation of the Caribbean islands persuaded Spain to look elsewhere for vital labour. The four voyages of Columbus had set in train a transformation of those islands first by destroying their native peoples and then by prompting the importation and settlement of peoples, animals and plants from the far corners of the globe. In Barry Higman's words the Caribbean became 'the testing ground for models of tropical colonisation, [and] the islands served also as a staging post for the Spanish-American empire.' What happened in Hispaniola was soon followed in Puerto Rico, Jamaica and Cuba. Spanish control, though resisted by the Taino people, was imposed by ferocious Spanish violence. Once established in the Caribbean, Spain

* Andres Resendez, *The Other Slavery*, p.13.

was able to move to new settlements in Florida, Mexico, Panama, Cartagena and then Peru – all from their springboard in the Caribbean. The new world order of the Spanish empire in the Americas came into being – but it did so on the bones of the Taino people.*

It might have been possible for the Taino people to repel the Spanish invaders. But they were awestruck – dumbfounded – by the arrival of European ships and men along with their fearsome firepower. When Taino resisted Spanish aggression, they were met by extreme violence – and enslavement. A famine – and the later impact of disease – weakened and then totally undermined the Taino people. A military Spanish campaign in Hispaniola in 1503 to 1504 destroyed Taino settlements, killing or relocating the population into towns, and by 1508 only those Taino who had fled remained outside Spanish control. They were, however, in precipitous decline, hastened by the Spanish labour demands in gold mining and agriculture. As Taino labour withered, Spain began to raid other islands for labour. The Lucayan people of the Bahamas were rounded up for labour and shipped elsewhere while similar raids in Florida and the Yucatan dragooned labour for Cuba. From one place to another, violent Spanish attacks greatly depleted local populations among a huge arc of societies from Trinidad in the south, to Florida in the north. In only a few years, the populations of Barbados and the Bahamas disappeared (at the same time, the Spanish populations of the new towns and settlements in Hispaniola expanded and thrived). There were places where Taino and their cultural habits survived – or survived by absorption into and adaptation to local Spanish life – often via

* B. W. Higman, *Concise History of the Caribbean*, pp.67–78.

marriage. But this has to be set against the disaster that swept across the Taino people in general. Spanish violence and killings, the excessively arduous labour demands of Spanish settlers and the collapse of indigenous food supplies produced a massive depletion of the native people of the islands. All this was completed by the later impact of disease.*

Historians have widely assumed that the demographic collapse in the Caribbean (and elsewhere in the Americas) was caused by the unconscious importation of diseases to which indigenous people had little or no resistance. The finger of blame has usually been pointed at smallpox. We now know, however, that the population collapse began *before* the impact of major diseases. Smallpox flared a full generation *after* Columbus arrived – and by then the population decline was already catastrophic. Las Casas, again, offers an eyewitness account. He arrived a mere decade after Columbus's first landing and believed that greed was why Spaniards 'murdered on such a vast scale' killing 'anyone and everyone who has shown the slightest sign of resistance.' He thought that the enslaved Taino were treated 'worse than animals.' Even King Ferdinand believed that native people died because of excessive work. Having no beasts to help them, settlers 'forced the Indians to carry excessive loads until they broke them down.' The figures tell a horrifying story. When the Spaniards first landed, the population of Hispaniola is thought to have been in the region of two to three hundred thousand. By 1508 (i.e. a decade *before* smallpox was recorded there) the population had slid to sixty thousand. Six years later it was only twenty-six thousand, and by 1517, the population stood at eleven thousand, i.e. a

* B. W. Higman, *Concise History of the Caribbean*, pp.75–78.

mere 5 per cent of the numbers when Columbus had arrived. The impact of smallpox shortly afterwards did not *cause* the population collapse, but 'appeared to deliver the coup de grâce.' The epidemics of 1518 and 1519 completed what Spanish settlers had set in train earlier. The end result was that, between 1492 and 1550, 'a nexus of slavery, overwork, and famine' killed more Indians than disease, and 'among these human factors, slavery has emerged as a major killer.' By 1570 there were only a few hundred Tainos left on the island of Hispaniola.*

A similar pattern was repeated on other islands across the Caribbean. The Indian people of Jamaica were turned over to the strenuous work required by the Spanish settlers, and by 1520 the island's indigenous population had vanished. But Spain had not yet finished with the enslavement of the Indian peoples of the Americas. As their empire expanded into North America, across Central America and south along the Pacific coast, they needed labour for a multitude of arduous tasks: to forge new settlements, towns and mines and to expand agriculture. The violent enslavement of local Indians was followed by their enforced movement, often on long distance and draining routes as they criss-crossed Spanish America. The numbers involved are, again, enormous, though the scale of the phenomenon has only recently been fully grasped. The most exhaustive study suggests that between 1492 and 1900 somewhere between 2.4 million and almost 5 million Indian people were enslaved across the Americas. In the Caribbean, where the process began, upwards of half a million Indians were enslaved. In North America – and starting much later – between 147,000 and a third of a million Indians were enslaved. By far the largest

* Andres Resendez, *The Other Slavery*, Ch.1.

numbers were to be found in South America where, excluding Brazil, an estimated 965,000 to 1.7 million Indians were enslaved. Brazil's enslaved Indian population was between 490,000 and 900,000. Even more striking are the figures (between 590,000 and 1.4 million) to be found in Mexico and Central America. This enslavement of Indian peoples began *before* the arrival of significant numbers of Africans and was to continue long after the Atlantic slave trade had ended. When we add together these astonishing figures to the numbers now available for the Atlantic slave trade, the role of slavery in the shaping of the Americas becomes ever more startling.*

The treatment of Indian slaves was every bit as brutal and savage as we find in the history of African slavery. Moreover, Spanish settlers were offered slaves by other native Americans. At first they handed over small groups of captives but that grew into larger gangs of enslaved people as predatory Indians acquired more powerful weaponry from the Spaniards and were able to attack and round up growing numbers of victims. Tens of thousands of Indians, for example, were dragooned for the booming silver mines of Mexico and Peru. The silver mines of Peru required such enormous supplies of labour that the Spaniards introduced a system known as the *mita* which imposed levies on two hundred Indian communities scattered across present-day Peru and Bolivia, obliging them to send one seventh of their menfolk to work in the silver mines of Potosi, Huancavelica and Cailloma.†

The use of Indian slaves in the guano industry in Peru was the origin of a massive industry which later spread to Pacific

* Andres Resendez, *The Other Slavery*, Appendix 1.

† Andres Resendez, *The Other Slavery*, pp.123–124.

islands in the nineteenth century and aided the agricultural development of both Australia and New Zealand.*

The enslavement of Indians was accompanied by all the features that were to become so common to African slavery: brutal treatment – to goad, to punish and intimidate – and the widespread use of shackles and chains, especially as gangs of Indians were being moved to their new homes and workplaces. Huge numbers were recruited in Chile then moved north to the labour markets of Peru and on to the mining regions. Paraguay and Tucuman yielded another rich source of Indian slaves, who were then moved elsewhere via the Rio Plata region. Further north, Indian slaves were captured in Colombia and Venezuela (where European traders were greatly assisted by the slave-raiding of local Indians). Northern Mexico yielded rich returns for slave raiders and traders (despite a formal legal ban on Indian slavery) with slaves being passed on to the mines and towns of northern Mexico – and south to Mexico City. But perhaps the largest region for the enslavement of native peoples within Spain's empire was much further afield – the Philippines. There, 'Europeans had stumbled on a dazzling world of slaves.' Some were born into slavery, others were victims of local warfare – but more were captured by slavers who fed the expanding Spanish appetite for slaves after the Spanish conquest. 'A variety of slaves were offered in the markets of Manila, and many were transported across the Pacific on the Spanish galleons bound for Mexico.'†

* Gregory T. Cushman, *Guano and the Opening of the Pacific World*, Cambridge, 2013.

† Andres Resendez, *The Other Slavery*, p.135.

There was in effect a massive network of slaving regions covering the whole expanse of Spain's enormous empire. Wherever Spaniards acquired their Indian slaves they were operating among people who had an *existing* slave system of their own. 'All of them had possessed traditions of Indian bondage harking back to pre-contact times.' Here was a reflection of what unfolded on the slaving coast of West Africa, with Europeans tapping into existing forms of trade and bondage, but transforming them into something quite different. Wherever Indian slavery thrived in Spanish America, there we find all the characteristics we see in the more familiar story of African slavery: the brutal dragooning of people over long distances, the commonplace use of violence as an essential element in control and labour, and the universal break-up of enslaved families whenever it suited the interests of the slave traders or slave owners. Similarly, the story of Indian slavery in Spanish America did not go unchallenged. It was a history marked throughout by resistance among the enslaved: individual flight, foot-dragging, violent reaction and outright revolt. The most striking of revolts was that of the Pueblo Indians of New Mexico in 1680 with 'an audacious plan of liberation.'*

The killing of some four hundred people – about 20 per cent of the Spanish population of New Mexico – and the flight of survivors left New Mexico to the Indians – but the Spaniards returned twelve years later. Though the revolt was directed primarily against Spanish officials, the church and priests, it was also paralleled by a growing unease about slavery among Spain's intellectual and religious elite. The total collapse of some Indian populations, the grotesque enslavement and

* Andres Resendez, *The Other Slavery*, pp.135–148.

brutalisation of armies of others – all and more fed an early Spanish abolition voice which, though unsuccessful in the main, thrived a full century before the better-known abolition campaigns in Britain and North America. By 1680, as the Spaniards fled New Mexico in terror, Indian slavery had taken root securely across the enormity of Spain's New World empire. And it was paralleled by the better-known slavery of Africans in the same regions.

By the time of the Pueblo Revolt of 1680, the Atlantic slave ships had delivered more than half a million enslaved Africans to the Spanish Americas. Although Spain turned to African slaves as a major labour supply, they continued to run both systems side by side: enslaved Africans and enslaved local Indians, often literally working side by side, in all major regions of Spanish America. They became part of the human fabric of that astonishing empire, working, settling alongside each other, mingling as fellow labourers, as social beings and as families, and bringing together the peoples of Europe, Africa and the Americas into a human mix that was to characterise the hemisphere down to the present day. (The precise chemistry of those combinations of people are, today, more easily and precisely explained by the emergence of DNA testing.)*

The European arrival in the Caribbean had heralded an astonishing transformation in the way the world's population was to develop henceforth. It pitched together indigenous peoples of the Americas with people from Europe, Africa, and later from Asia. It was a mixture from which there emerged cultures that were hybrid – creole: 'rooted in the Caribbean,

* Carl Zimmer, 'Ancient DNA Shows Humans Settled Caribbean in 2 Distinct Waves', *New York Times*, 23 December 2020.

but created from elements that were universal rather than localized.' It was a momentous change because this new settlement of the Caribbean was a driving force in a massive redistribution of global population. What was put in place in the Caribbean was soon to be replicated across the Americas, in localised form, with subsequent transformations in populations, social systems, agricultural systems and even in the very flora and fauna of the natural world.

***

Africans caught in the net of Atlantic slavery endured one traumatic experience after another and from which there seemed no escape. Much the same was true of their children, born into slavery in the Americas, who, though spared the nightmare of the slave ship, also fell victim to recurring threats. If we freeze the life of the enslaved at any one moment or phase of their lives, we can easily miss the *totality* of their experiences. The lives of the enslaved formed a continuing pattern of dangers which lasted a lifetime: from African enslavement (or childhood in the Americas) to old age. Each phase of their lives brought its own distinctive woes and dangers. Moreover, their lives were overshadowed, throughout, by a cloud of deep uncertainty: *they never knew what might happen next.* Not one of the millions of slaves throughout the Americas was safe or secure: no one could be certain that their life would not be convulsed – for the worse – and all in the blink of an eye. Slave families apparently safely rooted on a particular property, or an individual working at a particular task, could, in an instant, be uprooted, removed, sold and force marched hundreds of miles away. And all by the unpredictable change of circumstance among their owners: of death, ill-fortune, economic distress – or warfare. It is impossible to know how to assess this basic fact, but it is important to recognise that slaves, everywhere, lived out their lives in an atmosphere of insecurity. Not one of them could guarantee what tomorrow might bring. Often it brought upheaval and further grief.

It began in Africa with the confusion and terror of enslavement. People were enslaved via warfare, slave raiding, famine, debt bondage and more. Each person had their own individual horror story to tell, and all before being force marched to the Atlantic coast or to a riverside location where slave traders waited. The popular imagination has the Africans corralled into the slave forts, though in fact, many more Africans were passed onto the slave ships from beaches, barracoons (holding pens for the enslaved) or a variety of other coastal facilities. Moreover, for most enslaved Africans the first experience of the Atlantic was not on the slave ship, but on the canoes and small boats which ferried captives from the shore to the slave ship riding at anchor in deeper waters.

What happened on the slave ships remains a familiar and deeply troubling story: one which more than eleven million Africans survived. Even when a slave ship arrived at its American destination relatively untroubled by dangers and threats from the enslaved on board, the Africans had undergone a personal and communal trauma like no other. What happened immediately *after* their arrival in the Americas has gone largely unnoticed. Landfall may seem to have been the end of their sufferings – at least they were now spared further oceanic misery: back on terra firma, perhaps the worst was behind them. In fact, they were confronted by torments of a different kind. For most Africans, the initial landfall heralded merely a temporary respite:

a way station before the next leg of a journey that would see many of them taken *back* to sea, before landing at even more distant locations in the Americas. Africans spilled out of the slave ships only to be moved onwards, to the very edges of colonial settlement: from the high Andes to the Brazilian and North American frontiers. They were scattered along a vast network of riverine and sea routes, along overland trails, following in the wake of European settlement (and Indian destruction). It is as if the Africans had become the human flotsam and jetsam of European exploration and settlement in the Americas. The Africans shipped to Spanish America found themselves scattered enormous distances across that huge empire.

Spain's empire stretched from California to Buenos Aires. It was also the destination for the first (1505) and the last (1867) Atlantic slave voyage. After Brazil, Spanish America received more enslaved Africans than any other region in the Americas. More than one and a half million people landed there direct from Africa, while more than half a million arrived via other colonies, notably from Brazil and Jamaica. Recent scholarship has established beyond all doubt that the African presence was vital in the development of colonial Spanish America, before, say, 1800. In the nineteenth century, the arrival of yet more Africans, in Puerto Rico and Cuba, transformed the economies of both those islands. Spanish America thrived on enslaved Africans. Moreover, what happened to Africans and their descendants in Spanish America provides some of the most compelling evidence about the remarkable enforced onward migrations, and personal upheavals endured by Africans *after* they left the Atlantic slave ships.

Many of the Africans who were disembarked in what is now Buenos Aires and the River Plate region were moved, overland, across the vastness of the southern continent, high into the Spanish settlements of the Andes. There they worked alongside local Indians in agriculture and in mining. Others were landed in the Caribbean, in Santo Domingo, Havana, Vera Cruz and Cartagena.

The merchants involved in this trade *within* Spanish America, like those involved elsewhere, made intimate physical inspections of the African victims, choosing only those likely to survive the next, punishing journey. Despite their attention, disease inevitably attacked the African captives. Though the health risks of this Spanish intercolonial slave trade were much lower than on the Atlantic crossing, they were nonetheless real and terrifying. Little could be done about storms, shipwrecks, catastrophic maritime accidents (fires and explosions), to say nothing of African uprisings, or the damage caused by the capricious violence of the crewmen. The 360 Africans who arrived at Kingston in May 1729 on the *Freke Galley* were sold to agents planning to ship them to Cuba. One hundred and eighty had been transferred onto a sloop, the *Ruby*, when an accident with the ship's guns and powder led to a massive explosion which totally destroyed the vessel, killing sixty crew members and some 140 Africans. Most of the survivors were badly wounded and 'in a miserable Condition.'* Even without such catastrophes, the onward journeys into the Spanish empire were daunting and sapping both of moral and physical strength.† Yet this was the reality for those Africans scattered across Spain's vast empire. In truth, upheavals and enforced removals

* Gregory E. O'Malley, *Final Passages: The intercolonial slave trade of British America, 1619–1807*, Chapel Hill, 2014, p.12.

† Gregory E. O'Malley, *Final Passages*, Ch.1.

remained a feature of slavery everywhere: they were part of the very nature of slavery itself.

The geographic enormity of Spain's American empire, and the huge range and variety of its imperial economic activity, meant that enslaved Africans could be found in any number of occupations. Africans became an inescapable presence in all Spanish American towns and cities. In Lima, Mexico City, Quito, Cartagena and Bogota, anything up to 25 per cent of the population was made up of enslaved Africans. They worked as domestics and as artisans but were to be seen in their most eye-catching form as lavishly dressed retainers to government officials and the wealthiest of planters and merchants. In 1625, an Englishman reported that the prosperous in Mexico City:

> have their train of blackamoor slaves, some a dozen, some half a dozen, waiting on them in brave and gallant liveries, heavy with gold and silver lace, with silk stockings on their black legs, and roses on their feet, and swords by their sides.*

Much harsher work awaited the Africans turned into the sugar fields of Spain's Caribbean islands. Others worked on haciendas and even in Spain's textile factories in Peru – again, alongside local Indian labour. Africans could be found in gangs panning for gold in New Grenada (roughly today's Venezuela, Ecuador and Columbia), and in mines in Mexico. The mines of New Spain came to depend on enslaved Africans: as one local catchword had it:

* J. H. Elliott, *Empires of the Atlantic World*, New Haven, 2006, pp.100–101.

Bad to have them, but much worse not to have them.*

Even in the high-altitude silver mines of Potosi – the source of Spain's priceless silver and where Spain much preferred local Indian labour – African slaves were commonplace (though employed more in local agriculture and domestic labour than in the silver mines themselves). By 1600, Potosi's population was 120,000 (three times that of London), all developed in a mere half century. It was a city of incredible filth, hellish working conditions and cruelty which was appalling even by the standards of Spanish America. Potosi was thought of as 'the mouth of hell'. Yet for all that, the consequences of Potosi's silver (some 200,000 kilos per annum by the 1590s) were global – and swift. The world was suddenly awash with silver from Potosi with consequences for European manufactures, Chinese ceramics and Indian textiles. It also bankrolled Spain's wars in Europe and enabled them to defeat the Turks. To sustain the rapid development of that high-altitude city (at 4,000 metres) food and goods flowed in: labour, clothing, food and drink. African slave labour was vital for that mining city, not so much for mining itself, but for the host of industries – especially local agriculture – which fed the largely Indian enslaved labour force in the mines.† African slaves effectively fed the Indian miners. Indeed Africans, and their children, were similarly vital in the economy of Peru, especially in and around Lima and other urban areas, where they laboured in agriculture, tended cattle and acted as drovers and drivers in the local transport system.

* J. H. Elliott, *Empires of the Atlantic World*, p.101.

† Kris Lane, *Potosi: The Silver City that Changed the World*, Berkeley, 2021 edn.

Africans were, then, an integral presence in the emergent well-being of Spanish America, but their work was especially important in the plantation cultivation of export crops – notably of sugar in tropical and semi-tropical regions. Long before northern Europeans had secured their own viable settlements in the Americas, Africans and their children, enslaved and free, had become a visible presence in the human make-up of Spanish America. But the numbers involved seem small when we look at the one region which absorbed more Africans than any other – Brazil. African faces were not only ubiquitous and unexceptional – a living illustration of the human diversity that was rapidly transforming the Americas – but were central to the economic growth of Spain's massive American empire.

In the early years of Spanish expansion, roughly 1550 to 1650, many of Spain's settlements in the Caribbean islands, and along the Pacific coast from Panama to Lima, were home to more Africans than Europeans. By the mid-seventeenth century, there were important Black populations in Mexico City, in Colombia, Ecuador, Peru and Venezuela. All those communities emerged from people who had been moved vast distances, *after* stepping from the slave ships, though many of course subsequently mixed with indigenous Indian people and Europeans.*

The enforced travels of Africans destined for the far reaches of Spanish America were extraordinary. Slave ships arriving in the region of Rio de la Plata (Montevideo and Buenos Aires) brought Africans from as far afield as south-west Africa and

* Alex Borucki, David Eltis and David Wheat, 'Atlantic History and the Slave Trade to Spanish America', *American Historical Review*, April 2015.

Senegambia. Though the numbers involved were small (some sixty-seven thousand people) many of them were then force marched across the vastness of the southern continent, to Spanish settlements in the high Andes. Many more, however entered Spanish America after first landing in a British island (notably Jamaica) thence to Cartagena. From there, they were moved through rugged terrain to the south. Africans landing at Veracruz travelled onwards 200 miles to the Valley of Mexico – but rising 7,000 feet in the process. Worse still, Africans sold at Portobello were taken clean across the Isthmus to the Pacific coast, and there they embarked on yet another ship for a voyage south along the Pacific coast. A voyage of two to three weeks took them to Lima's main port of Callao, with others landed at Trujillo, before being marched to Lima, though some were sold at smaller towns en route south. Such journeys added upwards of five months to the time Africans had *already* spent on their odyssey from Africa – with all the added physical stress to health, and with deaths en route adding to the doleful litany of slave trading mortality.*

* Gregory E. O'Malley, *Final Passages*, p.68.

4

Slavery, Sugar and Power

PORTUGAL'S INITIAL TRADE in enslaved Africans had drawn heavily on Upper Guinea and Kongo, but their 'conquest' of Angola created an entirely new source of enslaved Africans. In the long subsequent history of the trade, Angola was to provide more enslaved Africans than any other region in Africa – and by a very considerable measure. There developed a massive flow of people across the South Atlantic, overwhelmingly to Brazil. What happened in Brazil had been presaged, in miniature, in São Tomé. That small island lies close to the African coast in the Gulf of Guinea, and it became the real commercial test case for using slave labour on sugar plantations. It was a lush island brimming with natural abundance, with plentiful water – and hence a natural stopping-off point for ships heading westward across the Atlantic. It also yielded plentiful supplies of fruit and other foodstuffs, and quickly became 'the main slave emporium of this whole region.' São Tomé's role as an important way station and refuelling point for ships heading into the Atlantic continued for the next three centuries.*

* Hugh Thomas, *Slave Trade,* p.364. See also Robert Harms, *The Diligent: A Voyage through the World of the Slave Trade,* Oxford, 2002, Part 9 'Atlantic Islands'.

Sugar cane had been planted by settlers on a number of the Atlantic islands, from the Canaries south to São Tomé, though in some islands other crops (grapes and wheat for example) proved more suitable. Sugar, however, had the most abiding and transformative effect. Long cultivated in the Mediterranean – in Palestine, Crete, North Africa and southern Spain – cane sugar had traditionally been costly and exotic, and was far beyond the pockets and aspirations of ordinary people. More often it was used as an extravagant display of power and wealth among Europe's ruling elites. Sugar confections of the most elaborate kind graced the tables and banquets of monarchs, clerics and aristocrats, to impress their guests (and rot their teeth). All that changed when sugar from the Atlantic islands, but especially from São Tomé, began to arrive at the docksides of Lisbon and thence to other European cities.*

By 1470 Madeira had become the West's main sugar supplier, its sugar lands worked by slaves from the Canary Islands – and from Africa. Financed by Flemish and Italian backers, the sugar plantations transformed the face of the island – and nurtured the West's growing appetite for sugar. By 1506 Madeira exported 2,500 tons, but the industry there collapsed as quickly as it had emerged, victim of the ecological destruction of the island's resources and, more especially, undermined by competition from the Portuguese settlement of São Tomé.†

São Tomé had fallen to Portugal in 1472, and followed the pattern established in Madeira and the Canaries. By the end of

* James Walvin, *Sugar: The World Corrupted, from Slavery to Obesity*, London, 2017, Ch.3.

† James W. Moore, 'Madeira, Sugar and the Conquest of Nature in the "First" Sixteenth Century,' *Review*, (Fernand Braudel Center), vol. 32, No. 4, 2009.

the sixteenth century, São Tomé's sugar economy boasted two hundred mills, servicing plantations which covered the island. Most of them were worked by enslaved Africans and in 1519 something in the region of four thousand Africans landed on the island. By mid-century, about two thousand worked there, while six thousand more were corralled in pens awaiting transportation elsewhere. Though the coast of Guinea was only a short sailing distance from São Tomé, Africans arrived on the island from more distant African locations – from Benin, Angola and Senegambia. In all of these places, slave trading had *already* been developed by the Portuguese. Here, in essence, was the prototype of the system that was soon to be developed in the tropical Americas. The sugar cultivated by this enslaved labour filled the sugar bowls, and moulded the sweet confectionaries (the 'subtleties') that graced the tables of fashionable Europe. Like Madeira before it, however, São Tomé crashed almost as quickly as it had emerged – swept aside by the emergence of a new and more productive sugar industry – in the new Portuguese settlements in Brazil.

Sugar had made a slow geographic progression westward, travelling with maritime adventurers and merchants on a protracted journey from its birthplace in Asia. Columbus had carried sugar cane on his second voyage in 1493, though it was soon apparent that if sugar were to thrive in Spain's new lands in the Americas – in the face of the catastrophic collapse of local people – labour had to be recruited elsewhere. Sugar seemed to offer a bountiful future – but only if suitable labour supplies could be found. Spanish officials in the Caribbean frequently wrote home that African labour was vital to the islands' development. Spain, however, had no means of its own of delivering the numbers of Africans required, though Portugal could – if given appropriate licences. Portugal had effectively perfected the early transatlantic transportation of Africans on what proved to be the quickest routes, between Africa and Brazil. And the aim was to provide labour for Brazil's new sugar plantations.

Though it is very difficult to generalise about Brazilian slavery because of the multiple and very different regions of Brazil, and the great variety of Africans involved, it is clear that sugar drove forward the initial development of Brazilian slavery. In the century 1580 to 1680, African slavery grew at an astonishing rate in Bahia – centred on Salvador – because of that region's sugar industry.

At first Africans worked alongside local Indian labour, but by 1600 half of Brazil's plantation labour force was African – and enslaved. Both on smallholdings and large plantations, sugar work was infamously hard and unrelenting – and often dangerous. But the finished product – crude cane sugar and rum – found a keen and expansive market, first in Portugal, thence to Europe at large. European sugar consumption marched in step with the expansion of Brazil's enslaved labour force. The more Africans arrived in north-east Brazil, the more sugar was shipped to Europe. As Brazilian sugar production flourished (thanks largely to the 'captaincies' granted by the Portuguese Crown to settle new lands) it was fuelled by the arrival of ever-increasing numbers of enslaved Africans. By 1600, two hundred thousand Africans had landed in Brazil.*

Sugar changed not only the culinary tastes of the West but it helped to transform the physical face of Europe's port cities

* Stuart B. Schwartz, *Sugar Plantations in the Formation of Brazilian Society: Bahia, 1550–1835*, Cambridge, 1985.

(much the same happened in the USA in the nineteenth century). The sugar shipped across the Atlantic had been crudely refined in simple factories which sprouted on bigger plantations, and required further refining in Europe. Sugar refineries and distilleries quickly proliferated in Europe's port cities; belching smoke and unpleasant smells, and causing a chorus of complaints from residents and city fathers. They also posed a major fire hazard. Nonetheless they increased rapidly and became the conduit linking the slave plantations of the Americas and the expanding market of Europe's sugar consumers. By 1550, Antwerp boasted nineteen sugar refineries: Amsterdam's increased from forty to one hundred and ten in the years 1650 to 1770. By 1753, London was home to eighty. By then, sugar was cheap and had become an everyday item among all sorts and conditions of people, sold in shops, by pedlars and at markets.*

In the process, cane sugar lost its luxury status and mankind's traditional sweetener – honey – was replaced by cane sugar cultivated by Africans in Brazil and the Caribbean. Sugar also found a role in medicine and pharmacology and was to remain an important ingredient in a range of traditional and newer medicine. From ancient Arabic medicine to the world of modern pharmaceutical giants, sweetness remains an important additive to a host of medicines.

Sugar's main impact the world over was of course as an additive to a range of food and drinks, notably and most spectacularly when added to the naturally bitter-tasting drinks of chocolate, coffee and tea. At first Brazilian sugar dominated the market, but that changed from the mid-seventeenth century

* James Walvin, *Sugar*, pp.37–38.

with the rise of the Caribbean sugar islands. The emergence of English and French global power and ambition had lagged well behind Spain, Portugal and Holland but by the early seventeenth century, both began to catch up. From the 1620s onwards a string of Caribbean islands fell to those emergent colonial powers, each keen to expand its commercial and political interest in the Americas (and elsewhere) and each seeking a viable economic base for their new acquisitions. With luck, they might even surpass the good fortune of their Iberian rivals in the riches which flowed back to the metropole from the Americas.

The early years of French and English settlement in the Caribbean involved trial and error with a range of tropical crops – tobacco, dyes, cotton, timber – before it became clear that the future lay with sugar. Other crops also provided profitable trade in the Caribbean and in North America (where rice, dye and tobacco flourished). They too used slave labour. But it was sugar which took hold in the Caribbean – helped by Dutch finance and by men experienced in sugar cultivation in Brazil – and the French and English Caribbean colonies took off. When the English seized Jamaica from Spain in 1655 the stage was set for a major leap in the sugar economy, though not without spluttering efforts with other commodities. Both Jamaica and its neighbouring French colony of St. Domingue – the western part of Hispaniola, now Haiti – were big islands, quite unlike most of the settlements in the eastern Caribbean which were small and offered little scope for growth and expansion. Although both islands were mountainous, there was plentiful land in inland valleys, remote regions, and large coastal stretches, and in both places, new sugar lands were still being brought into cultivation more than a century after the pioneering settlements. The islands' varied geography enabled the development of parallel industries, most notably coffee cultivation in mountainous areas: that too became a major slave activity.*

Jamaica and St. Domingue followed a trajectory that had already been seen in Brazil and on the smaller islands of the eastern Caribbean. As ever more land fell to sugar cultivation, that crop's progress was paralleled by the importation of African slaves. Pioneering smallholdings were worked by a mix of free, indentured and slave labour, but as landholdings became larger and required bigger labouring gangs, plantations grew in size and the labour force became increasingly African – and enslaved. The French and the English were, after a fashion, only the latest to follow a pattern marked out first in São Tomé, then Brazil – of fruitful tropical land being brought into profitable cultivation by back-breaking labour undertaken by increasing numbers of enslaved Africans.

The consequent rise in sugar output was massive. In 1580 Madeira had produced 23,000 arrobas† of sugar (337 tons) and São Tomé 20,000 (293 tons). But even at that early date Brazil produced 180,000 arrobas (2,644 tons). Thirty-four years later – in 1614 – on the eve of the onset of the eastern Caribbean sugar industry – Brazil had 'broken through to a new order of magnitude' producing 700,000 arrobas (i.e. c. 10,000 tons.)‡ By 1620, it was producing one million arrobas. This astounding output was soon rivalled by islands in the

* B. W. Higman, *Concise History of the Caribbean*, Ch.4.

† A Portuguese arroba was roughly 32 pounds.

‡ Robin Blackburn, *The Making of New World Slavery*, London, 1997, p.172.

Caribbean. By 1650 Barbados was producing 7,000 tons of sugar. Fifty years later, Britain's Caribbean possessions were exporting 25,000 tons of sugar and were already outstripping Brazilian production. By then, there were ten sugar exporting regions in the Americas, sending 60,000 tons of sugar to European and American markets. Fifty years later, the number of sugar producers had doubled and by 1750 were producing 150,000 tons. In 1770, of the 200,000 tons of sugar produced, 90 per cent came from the Caribbean.* All this was only possible because of the massive imports of enslaved Africans.

Spain, as we have seen, had dabbled with African slaves in its early Caribbean settlements but it had been Brazil which changed the very nature of slave labour and Atlantic slave trading. By the time the British and French began to settle their Caribbean islands from the 1620s onwards, more than four hundred thousand enslaved Africans had *already* landed in Brazil. Once sugar came to dominate the Caribbean economies, Africans were arriving in huge numbers. In the quarter of a century before 1775 more than one quarter of a million were landed in St. Domingue. By 1800, almost one million Africans had been landed in Jamaica, though many were promptly transhipped elsewhere in the region. The formula was simple: sugar and African slavery went hand-in-hand throughout the tropical Americas (with variations) from the early days of Portuguese settlement in Brazil through to the dying days of slavery in Cuba in the mid-nineteenth century.

Throughout this accelerating rush to ship ever more Africans to the Americas, no slave-trading nation found the trade ethically repugnant. None refused to take part. There were, it is

* B. W. Higman, *Concise History of the Caribbean*, pp.103–104.

true, important moral objections to slavery advanced by a range of philosophers and thinkers.* But such criticisms carried little weight in the rush to make money from slavery. For all the dangers involved – of oceanic travel, international conflict but above all the dangers posed by ships packed with angry captives – governments and complex coalitions of commercial interests hastened to fill ships with Africans. If people had doubts about the ethics or the irreligion of slave trading, their doubts were silenced or marginalised by the expectation of profit. The prospects of money-making silenced any qualms about slavery.

In the popular mind, the Atlantic slave system was simple: a geometric formula – 'The Triangular Trade'. Slave ships transported Africans to the Americas and returned to Europe with slave-grown produce. This, however, is a massive simplification of a much more complex trading system. In fact there was a multitude of trading systems which imposed on the Atlantic map a lattice-work of routes, east and west, north and south. What is often overlooked in this formula, however, is one vital leg of this trading system. Many thousands of ships arrived off the West African coast in search of enslaved humanity and each had left their home port for Africa loaded with cargoes destined for African markets. Those cargoes were carefully planned, selected, and purchased with an eye to the specific area of trading – and often to the specific African traders. The very early days of random, ad hoc slave trading (in effect scouring the coast for Africans who could be captured by brute force) – had given way to a more formal and highly organised trade. It was also a regimented trade which was firmly in place long *before* Europeans

* Keith Thomas, *In Pursuit of Civility: Manners and Civilization in Early Modern England*, London 2020 edn, pp.274–276.

diverted their slave trading across the Atlantic. Spain and Portugal had developed trade routes along the African coast, linking various African societies to each other, and connecting Africa to the Atlantic islands – thence to Iberian markets. From the first days of this Iberian system, the trade displayed all the features that were to characterise the transatlantic trade for the next three centuries: outbound ships left their home ports loaded with carefully selected cargoes designed to appeal to African traders who, in turn, had access to, or were in possession of enslaved Africans.

The voracious demand for slave labour in the American settlements initiated a massive growth in the slave markets of West Africa and an oceanic industry of unparalleled size and consequence. The trade effectively began after 1501 and continued until 1867 when the last slave ships landed Africans in Cuba. Over a period of four and a half centuries, an armada of European and American vessels made an estimated 42,500 voyages, and embarked twelve and a half million Africans.* A great variety of sailing vessels were used for the task. Tiny ones carrying a mere handful of Africans, and contemporary giants, packed with hundreds of people. The trade attracted all sorts and conditions of investors: rulers and governments, individual ship owners and large business syndicates. Some became international concerns with offices in Europe, Africa and the Americas. Most of them necessarily cultivated commercial contacts at all points of the Atlantic economy, and they did so under every major European and American maritime flag. The patterns of Atlantic slave trading reflected the rise (and decline) of the West's major commercial and maritime powers. Those with expanding slave empires in the

* All details of the Atlantic slave trade can be found in https://www.slavevoyages.org.

Americas went to the forefront of the Atlantic slave trade. Spain and Portugal dominated the trade until the mid-seventeenth century, when England, Holland and France entered the trade. A smaller but important trade also developed from North American ports. Finally, the last phase of the trade, in the mid-nineteenth century, was dominated by merchants from Brazil, Cuba and Spain. By then, however, slave traders were under serious attack from abolitionist powers – led by the British – whose new-found outrage about slavery seemed to overlook their own involvement in the trade in earlier centuries.

Throughout the entire story of the Atlantic slave trade, nature imposed its own patterns on it. The prevailing winds and currents of the North and South Atlantic were different, creating their own irresistible patterns on the flow, duration and direction on the trade. The currents of the North Atlantic system move clockwise, steering ships towards the Caribbean and thence to North America. South Atlantic currents flow anti-clockwise, driving sailing ships westward towards Brazil. Ships operating only within one of the systems enjoyed the fastest Atlantic crossings, but those crossing from one system to another endured more protracted voyages. The fastest crossings, say from Upper Guinea to the Caribbean and North America, could expect a voyage of six weeks. Ships leaving West-Central Africa for Brazil might also take six weeks. More protracted voyages, sailing from one weather system to another, were the most lethal. Vessels on the long haul from Mozambique, or those dropping south, from the Gold Coast and the Bight of Benin and Biafra, before heading westward, might take up to three months to reach their destinations.*

* See David Eltis and David Richardson, *Atlas of the Atlantic Slave Trade*, New Haven, 2010, Part IV.

In common with all other forms of maritime trade, the slave trade benefitted from man's changing understanding of the oceans that form the highways of global trade. Trial and error in early exploration, navigational innovation and improved ship designs and construction, all proved important (and had started in the Mediterranean *before* Europeans launched their global adventures). Marine charts which began as notes drafted by masters and pilots, were later printed and distributed, providing critical printed evidence about tides, coastal shelves and sandbars. New maps and charts of the Atlantic coasts and islands, printed descriptions of earlier voyages, almanacks compiled from all the available navigational evidence – all helped to create an expanding knowledge, in printed and graphic format, of the maritime world that formed the central experience of all slave traders – and of their African victims. Pioneering Portuguese instructions about the dangers of Atlantic sailing spread into all major European languages, and trading on the African coast was made easier (though still dangerous) by printed information about African coastal waters and the navigational dangers posed by Africa's major rivers (where Europeans also traded). This abundance of maritime literature ran parallel to ancient sailing skills – of assessing the colour and speed of the ocean, looking for seaweed, plumbing for depths, remaining alert for the sight of birds and fish, scanning the horizon for the sight of land or for signs of breakers (and their dangerous reefs).

In all this, the Portuguese led the way in the sixteenth century, followed by the Dutch in the seventeenth. Thereafter, French charts were unrivalled until the British naval dominance of the eighteenth century. Both the French and British used government-backed departments to perfect their charts and hydrography – to promote national interests, but greatly helped by the careful charting of coastal waters by both commercial and naval interests. Everywhere, however, trial and error played a part.*

The geography of Atlantic slavery was immense and it too generated a rich literature and cartography in all major European languages and seafarers learned about that ocean and its coastlines in literary and cartographic sources. Moreover, this world of printed knowledge was endlessly changing and being added to: improved by the latest news (and by regular maritime disasters). By the mid-eighteenth century, all involved in the slave economy had developed a practical understanding of navigating and transporting boats loaded with Africans. Merchants on the quaysides could point out the obvious risks to their ships' masters: which African coastal locations to avoid or to be aware of, which seasons to avoid, when to depart, and when and where to arrive. But no amount of literature could ever guarantee trouble-free success, and all voyages relied ultimately on the experience, or failings, of the master and his crew – and on luck. Time and again, experienced seamanship proved to be of no avail in the teeth of African insurgency, errors of navigation, planning and management – or the twists and turns of the weather. The crews arriving in Europe or the Americas after a prolonged slave voyage had much to give thanks for. The Africans who survived to landfall in the Americas had nothing to be grateful for, save perhaps for their escape from the seaborne nightmare that was the belly of a slave ship.

* J. H. Parry, *Trade and Dominion*, London, 1974, pp.307–313; J. H. Parry, *The Sea*, London, 1974.

Good, or bad, seamanship in the Atlantic had serious consequences for the African captives. The faster and safer the voyage, the better the outcome for the enslaved. On slower and more protracted voyages, shipboard conditions deteriorated, supplies ran short and levels of sickness and death rose. No matter how experienced a ship's master, however conscious he and the crew were of maintaining the physical well-being of the Africans (if only to make a profit when they were sold), they were always and everywhere at the mercy of the weather. They could simply pray for good weather and good fortune.

***

In the South Atlantic the trade, which accounted for almost half of the entire slave trade, was dominated by Portugal and Brazil, with many ships originating from Brazil. North of the equator, the trade was under the control of northern Europeans, who were joined, after 1730, by a growing number of slave traders from North America. This northern sphere of the Atlantic slave trade came to be dominated by the British, most notably in the form of the rapidly expanding city of Liverpool. By 1650, British ships had carried thirty-six thousand Africans across the Atlantic, but in the next century they transported more than 1.3 million. In the following seventy-five years, British ships carried a further one and three quarter million Africans. These staggering figures reflect the importance of the Atlantic slave trade to Britain's imperial and domestic economy. They also bear witness to the critical role played by slavery in the shaping of Britain's American empire.

The massive upsurge in slave trading in the eighteenth century was mainly to the Caribbean and Brazil. Dutch ships continued to be active in the trade which they had effectively entered from the mid-seventeenth century, and growing numbers of merchants from North America joined in. North American ships transported more than three hundred thousand Africans, while France shipped 1.3 million and Great Britain 3.25 million. But far and away the largest number of Africans – almost six million – were carried by Portuguese and Brazilian ships. These thousands of voyages, from all points of the Atlantic compass, scattered millions of Africans across the face of the newly settled Americas.

***

Throughout the entire history of the Atlantic slave trade, it lay at the heart of, and was often a fundamental element of, major global conflicts and warfare. European imperial rivalries generated military conflicts in all parts of the globe: in Europe itself of course, on the coast of West Africa (where the slave forts were both symbol of those rivalries and a lasting monument to the importance of the slave trade), in North and South America, the Caribbean, in India and the Indian Ocean. Europeans fought each other for imperial possessions, for valuable trading locations and for control of the maritime lanes that were the vital arteries of both military and commercial success. These conflicts determined which nations came to exercise dominance over particular stretches of the African coast. West Central Africa fell to the Portuguese, the British were dominant on the Bight of Biafra, and the French north of the Congo River. After 1807, when northern Europeans began to turn their back on the slave trade, the trade in enslaved Africans reverted to the nations which had pioneered it initially. Spanish and Portuguese merchants, based in Cuba and Brazil, developed yet another massive branch of this oceanic trade. Under abolitionist pressures, however (from British and US navies and from British diplomacy), they often used a variety of other nations' flags to circumvent international agreements – and the presence of the US and Royal Naval abolition patrols. Despite these obstacles, Spanish vessels transported three quarters of a million Africans (mainly to Cuba) and Portuguese/Brazilian ships almost two and a half million.*

These astounding numbers from the last phase of Atlantic slave trading leave us with some puzzling questions. Slavery thrived in Brazil and Cuba and continued to require fresh infusions of enslaved Africans, *at the very same time* the Western world was rapidly turning to abolition. Campaigns against the slave trade sparked outrage on both sides of the Atlantic just when slave ships carried more than three million Africans into American bondage.

***

The Atlantic slave trade linked all corners of the Atlantic world. Ships left for Africa from no fewer than 188 ports, though the great bulk came from only twenty ports. Six of the most important were in the Americas – the other fourteen were European. Ships from Rio carried 1.5 million Africans, while another 1.3 million travelled in vessels from Salvador. By far the largest European carrier was Liverpool, whose ships transported 1.3 million, rivalled only by London-based vessels with more than

* David Eltis and David Richardson, *Atlas*, Table 3, p.39.

eight hundred thousand Africans.* What underpinned these stark figures was a truly global economic enterprise: a complexity of investments, shipbuilding and outfitting, of insurance, labour, and an even more remarkable global cargo-system which focused on multiple locations in Africa. Most ships took Africans to their own nation's colonies with the exception of Spain which had contracted its slave trade to other carriers, via *Asiento* agreements.

The Portuguese–Brazilian axis was created, initially, by the expansion of the Brazilian sugar industry. Similarly, what propelled Britain's later rise to dominance in the North Atlantic was the emergence of sugar, and the insatiable demand of the Caribbean planters for ever-more Africans. There was, in addition, the thriving labour needs of the slave-based tobacco and rice industries in North American colonies. The British, however, shipped Africans not only to all their own colonies but also transhipped many onwards to other nations' colonies. France, Britain's greatest rival in the imperial contests of the eighteenth century (a rivalry not fully settled until the defeat of Napoleon in 1815) was also a prodigious slave trader. Between 1700 and 1791 (when the St. Domingue slave rebellion destroyed France's slave empire), French ships carried more than 1.3 million Africans to French colonies.†

So great was the demand for enslaved Africans, and so keen were investors to satisfy that demand, that new commercial groups emerged and flourished in a range of port cities on both

* David Eltis and David Richardson, *Atlas*, Table 3, p.39.

† David Richardson, 'Involuntary Migrations in the Early Modern World, 1500–1899', in D. Eltis, et al. *The Cambridge World History of Slavery*, vol. 3, Ch.22, Table 2.3.

sides of the Atlantic. Merchants pieced together networks of investors to organise, equip and man the slave ships, to buy and select suitable cargoes, and to organise the precise manner of trading on the African coast. The entire process was of course driven by the lure of successful commerce and profit. From one slave port to the next – some massive, others quite small – local merchants and investors developed their own links to Africa and the Americas. European slave traders tapped into existing financial and commercial systems in the port cities – notably Amsterdam and London – both to raise finance and to draw on existing trade for the cargoes destined for Africa. As the trade expanded, more ports emerged as major players in the Atlantic trade. Amsterdam, London and La Rochelle led the way, but they were soon joined by Middleburg, Nantes, Bordeaux, Bristol, Lancaster and Liverpool. The Portuguese trade from Lisbon was similarly paralleled by the rise of Brazilian ports. Brazilian involvement in the slave trade was also helped by the availability of goods from India which had landed first in Brazil, then were shipped onwards to Africa.* From the first, Asia was to play an important role in the Atlantic slave trade.

Wherever the slave trade took hold, it brought together new groups of merchants and investors who brought fresh ideas, energy and contacts to add to the local trade. This remarkable commercial story was not simply one of unfettered commercial enterprise – it was buttressed and directed by state involvement. It was clear from its early days that the slave trade was vital to the wider well-being of each slaving nation, and the state took an active interest both in its slaving fleets and their trading locations. Spain had heralded this interest via its *Asiento*

* David Eltis and David Richardson, *Atlas*, p.38.

agreements. Similarly, from the late seventeenth to early eighteenth centuries, monopoly trading companies were state-managed concerns promoting national slave trading. Of the first investors in the English Royal Adventurers (1660) one half were Peers or Royals. Even in its later, revised format, the Royal African Company (1672) had heavy royal, aristocratic and ministerial investment. Some of the Africans shipped by the Company were branded with the letters DY – Duke of York, the Company governor and subsequently James II.* Jean-Baptiste Colbert, the French Minister of Finance, initiated the French equivalent. But monopoly slave-trading companies proved incapable of providing Africans in the huge numbers required by the plantation economies, and independent traders demanded a more open trade, and a break with monopolies. There were quite simply many hundreds of people in Europe waiting to take over; people keen and able to sink their cash and experience into the business of buying enslaved Africans. By the early eighteenth century, whatever moral doubts people had about slavery were simply swept away by the prospects of lavish money-making.

Even when the slave trade was thrown open to competition, the state remained on hand with diplomatic and military support for the entire system. European navies provided essential protection for the Atlantic slaving system, guaranteeing security for their nation's vessels off-shore from Africa, in the Atlantic and the Americas. Naval power was vital, especially in the prolonged periods of European warfare in the eighteenth century, when

* For the Royal African Company, see William Pettigrew, *Freedom's Debt: The Royal African Company and the Politics of the Atlantic Slave Trade, 1672–1752*, Chapel Hill, 2013.

Britain and France were the main competitors for colonial assets and expansion. British Caribbean planters realised the importance of the Royal Navy in the region as a bulwark against French threats to supplies, and indeed for the very security of the islands themselves. Equally, navies were important as a means of crushing slave rebellion, by moving men and equipment between and around the islands. In 1760, the massive slave rebellion in Jamaica ('Tacky's Revolt') was only crushed by the ability of the Royal Navy to move men and equipment to endangered spots around the island. Contemporaries realised that slaves were terrified by the power of the Royal Navy:

> The Men of War . . . gives Them an Idea of the Strengh & Power of the English Nation & Strikes an awe & Terror into Them.*

The state's military power was an indispensable element in the continuing success of Atlantic slavery. (Nelson is perhaps the most famous naval officer to have learned much of his seamanship in Caribbean waters.) In 1776, British West Indian planters were dissuaded from joining their North America counterparts in breaking away from Britain by the knowledge that they needed British military muscle in the face of the persistent dangers posed by their disaffected slaves – and the French.† Tacky had come close to succeeding only sixteen years earlier.

* Vincent Brown, *Tacky's Revolt: The Story of an Atlantic Slave War*, Cambridge, MA, 2020, p.63.

† Andrew O'Shaughnessy, *An Empire Divided: The American Revolution and the British Caribbean*, Philadelphia, 2000.

From the first, then, slave trading in the Atlantic was closely tied to the military power and to the strategic interests of European states. Europe's various maritime states, their colonies in the Americas and the independent nations that emerged from those colonies, were acutely aware of the necessity of state power to sustain and advance Atlantic slavery – and to keep it in check. If we need a reminder of that intimidating power, simply travel through the Caribbean islands today, and visit the remains of European fortifications guarding harbour entrances or dominating the local topography. From the harbour of Havana, south through the islands to the signalling hill in Barbados, forts, castles, gun positions, naval dockyards, ammunition stores, barracks and more are surviving reminders of the need to keep enemies out and Africans in check. For all the vitality, innovation and enterprise of the commercial interests involved, they were dependent on state support and power. Indeed, it was only when that state power began to weaken, and was finally withdrawn, that the slave empires began to crumble.

Part Two

PEOPLE AND CARGOES

5

Bound for Africa: Cargoes

European merchants, their associates, backers, and ships' captains developed a crucial knowledge of what was required for successful trading for enslaved Africans on the African coast. They learned which areas yielded the best returns, which traders were the best to deal with and which commodities were most suitable for bartering for enslaved Africans. Though this trade changed a great deal over the years – shifting locations, developing new networks – the pattern remained similar across the centuries. The ships arriving at their chosen trading spot were filled with goods thought best suited to trade at that location. Their cargoes were critical to the entire voyage and they were put together to catch the eye of African traders.

Ships' owners were meticulous in assembling the right mix of goods. African traders were very choosy about what they wanted, and above all, they expected textiles, metal goods and cowrie shells – often mixed with supplies of tobacco and alcohol. Scrutinising those outbound cargoes to West Africa reveals not only the personal and commercial needs of African traders, but exposes the global nature of the Atlantic slave trade itself. Although the ships arrived off the African coast loaded with a great variety of goods for sale and barter, from the early days of the Portuguese trade, textiles were a major commodity. Moreover, the most striking of all those textiles came from India.

When the Portuguese settled the Malabar coast of India after 1498, they encountered a world of Indian textiles of a range quite unlike anything Europe was able to produce. The variety of those materials – from the roughest and crudest, to the finest, in colour and design, and in astonishing volumes – presented a golden opportunity to Portuguese traders. Huge volumes of Indian textiles soon began to flow back to Portugal – yielding handsome profits for the traders – and establishing a widespread popular taste for Indian materials across Portugal (and beyond).

Portugal's development of the sea route to India (and to Asia) quickly became a vital and lucrative trading system linking India to Europe. En route to the Cape of Good Hope, and on to India, it was inevitable that Portugal also developed trade along the west coast of Africa. In the process, the Portuguese realised that Indian goods which appealed to Portuguese consumers were equally attractive to African traders. Despite traditional African textile industries and fashions, the introduction of the colourful and multi-varied textiles from India proved just as irresistible to African consumers, as they were to the Portuguese. Thus it was, from the early encounters between European and African slave traders, that Indian textiles became part of the complex commercial web which saw imported manufactured goods exchanged, in West African markets, for enslaved Africans destined for distant locations. Indian goods became vital for the purchase of Africans destined for the Americas.*

***

* Maria João Ferreira, 'Asian textiles in the *Carreira da India*: Portugal Trade Consumption and Taste, 1500–1700', *Textile History*, 46, No. 2, 2015.

From the first, people who traded for Africans tended to be groups of merchants, often familiar with each other via earlier business ventures or family ties, who pooled resources to finance a voyage. It was a pattern of shared investment and risk that was to characterise the Atlantic trade throughout its history and was common from one country to another. Personal, commercial and political networks were critical to the entire enterprise.

In 1612, for example, Manuel Bautista Pérez, a Portuguese merchant and ship's master, embarked on a trading voyage to West Africa. He was backed by a group of relatives and friends, investors and partners who formed a network 'that stretched from the Iberian Peninsula, West Africa, India and America.' He had important contacts in Lisbon and Seville and a brother was based in West Africa (in what is today's Guinea Bissau). Pérez planned to acquire a cargo of Africans which he would then ship across the Atlantic and deliver to Cartagena, remitting the profits to Seville.* To do so, however, required formal government approval with *Asientos*, specifying in great detail how he could operate. The licences signify an astonishingly intrusive state bureaucracy – but provide the most revealing insight into the nature of the Iberian slave trade in its early years.

Pérez's ships – all of them tiny for such epic voyages – carried very mixed cargoes. The bulk of the outbound cargo consisted of different kinds of textiles and though they included cloth from North Africa and from Rouen, fully one half of the textiles

* Linda A. Newson and Susie A. Michin, *From Capture to Sale: The Portuguese Slave Trade to Spanish South America in the Early Seventeenth Century*, Leiden, 2007.

were Indian. There were cheap cotton and linen fabrics from Gujarat, alongside more expensive Indian cottons and silks. In fact, by 1612 Portugal had well-established trading bases in India, notably in Goa, and a range of Indian commodities – precious stones, spices and furniture – were regularly shipped back to Portugal and to Brazil, and Indian textiles had established themselves as a major item in the African slave trade.

Indian textiles were, by then, just one feature of Portugal's remarkable global trading presence. Portugal was actively shipping goods – and people – along protracted maritime trade routes from one corner of the globe to another. This early Portuguese trade also saw the movement of large numbers of Africans to Portugal itself. In the words of Theodore Rabb, Lisbon was 'the most globally connected and multicultural city on earth.' Portuguese ships traded in ports from Japan to Brazil, and anchored off the coast of West Africa.* Portugal now had a thriving commercial interest in both African slaves and gold, and its adventurous fleets looked far beyond West Africa. They sailed south, round the Cape and thence into the tempting commercial and strategic waters and locations of the Indian Ocean and beyond. African gold, and African slaves, were important factors in enabling Portugal to look eastward to the riches of India and China – and even to Japan. One result was that, by the early sixteenth century, Lisbon had become a city awash with the commodities, people and animals of Africa and Asia. Prosperous homes boasted artefacts from Africa, Ceylon, India and China: African spoons, Chinese porcelain, Ceylonese carvings. Moreover, there were more Africans (mostly enslaved)

* Theodore K. Rabb, 'Elephants on the Rua Nova', *TLS,* 12 February 2016.

on the streets of Lisbon than any comparable area outside Africa.

It is no surprise that other Europeans soon followed in the global wake of the Portuguese, shipping goods and people from one corner of the world to another.

Portuguese vessels heading home from India were usually prevented, by navigational reasons, from stopping in West Africa. Most European ships sailing home from the Indian Ocean headed round the southern tip of Africa, then north-west towards Brazil – before shifting north-east to Europe. The Indian textiles destined for West Africa had thus been shipped enormous distances: across the Indian Ocean, across the South Atlantic, before eventually sailing north-east back to Portugal. And there they were transhipped for yet another oceanic voyage: loaded into the hold of a vessel destined for the slaving locations of West Africa. The textiles of Gujarat had travelled an astonishing 12,000 miles to reach the slave market of Africa.

Of course, this was not the first time goods had been transported enormous distances, from one continent to another. The ancient silk roads had seen a wide range of items traded across thousands of miles between Europe, Central Asia and beyond. Any number of major empires – Rome, Viking, Moghul and others – spawned trade and human migrations along protracted tentacles of empire, war and peaceful commerce. There had, however, been nothing quite like the geographic reach of the trade and commerce that emerged in the wake of Western Europe's sailing and navigational break-out to the wider world, from the fifteenth century onwards. In a relatively short period, many people from around the habited globe had been brought into contact with each other via European trading ships. China and Japan, each with their own history of long-distance trade routes, were now linked to Manila, thence via Spanish ships onwards to Acapulco. From there, they connected to the economies of Central and South America. And it was here, in the Americas, that the entire story was utterly transformed by the arrival of African slaves, many of them purchased by the exchange of commodities from Asia. These were the self-same goods carried on board Pérez's ships casting off from Lisbon after 1612.

***

The northern Europeans were swift to follow the pioneering trail of Spain and Portugal. The Dutch soon developed their own trading system that linked Japan, Indonesia and Brazil. They too devised elaborate means of raising slaving investments, centred increasingly on Amsterdam, but embracing large numbers of backers and merchants who were experienced in older trade (to the Baltic and southern Europe, for example).* By the late eighteenth century when the British had come to dominate the North Atlantic slave trade, a similar pattern was at work. Groups of backers and financiers invested in slave voyages, some from London, the centre of British finance, others from the port cities themselves and their immediate environs. Ships from Liverpool (the major slave port of the period) were funded by a remarkably wide range of local and regional backers: merchants, traders already active in the Africa trade, local shopkeepers and artisans (a barber, cooper,

* Catia Antunes and Filipa Ribeiro da Silva, 'Amsterdam merchants in the slave trade and African commerce, 1580s-1670s', *tijdschrift voor sociale en economische geschiedenis*, 9 [2012] nr. 4, pp.3–30.

carpenter, grocer and innkeeper – even a cleric). Wherever we turn, the financial investment in slave ships reveals a widespread and complex system which lured people of all sorts and conditions, from a range of locations, to invest in a slave voyage. Europeans (later Brazilians and North Americans) of the most diverse backgrounds, faiths and persuasions, saw the slave trade as an attractive and unquestioned world for investment. Slavery was sustained by legions of people, from all corners of European and American societies.

One key factor which underpinned these various slave ship partnerships – and which helped their commercial success – was the obvious level of *trust* which developed between the people involved. This was true throughout the history of the slave trade. Existing business dealings, family ties, tried and tested friendships – all were important ingredients in bringing people together in the risky and dangerous world of slave trading. No less important – as we shall see – was the trust which investors placed in the master of the ship heading out to Africa and the Americas.

***

Though the cargoes dispatched to Africa by different European slave traders varied, textiles were highly valued universally on the slaving coast, and remained a core European export for centuries. Some places, however, demanded more jewellery, others more metalware, but whatever the specific nature of local African demand, it was for goods that had been brought together on the slave ships from distant locations. Dutch, English and French cargoes were, like the Portuguese before them, mixed: gathered from a slave port's economic hinterland, from other parts of Europe and from the far reaches of that nation's trade or empire. From India and China, from islands in the Indian Ocean and, in time, even from the Americas. The world of Atlantic slavery quickly became an integral element in the wider global commerce of all of Europe's major powers. Which meant, in time, that slavery became a major factor in the global strategies and decisions of Europe's global affairs. What happened in India had consequences for slaves in the Americas, and, conversely, what happened in the slave colonies had ramifications at the far edges of European imperial and commercial networks.

***

India was later to become imperial Britain's centrepiece, at the heart of its status and self-image, but at first its dealings were led by a simple trading company – the East India Company. The rising power exercised by that company on the Indian subcontinent from the mid-eighteenth century opened up the riches of the subcontinent, notably of Bengal, alongside the huge range of Indian textiles. Here was an ancient industry which yielded all sorts and conditions of materials, from the most costly and luxurious, through to the cheapest of calicoes. Moreover, all was available in an unrivalled range of designs and colours, and all unavailable elsewhere in such abundance and at such prices. Like the Portuguese before them, the British opened up the markets of West Africa to Indian textiles. Slave traders effectively swamped West Africa with Indian goods, to the extent that European textile entrepreneurs, keen to break into the lucrative African market, went out of their way to *copy* Indian styles and colours. They even gave names to their products that made them appear to be Indian. Indian textile names became part of the English language. In the words of William Dalrymple:

> Not for nothing are so many English words connected with weaving – chintz, calico, shawls, pyjamas, khaki, dungarees, cummerbund, taffeta – of Indian origin.*

British ships left their home ports packed with Indian textiles. When the ship *Ann* sailed from Liverpool to Sierra Leone in 1779, she carried Indian goods valued (in pounds, shillings and pence) at £875/2/0. The Manchester textiles on board were much less valuable at £517/2/1.† These Indian textiles had *already* travelled from India to Liverpool, whereas the Manchester textiles stored below (doing their best to appear Indian) had travelled a mere thirty miles to the Liverpool quayside. Here was a trade, in search of enslaved Africans, which straddled not only the nations and economies of the Atlantic world but was sustained by tentacles of trade stretching across the Indian Ocean. When we look closer, other – even more surprising – tentacles of global trade become apparent.

Europe's colonial settlements and trade routes brought the commodities of India and Asia to the marketplaces of Europe, West Africa and the Americas. In time, American commodities (notably tobacco and rum – both cultivated by slaves) also

* William Dalrymple, *The Anarchy: The Relentless Rise of the East India Company*, 2020 edn, p.14.

† 'Voyage of the Ship *Ann*, 1779', William Davenport and Co., Liverpool Account book relating to ships' voyages to Africa and the West Indies, 1777–1784. Huntington Library mss HM 82854. I am grateful to John Styles for bringing this to my attention.

joined the list of cargoes destined for the African slave coast. Goods from India and Asia, from the Americas and from Europe, jostled for space in the holds of ships destined for Africa, and ultimately for the attention of African slave traders who offered enslaved people in return. Ships arriving off the African coast disgorged French wines and textiles, Swedish metalware, Lancastrian and Yorkshire textiles, firearms from Sheffield and Birmingham, tobacco from the Chesapeake Bay and Brazil, and rum from the Caribbean slave islands.

Ships converged on the slave coast not only from Europe. They arrived from North and South America and from the Caribbean islands. Rhode Island, for example, dispatched a relatively small number of slave ships to Africa despite having no substantial resources to trade in an export market. What Rhode Island had in abundance, however, was rum. Local ports teemed with distilleries – converting molasses imported from the Caribbean into rum, for onward sale and export, mainly to other parts of North America. But rum was also exported, on the slave ships, to West Africa. In return for their cargoes of rum, vessels from Newport and Providence acquired enslaved Africans (some 131,000 in all) mainly on the Gold Coast, at Anomabu and Cape Coast.* This was, again, not without irony because the rum was derived from sugar cane, cultivated and processed by slaves in the Caribbean. What was described as 'the rum trade' – the direct trade between the Caribbean and West Africa – had been a striking feature of trade under the Royal African Company from the late seventeenth century. Rum from Barbados, Antigua and Jamaica was shipped to Africa in part exchange for enslaved Africans. By the first years

* David Eltis and David Richardson, *Atlas,* Map 42, p.21.

of the eighteenth century, this direct trade between the Caribbean and West Africa was thought to be one of the most profitable of that company's endeavour.* This was, however, relatively small scale compared to the trade that developed between Brazil and Mina in West Africa.

The expansion of Brazilian slavery created a flourishing trade in tobacco, between Bahia and Mina. Because of its distinctive climate and soil, the tobacco region of Bahia produced three harvests annually. The first went to European markets; the second crop of inferior tobacco was unpopular in the European market – but was eagerly bought on the Mina coast. Brazilian tobacco planters gave their Africa-bound tobacco a special flavour by soaking it in molasses. Here, then, were *two* slave-grown commodities – tobacco and molasses – shipped to West Africa as the major exchange commodity for enslaved Africans.

As slavery in Bahia expanded, so too did the export of Brazilian tobacco to Africa. Some 160,000 pounds were shipped to Mina in c. 1700: by the 1720s that had grown to two million pounds, reaching four million by mid-century. At much the same time, more than six million pounds were shipped to Lisbon (70 per cent of which was re-exported to other parts of Europe). Mina was not the only African market for Brazilian tobacco: it was also transported to Angola, São Tomé, Principe and Benguela, in present-day Angola, though only one third of the volume of Mina's imports went to those places. Even more extensive, however, was the trade in Brazilian tobacco to Asia. That tobacco was different again from the Africa-bound variety (it was cured differently) and was shipped to Goa, Macao and

* Joseph E. Inikori, *Africans and the Industrial Revolution in England*, Cambridge, 2002, pp.229–230.

Timor. The Chinese much preferred tobacco from Brazil, but it also won over the native Indian peoples of the eastern North American colonies. It was yet another quirk of the system, that those Indian peoples preferred Brazilian tobacco (bought initially from French traders who had acquired it in Lisbon) to tobacco cultivated by slaves in the Chesapeake region. Slaves working in Bahia's tobacco fields cultivated a commodity which became a major item of trade from the North American frontier, in Europe, West and Central Africa, and onwards to Asia. Laced with slave-produced molasses, Bahia's slave-grown tobacco helped to underpin the vital slave trade from the Mina coast of Africa to Brazil.*

Slave-grown Brazilian tobacco criss-crossed the world's major oceans and was enjoyed by people in the Americas, Europe, Africa and Asia. African consumers had acquired the habit of smoking Brazilian tobacco via a complex trading system which spanned the South Atlantic, and which enabled Brazilian merchants to pack their ships with still more Africans heading for slavery in Brazil.

The Atlantic trade was, then, anything but triangular. It was, in effect, a global trade which had its focus on the Atlantic coast of Africa, but which was made possible by the ability of the seaborne visitors to gather commodities from all corners of their increasingly expansive global trading empires. Trade and empire not only enriched the imperial motherlands, but they provided the necessary means for acquiring enslaved Africans.

***

* Jordan Goodman, *Tobacco in History: The Cultures of Dependence*, London, 1993, pp.163–165.

Manufactured goods played a major role in the British trade to West Africa in the era of the slave trade, but as early as 1650, some 85 per cent of all those exports to West Africa consisted of items manufactured *outside* of Britain. Even in the early years of the nineteenth century, the figure stood at 41 per cent.* These were goods imported into Britain before being transhipped to West Africa. Paramount among all those goods were textiles, as we have seen. In the course of the seventeenth and eighteenth centuries, something like one half of *all* the goods shipped to West Africa consisted of textile goods. Ships naturally carried textiles from their home industries (British ships carried items from Lancashire, Yorkshire, Scotland and Ireland while other nations' ships carried their own nation's textiles). All of them also carried textiles from other parts of Europe as well as from the far reaches of Europe's trading systems. As early as 1526, the Portuguese ship *Santiago* sailed for Sierra Leone (leaving with 125 enslaved Africans) carrying various Portuguese textiles: 1,600 lengths of yellow cloth, 357 of material for handkerchiefs and hemp for making sacks. Between 1613 and 1618, Portuguese vessels landed the following textiles on the Upper Guinea coast: linen from Holland, Indian cotton which had been dyed in Holland, serge from Flanders and England, woollen cloth from Spain and Rouen. Other textiles came from Gambia, calico from Gujarat, handkerchiefs and scarves made in Bengal and Surat, silk from Persia, cotton cloth from Sindh, woollen cloth from North Africa, and shawls from Southern India.†

* Joseph E. Inikori, *Africans and the Industrial Revolution*, Appendix 9.2, p.512.

† Linda A. Newson and Susie A. Michin. *From Capture to Sale: The Portuguese Slave Trade to Spanish South America*, Appendix A.

When British textile manufacturers learned of the African demand for cheap Asian cotton materials, they began to manufacture their own varieties to compete. Indeed, throughout the entire history of British involvement in the slave trade, the nation's textile manufacturers imitated Indian materials – copying their designs and patterns – to tap into the African demand for Indian materials and fashions. Textiles from widely dispersed Indian societies were shipped to Europe to be reprocessed, dyed, printed – and copied – before being shipped onwards to West Africa for the purchase of enslaved Africans. This was an important trade for the East India Company, and by the end of the eighteenth century, one quarter of *all* Indian textiles imported into London was re-exported to Africa. The world of trade (and conquest) in the Atlantic was clearly intimately linked to its counterpart in the Indian Ocean. In addition there was a major export textile trade to the Caribbean and North America, much of it for use on the slave plantations. This trade in Indian textiles helped to clothe the peoples of West Africa and the enslaved Africans on plantations in the Caribbean and North America.

***

For all the dominance of textiles, the merchants and captains of slave ships had to remain alert to the changing whims and tastes of the African traders in the regions they sailed to. Goods which were highly valued in one place, might be worthless elsewhere. Though a great variety of goods were used in exchange for slaves (at Elmina in 1618, no fewer than 218 items were traded for slaves) certain goods were in great demand at particular locations. In 1721, a British naval surgeon noted that 'Iron bars which are not asked for to the leeward are a substantial part of the windward cargoes.' Some goods, however, were welcome everywhere. 'Arms, gunpowder, tallow, old sheets, cottons [Indian] and English spirits are everywhere called for.'* At one location, a slave might be had for a single item of exchange, or for a number of goods: a specific amount of whisky or a certain number of cowrie shells, a number of guns, particular lengths of material, or a fixed quantity of iron bars. Yet from this great welter of goods used to acquire enslaved Africans, textiles stood out as *the* most popular.

There was of course an ancient tradition of African textile manufacture. From one location to another along the coast, colourful and varied African cloths were popular among local people. Long before the arrival of the European ships, spinning, weaving and dyeing were well-established African skills and some African textiles were bought and traded by Europeans. Often too, Africans dyed and refined the textiles bought from Europeans. But the slave traders were able to offer a much greater variety of textiles – and in greater volumes – because of their access to Indian textiles.

As the European interest in slaving gathered momentum in the course of the seventeenth century, an enormous range of textiles flowed into West Africa. African traders were offered textiles from northern Europe: English woollens were in demand as blankets and for clothing against the cold winds in the Gulf of Guinea; so too were the sturdy cloths manufactured in northern France (using wool from Spain, Scotland and Germany). When the Royal African Company's ship *Mary* sailed for Africa in 1684, though her cargo included firearms,

* Hugh Thomas, *The Slave Trade*, pp.315–318.

iron bars, manilas, beads and spirits, brassware, tallow and blankets, almost 80 per cent of the total cargo consisted of textiles.*

These apparently arcane details of ships' cargoes reveal a story of enormous geographic and economic complexity. Myriad African societies absorbed goods from locations which were far beyond their immediate trading reach. It also had a damaging impact on Africa. The manufactured goods shipped to West Africa retarded local economic development for centuries. The seaborne slave traders only wanted African *people*, not African goods (with the obvious exception of gold) and their demand for enslaved people, rather than goods, held back the growth of the regions involved. It is just one example of the way West African history was transformed by the impact of the external demand for slaves.

***

Cowrie shells

The most beautiful of cowrie shells are widely used today as decorative items, to adorn the hair, worn as necklaces and bracelets or incorporated into clothing. Commercial companies specialise in selling them, especially to African-American consumers, for personal decoration and as an unmistakeable assertion of African-American identity. Yet these shells have a

* Joseph E. Inikori, 'Transatlantic Slavery and Economic Development in the Atlantic World: West Africa, 1450–1850', *The Cambridge World History of Slavery, vol. 3*, David Eltis et al., eds., pp.650–674.

much more complex history than mere items of decoration. In 1693, Captain John Phillips on board the slave ship *Hannibal*, wrote that:

> The best goods to purchase slaves here are cowries, the smaller the more esteemed: for they pay them all by tale [account], the smaller being as valuable as the biggest.*

Cowrie shells had an ancient history as currency in any number of societies. Indeed it has been claimed that the cowrie shell was 'the most widely used primitive currency in world history.'† They had been used as currency in India at least from the tenth century and there is evidence they were in use in Africa from the eleventh century. Commonplace in Niger in the medieval period, by the thirteenth century they had spread via the marketing system into the empire of Mali, and by the sixteenth century cowries were in use in Timbuktu, on the Gold Coast, in Arda and Benin. Cowrie shells were, then, part of West Africa's market economy long before the seaborne arrival of Europeans, and well before the Europeans incorporated the cowrie shell into their own global trading system. They were used as loose change, and as currency for paying tolls and taxes, for bribing officials and to calculate measurements of commercial and financial value (especially of slaves).‡ The burial sites of Chinese rulers contained hordes of cowries, buried alongside jade and other precious items. They were also imported, at least

* Quoted in Simon Gikandi, *Slavery and the Culture of Taste*, Princeton, 2011, p.80.

† Mary Ellen Snodgrass, *Coins and Currency: An Historical Encyclopaedia*, London 2003, p.122.

‡ Toby Green, *Fistful of Shells*, pp.166–169.

from the thirteenth century, on dhows trading from the Maldive Islands to East Africa, and they appeared on the trans-Saharan trade routes.

The use of cowries was totally transformed, however, from the sixteenth century onwards by their adoption by seaborne European traders. These beautiful shells were an ideal currency: they were easily carried on the person, could be readily moved in bulk, and they could not be copied. They were quickly established as an important feature of the Atlantic slave trade and form an extraordinary example of slavery's global reach and importance.

The geography of this story is one of the most astonishing features of Atlantic slavery. To reach West Africa, cowrie shells travelled many thousands of miles: first from the Maldives, to India, thence as ballast on ships rounding the Cape of Good Hope, bound for Brazil, Europe and West Africa. As early as 1520, cowrie shells were being used on São Tomé to buy Africans who were then shipped to Elmina.

By the late seventeenth century, the shells had become a standard item in European trade in West Africa. Jean Barbot, who worked for the French African Company between 1675 and 1681, noted on his second voyage to West Africa that the French transported 'Cawries . . . or shells . . . by the French called Bouges.'* The English trade was equally committed to cowries, and as early as 1680 the Royal African Company was shipping huge quantities of shells from London to its agents at their commercial centres in the Gold Coast castles (European trading posts and defensive positions). The *Mary* carried fifty

* Elizabeth Donnan, *Documents Illustrative of the Slave Trade to America*, 4 vols, Washington, 1930–35, I, 282.

barrels of cowries in August that year.* Ten years later the *Arminian Merchant* loaded forty-six barrels of cowries, weighing more than 97 hundredweight.† By then, all the major north European slave-trading powers – British, French and Dutch – loaded large volumes of cowries onto vessels bound from their home ports to West Africa. Though the Europeans had not introduced the shells to West Africa, as with so many other features of their trading presence, they totally transformed the scale, significance – and consequences – of their use, much as their voracious appetite for enslaved Africans transformed trade and society across vast reaches of Africa.‡

Europeans trading in the Indian Ocean quickly appreciated the shells' great virtue as a means of international exchange. Though the English were relative latecomers to the cowrie trade, they became great users of the shells in their trading economy. The *Norman* departed from London in January 1714, bound for Sherbo on the African coast, carrying what had become a typical Africa-bound cargo. Alongside its arms and provisions for the officials of the Royal African Company, she freighted an array of items from Britain, Europe – and the far corners of the world: textiles from India, tobacco from North America, sugar from the Caribbean – alongside fourteen barrels packed with more than twenty-eight hundredweight of cowrie shells.§

By then, the cowrie shell was firmly embedded as a key item in the complex transactions of securing enslaved Africans. Slave

* Elizabeth Donnan, *Documents*, I, 262.

† Elizabeth Donnan, *Documents*, I, 371.

‡ Joseph E. Inikori, 'Transatlantic Slavery and Economic Development: West Africa, 1450–1850', *The Cambridge World History of Slavery*, vol. 3, David Eltis et al., eds., pp.657–658.

§ Elizabeth Donnan, *Documents*, II, 181.

traders assembled what they called a 'parcel' of goods to trade for Africans: an assembly of metalware (guns especially), tobacco, alcohol and textiles – along with varying volumes of cowrie shells. Cowries were even used as wages in some parts of Africa's slaving coast and were paid to Africans for particular tasks. At Whydah the local currency was calibrated by its equivalence in cowries.* Elsewhere, the cowrie shell itself became the favourite item of currency exchanged for Africans. At Arda (in present-day Benin) African traders offered to sell their slaves for prices that were calculated half in cowries, half in European goods.† Often too, cowries were used as a means of calculating the value of other imported items. In the words of Jean Barbot:

> The proportion of trade is commonly adjusted by the two standards of iron bars and Cauries, for valuing of all other commodities.‡

In some places it was impossible to trade for slaves *without* offering cowries shells.

Cowrie shells had a long history as decorative items: to adorn clothing and hair, as jewellery on necklaces, bracelets and clothing; but by the early eighteenth century, this simple shell had become a much-valued element in a global trade which bound together the economies of the Indian Ocean, Africa, Europe and the Americas. In the process, astounding volumes of shells were shipped enormous distances. The Atlantic slaving system had transformed these shells into items with global power and

* Elizabeth Donnan, *Documents*, II, 531–533.

† Elizabeth Donnan, *Documents*, II, 531–533.

‡ Elizabeth Donnan, *Documents*, I, 292–295.

importance. Shells used to purchase Africans had travelled 16,000 miles: from the Maldives, to India, to Europe, thence to West Africa. Accumulated in mounds along the Maldives shoreline, they were packed – twelve thousand at a time – into large nets and barrels, loaded onto the trading ships destined for India – thence the wider world. The volumes involved were astonishing: historians calculate that ten *billion* shells were shipped to West Africa between 1700 and 1790 – mainly along the coast between Accra and present-day Nigeria.* And there they embedded themselves into a variety of local economies, seeping deep into an interior that was largely unknown to the Europeans trading on the coast.

Some shells inevitably crossed the Atlantic along with the enslaved Africans and their owners, becoming, in turn, a feature of the aesthetics of the enslaved people of the Americas. Today, it seems strange, at first glance, that an apparently insignificant seashell (found all over the tropical world, but at its most voluminous and accessible along the shore of islands in the Indian Ocean) should become so central a feature of the trade in African slaves. But as a form of currency, easily used for personal and large-scale commercial use, it became the ideal means of exchange in the massive global trading system that was slavery. The shells were, after a fashion, not unlike a bill of exchange – or a traveller's cheque – accepted throughout the international web of trade: recognised and used in India, Europe and Africa to acquire goods and people. How

* Marion Johnson, 'The Cowrie currency of West Africa. Part I', *The Journal of African History*, vol. 11, No. 1, 1970; Jan Hogendorn and Marion Johnson, 'A new money supply series for West Africa in the era of the slave trade: the import of cowrie shells from Europe', *Slavery and Abolition*, vol. 3, No. 2, September 1982.

strange it now seems, that the beautiful shells which sit on the bookshelf behind me as I write, take us right to the heart of Atlantic slavery.

***

Metalware

Not all goods shipped to West Africa were as innocent or harmless as textiles or cowrie shells. Ships bound for West Africa also carried great quantities of metal goods – notably weapons. Today, Ghana's major slave forts are ringed with a fearsome display of ancient heavy weaponry. Massive cannons greet the visitors at Cape Coast Castle, and both there and at Elmina, the lines of gun ports are manned by rows of eighteenth-century cannons. Most are corroded and decayed – thanks to centuries of saltwater damage from the Atlantic Ocean below. They are an instant reminder not only of the bellicose nature of the slave traders' presence in West Africa, but also of the role of Western weapons in the history of the slave trade. The metal industries of the West thrived on the demand from the slave ships and of the traders at work on the African coast.

The Atlantic slave system relied on Europe's metal industries for incalculable volumes of chains, iron bars, guns, and other metal export goods for the outbound slave ships. Even the massive expansion of the merchant fleet itself boosted the metal industries in Europe and the Americas. Though the sailing ships were wooden, they were held together by thousands of metal nails, screws and bolts, and all defended themselves with an array of heavy weaponry. Today, this provides rich evidence for marine archaeologists working on the wrecks of slave ships.* Slave ships departed from their home ports equipped with a fearsome array of metal weaponry, chains and fetters, vital for keeping imprisoned Africans in place. From the mid-eighteenth century onwards, after successful experiments by the Royal Navy, copper sheathing was widely adopted on sailing ships, to prevent the damage caused to their wooden hulls by the teredo worm in tropical waters. It was soon adopted by slave ships, needing some 15 tons of copper per ship. The prosperity of Britain's copper industries, in the West Country and North Wales, was closely linked to their proximity to the major slaving ports of Bristol and Liverpool.

Slave ships also carried enormous volumes of metal goods to Africa. The most striking items were simple bars of iron which were in great demand to be reworked by African craftsmen into a variety of implements for everyday usage. Ships also carried large numbers of copper items, mainly pans and kettles, to Africa. It was no accident that those copper and brass industries located close to major slaving ports thrived, feeding that trade's appetite for pans and kettles. Indeed, copper utensils came to be known as 'Guinea pans' and 'Guinea kettles.'

Of all the metal goods shipped to West Africa, the best remembered – and most sinister – were the metal restraints which came to symbolise slavery itself and which enabled the entire system to function. On a fully laden slave ship, Africans greatly outnumbered the crew and no slave ship could hope to survive, still less cross the Atlantic, without the physical means

* Jessica Glickman and Dave Conlin, 'The Maritime Archaeology of Slave Ships: Overview, Assessment and Prospectus', *The Digital Archaeological Record*, 2016.

of subduing and controlling the ranks of disaffected Africans. Every slave ship needed manacles, fetters and many yards of chains to keep the Africans in place. They also needed guns.

Slave ships also exported huge volumes of armaments. The Portuguese had initially banned the export of weapons to Africa, but that had changed by the mid-seventeenth century with the emergence of competition on the African coast from other European powers. The British iron industry (and its Swedish counterpart which exported iron to Britain) thrived on the demands from the slave ships. By the late eighteenth century almost one half of England's iron exports went to Africa – and much of that took the form of armaments – mainly from Birmingham. Birmingham's gun and cutlass industry, and the local metal and coal industries, developed a lucrative trade with West Africa.*

Not unlike the present-day version, the arms trade to Africa clearly benefitted the manufacturers but had enormously destabilising and damaging consequences for the importing regions of Africa. Though Islamic traders may have been the first to introduce firearms to East Africa, the European export of firearms to West Africa was of an entirely different order. Guns and gunpowder arrived first as items of barter with coastal traders and governing elites but subsequently spread via warfare and violence waged by predatory groups extending their fiefdoms. Often, too, they were in search of slaves, to pay for their imported weapons. Wherever they traded, Portuguese, Dutch, English and French slave traders supplied weapons. In Madagascar, by 1650, guns and powder had become a 'prime commodity' offered by Europeans for enslaved Africans. In places, guns constituted 30 per cent of the

* Joseph E. Inikori, *Africans and the Industrial Revolution*, pp.459–460.

trade, though overall it is estimated that perhaps only 10 per cent of the trade took the form of armaments. Such data, however, can deceive: it can also hide the profound consequences of the arms trade within Africa. The rise and fall of states and rulers, and social changes set in train by the resulting conflicts were often linked to this arms trade. Imported weapons brought prestige as well as power. The conflicts spawned by the arms trade also yielded enslaved victims. But since many of them had had military and combat experience, they proved a mixed blessing to a number of slave societies in the Americas. Tacky's Revolt in Jamaica in 1760 and the Male rebellion in Brazil in 1831 had their origins in such internal African conflicts.[*] Time and again, African heads and slave traders would present themselves to outsiders clutching firearms, often in the company of guards and military attendants who also sported imported weapons. It did not matter if the weapons functioned properly or were serviced adequately: the sight of men armed with Western guns bestowed a power and status, creating fear and respect among opponents and outsiders.[†]

Europe's growing trading presence on the coast enhanced the importance of firearms, and as long as the Atlantic slave trade continued, guns – in a great variety of forms – remained a substantial export to West Africa.[‡] African rulers came to recognise the value of the imported weaponry, even though

* Vincent Brown, *Tacky's Revolt*, Ch.5; João José Reis, 'Slavery in Nineteenth Century Brazil', vol. 4, *Cambridge World History of Slavery*, David Eltis et al., eds., p.150.

† Peter Kneitz, 'The Lords of Muskets', *Anthropus: International Review of Anthropology and Linguistics*, 114 (1):2019, pp.119–144.

‡ Joseph E. Inikori, 'Transatlantic Slavery and Economic Development: West Africa, 1450–1850', *The Cambridge World History of Slavery*, vol. 3, David Eltis et al., eds., pp.668–669.

many of those weapons did not fare well in the tropical climate. They always posed a fearsome prospect, and it was one which Europeans did not hesitate to use against Africans. European bases and trading posts, their castles and their sailing ships, were girded by fearsome weaponry which played havoc with African attackers. Merely to be in possession of such weapons emboldened African rulers and merchants who promptly equipped their military and followers with a variety of imported weapons. The 'Angola' gun (a long-barrelled musket), shorter French guns, cheap 'Bonny' guns, all and more flooded into the slave-trading markets of West Africa. In 1700, Willem Bosman recorded that, for some time:

> . . . we have been selling many weapons. We are obliged to do this in order to remain at the same level as the foreigners and interlopers.*

Bosman deplored this arms trade to Africa and feared its consequences, but it proved irresistible because it was so lucrative. In 1709, the gunmakers of London stated that they had 'been very much supported by Sale of their goods, usually exported by the Royal African Company.' Arms manufacturers were not alone, that year, in petitioning Parliament to safeguard their trade to Africa. Petitions came from merchants in Edinburgh, textile merchants in London, from shipwrights and weavers, from Birmingham ironworkers – alongside a range of craftsmen and merchants scattered across Britain.†

* Hugh Thomas, *The Slave Trade*, p.324.

† 'Petitions to the House of Commons, 1709', Elizabeth Donnan, *Documents,* II, 96–99.

It was clear enough, by the early eighteenth century, that domestic trade and manufacture in a range of industries thrived on the African trade. Domestic British prosperity was already closely tied to the continuing buoyancy of the slave trade, and was evident from one city to another. By 1765, Birmingham exported some 150,000 guns to Africa annually. A Liverpool merchant claimed that armaments were, a 'necessary part' of a slave ship's cargo. In that one city, thousands of men worked in the local industry supplying the slave ships with guns.* Gunpowder, of course, was an equally important export. One Liverpool ship's captain claimed in 1765 that gunpowder was 'an article of which there is the greatest gains of any in the trade.' The volumes exported rose dramatically in the late eighteenth century and by the 1770s and 1780s, more than one million pounds were exported annually, rising to two million by 1790. No wonder then that gunpowder was known in Liverpool as 'African powder.'†

Some African societies became much larger and more militaristic on the back of their new weapons, extending their borders, subduing neighbours – and acquiring more captives for the slave markets. In its turn, this created new layers of local economies and government, with new groups involved in seizing slaves, moving them onwards, while others benefitted from the expansion of slaving by imposing levies and dues on the movement of enslaved Africans through their jurisdiction.‡

* Hugh Thomas, *The Slave Trade*, p.324; J. Longmore, 'Cemented by the Blood of a Negro? The impact of the Slave Trade on Eighteenth Century Liverpool', in David Richardson, Suzanne Schwarz and Anthony Tibbles, eds., *Liverpool and Transatlantic Slavery*, Liverpool, 2007, p.243.

† Hugh Thomas, *The Slave Trade,* p.325; David Richardson, et al., *Liverpool,* p.130.

‡ Marcus Rediker, *The Slave Ship*, London, 2007, p.77.

By the end of the eighteenth century, West Africa had also become a dumping ground for substandard, inferior armaments, a fact widely accepted among arms manufacturers, and also in government circles. Guns rejected by the British Ordnance Office found their way to Africa. When the British slave trade was abolished in 1807, gun manufacturers complained that they were no longer able to get rid of their substandard products – as they had in the past, by exchanging them for slaves.*

In the decades immediately before abolition, the volumes of armaments shipped to West Africa provided 44 per cent of Britain's entire iron exports.† On top of this, British arms manufacturers sold considerable volumes of firearms to European merchants who – in their turn – shipped them onwards in their own ships heading to West Africa. There were disputes and complaints about the poor quality of many of those weapons sold to Europe but African demand for guns – in exchange for slaves – continued. At times, demand for weapons was so great that manufacturers simply could not meet their promised quotas. Problems with labour hindered expansion, competition for labour sometimes meant that workers were enticed to work elsewhere – with all the resulting problems of strikes, wage disputes and even rioting. Not surprisingly perhaps, some of Birmingham's major gun manufacturers left considerable fortunes at their death, having used the lucrative African trade to diversify into a variety of other businesses (banking and canals, for example). When Samuel Galton, a major Birmingham arms manufacturer, died in 1832, his

* Joseph E. Inikori, *Africans and the Industrial Revolution*, p.459.

† Joseph E. Inikori, *Africans and the Industrial Revolution*, pp.459–460.

fortune was estimated at £300,000 (about £35 million in today's value). He had properties scattered across Britain, held substantial shares in various canal companies, held stock in the East India Company and the Bank of England.* By then, no one seriously doubted that prosperity and industrial progress had been generated by the Atlantic slave system. All this was readily available by simply looking at ships' cargoes bound for Africa.

* Joseph E. Inikori, *Africans and the Industrial Revolution*, pp.464–465.

6

The Dead

We know a great deal about the millions of Africans survivors who stumbled ashore from the slave ships to enter a lifetime's servitude in the bewildering world of the Americas, but we know much less about those who did not survive the Atlantic crossing, still less about those who did not even survive the journey from their homelands to Africa's Atlantic coast. Huge numbers – more than one million – died on board the slave ships (shipboard deaths ranged between 12 and 15 per cent*) and the paperwork of slavery is burdened with misery and death among the enslaved shackled below decks. To the men who ran this business, however, the casualties were mere debits in their economic calculus: numbers to be struck off as losses in their trading data. Occasionally luck was on the side of the slave traders (and the Africans) and the protracted voyages passed with relatively few deaths. Much more common, however, was a regular mournful litany of

* B. W. Higman, 'Demography and family structures', Ch.19, *Cambridge World History of Slavery*, vol. 3, David Eltis et al., eds.; Marcus Rediker, *The Slave Ship*. p.5.

African mortality which we find dotting the pages of the surviving evidence.

The surgeon on the slave ship *Elizabeth* left us with one such account in 1719:

March 11	'Woman apoplexy'
March 14	'Boy convulsions'
March 24	'man stubborn and w[ould] not eat'
April 5	'man, flux'
April 8	'man, of flux and astma [*sic*]'
	'woman of consumption'
April	'negro man, flux'
April 13	'man, flux and malignant fever'
April 28	'boy, consumption and astma [*sic*]'*

Men, women, boys . . . so it continued: a tabulation of grim mortality as the *Elizabeth* made its way across the Atlantic, with African deaths tumbling from the pages every few days. The longest gap between fatalities on that voyage was little more than two weeks and the victims were simply pitched overboard – a feast for the trailing sharks. Sailors in tropical waters regularly noted the presence of sharks following their ship, or circling when the vessel was at anchor. All ships dumped plenty of items overboard for the predators, but slave ships were especially attractive to sharks. Numerous trading locations on the African coast lacked safe anchorage or quaysides, and the enslaved Africans were ferried out by canoe or small boats to the slave ship anchored in deeper water – clear of the shoals or breakers. Buffeted by Atlantic rollers and rapid changes in tides and currents, canoes were at risk and the

* David Eltis and David Richardson, *Atlas*, p. 211.

Africans were victims in regular canoeing accidents. Sailors dreaded the ever-present sharks, and when they buried a shipmate at sea, they took the precaution of wrapping the corpse in a shroud weighted with ballast. But sharks were not easily deterred. The misery of a shipboard death was often followed by the horror of witnessing the cadaver torn apart by sharks only seconds after it had been pitched into the ocean.

It was worse – more squalid and savage – when Africans died. When slave ships gathered at major trading locations, sharks gathered in large numbers, to feed off the inevitable victims. Sharks 'in almost incredible numbers' swarmed around the ships at Bonny:

> Devouring with great dispatch the dead bodies of the negroes as they were thrown overboard.

Willem Bosman in 1705 told of a feeding frenzy as sharks fought each other for a share of the spoils. Slave captains reported sharks following their ships right across the Atlantic. More were waiting for them in the Americas. In 1785, a Kingston newspaper called them, 'The consistent attendants on the vessels from the coast.' When a large number of ships arrived in Kingston harbour, so too did 'a number of overgrown sharks.' There were even times when captains or officers baited sharks – luring them to follow the ship, thus spreading fear and horror among both the crew and the slaves. There are no statistics for this terrible story, but the evidence we have is chilling: that sharks learned that the slave ships provided a feast, off the African coast, in mid-Atlantic and in the tropical waters of the Americas.*

* Marcus Rediker, *The Slave Ship*, pp.37–40.

Though the great majority of Africans embarked onto the slave ships survived to landfall, as we have seen, large numbers died en route. Scholars have recently begun to give serious attention to the nature and extent of death on the crossing from Africa to the Americas: to plot its deadly path and to pinpoint the patterns of mortality as ships crossed the ocean.* Moreover, many of those survivors died within their first years in the Americas. This 'grim period', known as 'seasoning' to the slave owners, was the time when the newly arrived Africans struggled to adapt to life in a different environment, learning to bend to the rigours of their new labouring life, especially stressful in sugar and mining. As high death rates blighted the slave quarters, something like one in ten of newly arrived Africans died in their first year. When we add together the distinct phases in the lives of the enslaved Africans – the initial enslavement in Africa, the misery of life on the slave ship, followed by the wretchedness of adapting to life in the Americas – it forms a continuum of suffering and death. Though it is true that *most* survived to settle down into the life of the enslaved in the Americas, they left in their wake an army of lost souls: people killed by enslavement, by oceanic transportation and by adjustment to the Americas. It forms a litany of suffering and death – a way of death – which scarred the survivors with memories of dead companions, and which passed into slave folklore: stories told by old Africans to their children born in the Americas.

The paperwork of slavery is littered with the details of this suffering, though much of it goes unnoticed because it takes the

* Andrew Sluyter, 'Death on the Middle Passage: A Cartographical Approach to the Atlantic Slave Trade', *Esclavage et Post Esclavage*, (3), 1 January 2021.

form of simple economic data: numbers deleted and values lost. We can readily recall the survivors – it is much more troublesome to recall the dead. Yet more than one million died on the slave ships. If those people could be memorialised, they would form a floating reminder – a string of signposts – across the vast Atlantic. We know what killed them, because captains and surgeons dutifully recorded the details in their paperwork. Sometimes, an African seemed doomed from the moment he or she stepped on board (despite the traders' efforts to weed out the sick before purchase). John Newton accepted one African 'tho she had a bad mouth. Could have bought her cheaper.' She had no name and was simply numbered 47: just another number in the remorseless accountancy of slave trading. In the eyes of the slave traders, Africans died as they lived – nameless:

> In the morning buried a buy slave (No 66) who was ill with a violent flux the 3rd day after he came on board. Some time later, the crew buried a man, number 33 having been a fortnight ill of a flux, which has baffled all our medicines.*

The core experience at sea for every single African was the terror of sickness and death.†

The physical conditions endured by all Africans below decks were vile beyond words, especially in bad weather when they were shackled below as the crew struggled to maintain the ship against the elements. Even the most callous and experienced of ships' doctors were reluctant to step below into the belly of the ship to

* *The Journal of a Slave Trader, John Newton, (1750-1754)*, Bernard Martin and Mark Spurrell, eds., London, 1962, pp.26, 46.

† Marcus Rediker, *The Slave Ship*, p.273.

tend to the Africans – forced to wallow in the communal filth, the dead and dying side by side – until crewmen could be spared to remove the dead and clean out the decks. Though it was in the crew's interests to keep the Africans alive and fit for sale in the Americas, such resolve often vanished in the pressing demands of manning a sailing ship battered by a storm. (The crew might also be badly affected and depleted by ailments picked up on the African coast.) In time, though the increased experience of handling large numbers of enslaved Africans at sea served to reduce the levels of sickness, nature had its own way of intervening and playing deadly havoc. It was well known that the *duration* of an Atlantic crossing was the key to a uneventful voyage: the swifter the crossing, the lower the death rate and sickness. The ideal of a speedy and trouble-free voyage could never be guaranteed. Even though conditions improved as the trade developed, and as mortality rates fell in the eighteenth century (though they peaked again in the nineteenth century), the trauma of sickness and death haunted every African on board every slave ship.

Africans were packed below decks in filthy proximity. When the early abolitionists began to instruct the public about the inhumanity of the slave trade, they focused precisely on this point: on the visible overcrowding of imprisoned Africans. The crowded slave ship proved to be one of the most effective – and durable – of propaganda images: an image used time and again right down to the present day. It is an image that quickly embedded itself in the public imagination. It was (and remains) an image which establishes an essential fact: every African captive endured an experience of contagious, filthy and enforced intimacy with a crowd of other people. It was utterly unlike any previous experience, and formed a concoction which produced physical sickness and mental trauma.

The physical filth of the slave ships could be smelled miles downwind. For those incarcerated below decks, there was no escape. In the sweltering gloom of a crowded slave ship in the tropics, the enslaved Africans rapidly dehydrated. Water supplies were vital: barrels of water took up more physical space on a slave ship than the enslaved Africans themselves. A contagious slave would quickly infect others, most commonly with the 'bloody flux'. Dysentery was the plague of the slave ships, and was as commonplace as the onboard rats (another torment for the Africans). The flux quickly polluted the slave decks, spreading easily via communal eating and drinking utensils and – most horrifying of all – spreading via the human waste from sick Africans to others close by. Doctors who worked on the ships, or who visited the ships when they first docked in the Americas, all told the same tale across the centuries: of Africans kept in conditions of overpowering filth.

While early scrutiny of the slave trade confirmed dysentery to be a major killer of Africans on the slave ships, there were others, much dreaded because there was no real defence against them. Malaria, yellow fever, measles, smallpox, influenza – all could surge through the ranks of the imprisoned Africans with little warning and with devastating consequences (for the crew as well). Furthermore, they continued throughout the long history of the Atlantic slave trade, up to the 1860s.*

Some of the most terrible accounts of conditions on slave ships belong to the very last phase of the trade. Ships bound for Brazil in the nineteenth century were packed as rarely before, their masters paying little attention to the Africans' well-being. The scenes of crowded misery and of rampant on-board disease appalled doctors and naval officers who encountered the ships

* Manuel Barcia, *The Yellow Demon of Fever*, New Haven, 2020.

and who might, themselves, be abolitionists. Scenes of mass suffering were being played out regularly in the nineteenth-century Atlantic, and were repeated time and again by eyewitnesses. Africans had their own stories to tell. An African child, shipped to Brazil in 1830, later recounted his experience, of being in the midst of others dying around him 'in consequence of the excessive heat and the want of water.' They lived 'the same as pigs in a sty.' A British doctor who attended Africans landed in Brazil between 1841 and 1843 gave his own graphic account. Though accustomed to 'a scene of disease and wretchedness' he was nonetheless stunned by one vessel, packed with 362 Africans 'with disease, want, and misery stamped upon them with such painful intensity as utterly beggars all powers of description.' Many were blind, all were emaciated, naked in their wretchedness, with women holding children to their empty breasts. The stench was overpowering. Yet such scenes were regularly encountered and described by doctors and naval officers when they boarded 'illicit' vessels (those ships which contravened the various agreements to ban slave trading after 1807) bound for Brazil in the nineteenth century.*

Not surprisingly, in the midst of such horrors, many Africans simply lost the will to live, slipping into a catatonic gloom and fading away, refusing to eat and drink. Some, given the chance, leapt overboard and took their own lives. Many others, however, refused to accept the world they had been plunged into: refused to be treated like beasts in transit and resolved to fight back and to resist as best they could. The history of the Atlantic slave ships

* Robert Edgar Conrad, *Children of God's Fire*, pp.37–39: 43–48. Mary Wills, *Envoys of Abolition: British Naval Officers and the Campaign Against the Slave Trade in West Africa*, Liverpool, 2019.

was peppered by African rebellions. Fear of African violence and insurgency haunted the crew quarters. Something like one slave ship in ten experienced some form of slave resistance, and acts of individual or communal violence against the crew were common – and were always anticipated. Most of those outbursts erupted off the African coast (where escape back to the land was most realistic). Some succeeded, but ships overwhelmed by insurgent Africans were generally lost: who could sail a complex sailing ship when an experienced crew had been vanquished and killed? Much more common after a shipboard rebellion was defeat followed by bloody reprisals. When, from the late eighteenth century onwards, the grotesque details of shipboard conditions began to receive widespread publicity, there was growing outrage at the violence involved. Moreover, the outrage was expressed by people who were accustomed to the grim punishments doled out by the contemporary penal code. What happened on board slave ships took revenge to an entirely different level.

There was of course a purpose behind the excessive violence used, and the excruciating killings suffered by rebellious Africans on slave ships. Executions and dismemberments were designed to terrify and intimidate the survivors. Africans were brought on deck to witness (and to remember) exactly what happened to Africans who rebelled. Execution, whipping, mutilation, dismemberment, beheading: all and every means of inflicting excruciating pain and instilling fear in onlookers, was doled out to unsuccessful slave rebels. Jean Barbot urged slave ship captains to:

> Spare no effort to repress their insolence and, as an example to the others, sacrifice the lives of all the most mutinous. This will terrify the others and keep them obedient . . . the

> form of punishment that scares the Africans most, is by cutting up a live man with an axe and handing out pieces to the others.*

With African resistance suppressed, slave captains often had to decide what to do with wounded survivors. The slave markets of the Americas had no place for wounded or badly impaired Africans, still less for those known to have been rebellious at sea, and likely to be troublesome on land. One merchant complained that the Africans fresh from a rebellious ship 'had wounds on their bodies which gave an unfavourable impression.'† Some captains solved the problem by simply killing the wounded. One Bristol captain, concerned that his wounded Africans would be worthless on arrival, simply pitched them overboard. A revolt on the ship *Nassau* left a number of Africans with gunshot wounds: the more severely wounded were thrown over the side. Such losses on British ships could be claimed as a loss on the ship's cargo insurance. This was explained in the major legal text defining the law of insurance:

> The insurer takes upon himself the risk of the loss, capture, and death of slaves, or any other unavoidable accident to them: but natural death is always understood to be excepted – by natural death is meant, not only when it happens by disease or sickness, but also when the captive destroys himself through despair, which often happens, but when slaves are

* E. R. Taylor, *If We Must Die: Shipboard Insurrections in the Era of the Atlantic Slave Trade*, Baton Rouge, 2006, p.113.

† James Walvin, *Crossings: Africa, the Americas and the Atlantic Slave Trade*, London, 2013, p.118.

> killed, or thrown into the sea in order to quell an insurrection on their part, then the insurers must answer.*

English maritime insurance was clear. Slaves who died of natural causes, or who killed themselves, were *not* covered by insurance: those killed during a revolt or in its aftermath, *were* covered. What the law did *not* cover – and what it did not have to deal with as a legal issue until the infamous *Zong* case in 1783 – was the question of a massacre of Africans at sea.

Every African who reached the Americas had endured a traumatic ordeal like no other. Many had seen shipmates die in the misery of their own filth. Many had also witnessed what happened to slaves whose defiance had flared and failed. No African could have been under any illusion about the nature of the power and dominance of the people who controlled them. They were in the hands of people for whom violence was the very lubricant of daily life.

Throwing dead Africans overboard was, then, part of every slave voyage. What shocked outsiders, in the late eighteenth century, was the revelation that occasionally Africans were also jettisoned *when they were alive.* They were thrown overboard in battles with the crew: wounded survivors – now worthless because of their wounds – were likewise thrown into the sea. We also know of shipwrecks, or when a vessel ran aground, when Africans were left to die, locked below decks, when the crew abandoned the doomed vessel. Such terrible incidents were perhaps unusual but were sufficiently well known in seafaring circles. Such horrors came to light in the *Zong* case,

* John Wesket, *A Complete Digest of the Theory, Laws and Practice of Insurance,* London, 1781, p.525.

heard before Lord Mansfield in 1783. One hundred and thirty-two Africans had been murdered – pitched from a Liverpool slaver, the *Zong*, which had lost its way en route to Jamaica. As the ship's water supplies ran low, the crew were persuaded to kill some of the Africans in order to save the rest. Or so the ship's Liverpool owners argued when they claimed on the insurance for the dead Africans. The outrage at the killings was compounded by the cold-blooded insurance claim. When Lord Mansfield and two fellow judges heard an appeal in the case, they were obliged merely to consider the case as one of contested insurance. They were not asked to sit in judgement of a mass murder. The law was clear enough: Africans were insured for loss in transit, much like any other form of cargo. But this was obviously *not* an ordinary insurance case: the Africans had *not* been lost to insurrection or shipwreck but had been murdered in cold blood.*

Although the legal issues were never fully resolved, the *Zong* case prompted political and social outrage in Britain, galvanising a horrified public to speak out against the slave trade. Among the most vociferous were Africans living in London who added their personal testimony to the growing outrage that slowly coalesced into the early campaign against the slave trade.

There was, however, a glaring irony here. Everyone closely involved in the Atlantic trade – and especially the men who manned the ships, and those who tallied the ships' documents – was fully aware that Africans were periodically killed on the slave ships. Though the aim and purpose of that trade was to keep the African captives alive, in order to sell them at a profit

* James Walvin, *The Zong: A Massacre, the Law and the End of Slavery*, London, 2011.

in the Americas, there were times when killings were thought to be unavoidable and even necessary. It was the ultimate safeguard for the crew and the ship itself at times of greatest danger.

The public outrage caused by the *Zong* murders did not bring such shipboard killings to an end. In fact, even worse examples came to the public's notice in the nineteenth century. Despite a number of abolitionist diplomatic treatises and conventions, there was, as we have seen, a continued thriving trade in enslaved Africans across the South Atlantic, mainly to the coffee and sugar plantations of Brazil and Cuba. Despite abolitionist patrols by the US and British navies, formed after the abolition of the slave trade in 1807 and 1808, more than four million Africans landed in Brazil, and more than seven hundred thousand in Cuba. It was in this last phase of the trade that some of the worst recorded examples of killings on slave ships took place. It was also the period which saw the most shocking of shipboard sufferings among the Africans.

The Atlantic slave trade continued to have strong support. The French resented and resisted British abolition pressure, but Spain and Portugal were especially hostile because both Brazil and Cuba demanded ever more African arrivals. Despite the punitive measures taken against offending ships caught by the abolitionist patrols, the flow of enslaved Africans across the Atlantic continued. With vessels under pressure to load as many Africans as possible, before they made a dash for Brazil or Cuba, hundreds of Africans were hurriedly packed onto overcrowded ships in numbers which far exceeded the eighteenth century levels. One ship of 180 tons (which, under the British restrictions laid down in 1787, would have been allowed only 270 Africans) took on board 530 Africans. Another carried 642 Africans, compared to the 410 permitted by the 1787 law. The inevitable casualty rates were enormous. One vessel lost 120 of its 530 Africans, another lost 140 out of 642. In 1818, *The Protector* embarked an astonishing 807 Africans – but 307 of them died.*

It also emerged that some slave ship captains, facing capture and loss of their vessel to an approaching abolitionist naval patrol, preferred to pitch the Africans overboard rather than face conviction. As a result, Africans were jettisoned at all points of the Atlantic trade: at embarkation in African waters, in mid-Atlantic and in American waters. In the words of one commentator:

> Persons who make a trade of human misery are not likely to trouble much about human life.†

The threat from the abolitionist navies (however limited their abilities) may, paradoxically, even have exacerbated the basic problems of overcrowding and cynical killings. Similar killings had almost certainly taken place in earlier phases of the Atlantic slave trade, but in the nineteenth century, the political and social mood among large sections of Western opinion had changed, and these shipboard killings took place in a totally transformed cultural climate. The abolitionists were gaining momentum, in Britain, the USA and Brazil – notwithstanding the boom in slavery on the back of cotton and coffee – and found plenty of evidence for their campaign in the horrors

* *A View of the Present State of the African Slave Trade*, Philadelphia, 1824, pp.59–61; *Foreign Slave Trade: Abstract of Information*, London, 1821, p.37. Both in Slavery Pamphlets (1826), Beinecke Library, Yale University.
† James Walvin, *Crossings*, pp.180–181.

revealed from the illicit trade. Reports from naval officers (many of them committed abolitionists), from doctors and businessmen working in Brazil, filtered back to Europe and the USA. Formal reports to government departments were leaked to the press, with details of the killings on slave ships quickly finding their way into the public domain to become grist to the abolitionists' mill. They helped to persuade ever more people that the slave trade (and the institution of slavery which was the engine behind the entire problem) was an abomination – and must be stopped.

***

The end result of this terrible story is that more than one million Africans, destined for the Americas, were consigned to a watery grave. Some were thrown into Africa's mighty rivers, some died off the African coast. Others were pitched overboard off the Americas. More were consigned to the swallowing depths of the Atlantic. Today, in Africa, the Americas and Europe, there are plenty of physical memorials to the people who became the enslaved labouring force of the Americas. But who recalls those left behind in the wake of the slave ships? Who remembers the dead, cast into the ocean as slave ships sailed west with their crowded, human cargoes, heading for a lifetime's bondage in the Americas? Modern geographers have made a start, by extracting information from slave ships' logs to plot the geography of these deaths at sea. The maps they have created provide an initial mournful visual reminder – dots along the transatlantic trade routes – of the last known resting places of more than one million Africans. They stand as memorials to people who did not survive to landfall in the Americas.

Part Three

INTERNAL TRADES

7

Upheavals

IN NOVEMBER 1755, three hundred Angolan captives sailed into the Caribbean on board the French slave ship *L'Aimable,* destined for the booming French colony of St. Domingue. The vessel was seized, however, by a marauding British naval squadron (it was in the midst of what became the Seven Years' War) and diverted to Barbados, where a small group of Africans was put ashore and sold. The British admiral in charge was entitled to forty-six Africans as his share of the prize money, and he struck a deal to ship the remaining Angolans to South Carolina (where slaves were known to be in great demand). Shipped onwards, on a vessel which was in a poor, battered condition, the Africans endured a dangerous and water-logged voyage north to Charleston, stopping en route at Anguilla for repairs. As they sailed north, the weather turned colder, and the Africans suffered badly. Six died on arrival at Charleston's Sullivan's Island, and many more were in a miserable condition. Even before the Angolans had cleared quarantine, they were advertised in the local press, but sickness was rife and the slave trader could bring only 105 of the 127 survivors to the sale. Even then, prices were disappointing.

The Angolans' travels had not ended, for they had now to

trek onwards to their new homes in South Carolina – some tramping several days to remote properties. A small group of the remaining Africans in Charleston proved difficult to sell, and were returned to yet another vessel and shipped 60 miles along the coast to Georgetown. The last two were sold six months after they had arrived.*

This one group of Africans, despite having been intended for St. Domingue, were now scattered between Barbados and South Carolina. They form one simple example of a pattern that was repeated time and again over the centuries: of Africans being transhipped and marched huge distances *long after* they made first landfall in the Americas. Some of the initial group embarked in Africa had died on the Atlantic crossing, others succumbed at different points on the subsequent protracted journeys: in another ship, in a merchant's yard or soon after settling in a new home. Such upheavals form a common pattern we find across the slave colonies. When Sir Charles Price bought two groups of Africans for his Jamaican plantation in 1792, more than half died within four years. The alarmed sugar planter shifted the Africans to a new location which, he hoped, would be healthier for them. But still they died; two of them poisoned themselves (though twenty of the survivors lived for another forty years).† It is clear that many Africans who died in their early years in the Americas succumbed to ailments contracted in the squalor of the slave ships, lingering in great distress until the illness contracted at sea finally killed them.

***

* Greg O'Malley, *Final Passages,* pp.1–5.

† Michael Craton, *Searching for the Invisible Man: Slaves and Plantation Life in Jamaica*, Cornell, 1978, p.200.

By any standards, the enslaved made epic journeys, clouded by fear and uncertainty – worries that did not diminish as the journey progressed, from Africa, to landfall followed by yet further upheavals and travels in the Americas. On top of all this, Africans often found themselves caught up in the terror of warfare and seizure, as European and later American states fought each other on land and at sea for the expansion or defence of colonial possessions and global trade. Shipping – the lifeline of empire – offered rich pickings for privateers and naval ships: slave ships, packed with valuable enslaved Africans, were a prize target – not unlike the Spanish treasure ships of the sixteenth century. Attacking a slave ship, seizing its human cargo and diverting it to a different destination, provided wealth for the captors – but compounded the perplexed fears of the Africans. We have seen that that happened to the three hundred Angolans on the French slaver *L'Aimable* in 1756. It also happened to 244 Africans on board the Dutch slaver, the *Zorgue,* seized by the British off the African coast in 1781. Bought by Liverpool merchants, the vessel lingered on the coast, eventually heading west with 442 enslaved Africans. When the vessel was seized by the British, its African prisoners had *already* been imprisoned at sea for at least seven months. Renamed the *Zong*, the ship is today infamous for the mass murder of 132 people on board late in the voyage to Jamaica.*

Though the massacre of the Africans on board the *Zong* was exceptional, in many respects it represented, in an extreme form, experiences common to untold numbers of African captives. Having lingered on the coast of Africa for months on

* James Walvin, *The Zong*; Jeremy Krikler, 'The Zong and the Lord Chief Justice', *History Workshop Journal,* No. 64 (autumn, 2007), pp.29–47.

end, victims of European conflict as vessels clashed and changed hands, the Africans then fell victim to navigational mismanagement – and a murderous onslaught. The survivors of the *Zong* massacre landed in Jamaica in a wretched physical condition, having endured terror and distress on an epic scale.

Many Africans crossed the Atlantic with people from their own kin, people they recognised from their home region and with whom they shared a language and cultural ties. Others acquired 'shipmates' on the voyage – friendships that sometimes survived to the slave quarters of plantations. Africans created – and maintained – networks and relationships that were forged in Africa, on the slave ships and at different points in the Americas. In Catholic America, when the enslaved wanted to marry, they had to provide proof and witnesses to their single status. The resulting Church records provide some astonishing evidence. When in 1777, Pedro Antonio, a man born in Angola, wanted to marry Ana Maria, born in Rio – both then living in Montevideo – Pedro's first witness was Domingo – a man from Benguela. They had known each other for six years and had travelled from Rio to Montevideo. A second witness, also named Pedro, had known Pedro Antonio for ten years, having first met in Angola, later in Rio, before finally meeting up in Montevideo.*

Too often though, all such bonds were broken by sale at the markets of the Americas. In Kingston (the major point of arrival for Africans landing in the British Americas) most Africans were bought by a small group of local merchants who

* Alex Borucki, 'Shipmate Networks and Black Identities in the Marriage Files of Montevideo, 1768-1803', *Hispanic American Historical Review*, 93: 2, 2013.

then sold them on in batches or individually. There was in effect a retail sale of Africans, normally conducted in merchants' yards in Kingston. Some Africans were held there for very long periods before they were sold again – and moved on once more. In February 1769, the last Africans from the slave ship *Plumper* were sold ninety-nine days after they had landed on the island. In merchants' yards – as on the slave ships – whatever relationships that existed among the Africans were again destroyed by sale and onwards movement. It was a life of 'constant flux, disruption and misery' long before they reached a plantation.*

Stepping from an Atlantic slave ship was, then, just the first step of many in the Americas, as Africans were scattered to different islands, to a distant American frontier and often to a sick and meagre survival in a place intended to be their final destination. Too often, it soon proved to be their final resting place.

Such cases are not unusual or exceptional stories. On the contrary, they expose the realities that shaped the lives of huge numbers of Africans. We know for example that of the 2.7 million Africans landed at ports in the British Americas before 1808, some three hundred thousand were promptly shipped onwards to other regions. Some two hundred thousand went to French and Spanish colonies and fifty thousand were moved from one British island to another. Even those Africans who remained in the colony where they first landed, faced further upheaval and travel. Local slave traders bought them, kept them in their yards close to the docks and offered them – via advertisements in the local

* Trevor Bernard and P. Morgan, 'The dynamics of the slave market and slave purchasing patterns in Jamaica, 1655-1788', *The William and Mary Quarterly*, vol. 58, 2001, p.224.

newspapers, on handbills posted round the town and by word of mouth – to planters and other slave owners across the colony. Although these later stages of an African's journey might perhaps seem mundane after the horrors of the Atlantic, they too were often prolonged, debilitating and dangerous.

Wherever Africans finally settled, they had entered a totally unfamiliar world, utterly unlike their homelands. Many, perhaps most, had been damaged by the experiences endured en route. The newly arrived were usually in poor physical and mental condition. Yet they were about to face a lifetime of unrelenting toil – normally of the most severe and taxing kind.

***

The slaves' fears about upheaval were not laid to rest, even after they had settled into their final destination. In the Americas, as they had been on the slave ships, the enslaved remained chattel – items of trade. They formed a valuable item in their owners' portfolio of material goods. When we look at slave owners' papers, we find the enslaved listed alongside other assets: the land, the buildings, equipment and the beasts of the field. Like all those other possessions, the slaves could be transferred, at a moment's notice (and normally without any warning): sold and passed into other hands along a chain of ownership. Huge numbers of slaves were torn from loved ones and dispatched (they knew not where) to new locations and new owners. Slavery proved to be a bewildering world of uncertainty.

Slave owners themselves often moved on. As new lands and new economic opportunities became available, early settlers left their initial locations – normally close to coastal or riverside places

– for more distant regions. Their enslaved labourers travelled with their migrating owners – or were sold to distant settlers. Demands from such frontier settlements created a new breed of slave traders: men and businesses specialising in acquiring slaves from older established regions and transporting them by land, river or sea, to the expanding frontier with their new slave-based industries. This new breed of slave trader closely resembled the better-known maritime slave trader: tough men, not too sensitive about manhandling humans and generally free with the whip or simple physical assault both to acquire and to keep the slaves subdued as they moved onwards towards a new home.

Such transfers of slave labour *within* the Americas were a feature of *all* America's slave societies. When the US abolition movements emerged in the nineteenth century, campaigners made telling use of the upheavals taking place in slave communities. They regaled their readers and audiences with countless examples of individuals removed huge distances against their will and of the resulting destruction of slave families. Moreover, these distressing incidents were highly visible, as groups or individuals shuffled, sometimes in chains, through towns, as they headed elsewhere. They could also be seen in the advertisements which littered contemporary newspapers. Long before the development of the massive movement of slaves in Brazil and North America in the nineteenth century, there was a 'domestic slave trade' operating throughout the Americas. For all that, slave networks of friendships and family survived, or were created anew. Africans created, and maintained, networks and relationships that were forged in Africa, on the slave ships and at different points in the Americas.

***

In 1821, Bushrod Washington, nephew of George, was facing hard times on the family plantation at Mount Vernon. He sold fifty-four of his enslaved Africans for $10,000 to two men from Louisiana.* Washington's hope of keeping the sale secret were unrealistic: how could you disguise a line of manacled Africans shuffling their way south to a new life in Louisiana? This single example, from the Washington family, was one of countless slave sales and migrations in nineteenth-century USA. In fact, the numbers uprooted in this fashion were astonishing. Something like one million slaves were uprooted and moved, in the years 1790 to 1860. In the thirty years to 1840, 350,000 slaves left Delaware, Maryland, Virginia and the Carolinas for other parts of the USA. These massive migrations had devastating consequences. An estimated one third 'of all first slave marriages in the Upper South' were destroyed by this internal slave trade.† This severed links between spouses, between parents and their children, and separated siblings from each other. The US domestic slave trade battered family life among the nation's enslaved people.

Before 1820, US slaves tended to be uprooted when they moved along with their owners. But after the abolition of the Atlantic slave trade, in 1808, when Southern planters found it increasingly difficult to secure fresh enslaved Africans, they looked north for additions to their enslaved labour force. More striking – and new – was the rise of specialised US slave traders: men who scoured the old slave states for victims and who

* *Lives Bound Together: Slavery at George Washington's Mount Vernon*, Exhibition, 2016–20.

† Michael Tadman, *Speculators and Slaves: Masters, Traders, and Slaves in the Old South*, Madison, 1996 edn, pp.169–171.

moved them, often in chains, along protracted and painful marches south, to the auction blocks and plantations of the expanding cotton economy. This domestic slave trade was blatant and brutal and had devastating consequences for the victims – and for those left behind.

When settlers moved from an old property in the company of their slaves, the enslaved walked huge distances though sometimes the less able were allowed to ride on carts. Migrating planters often tried to keep slave families together, realising that family break-ups were bad for morale (and therefore for productivity). Others also realised that chaining slaves as they travelled was both distressing and bad for their spirits. In these resettlements, slave owners had to decide: which slaves were fit for such exhausting treks – and for the heavy labour that was to follow – and which ones should stay behind permanently, or be left to wait for a more suitable time to be moved on. Time and again this was a story of carefully thought-out plans; of how best to move enslaved labour, how best to rearrange the slave gangs and who was best suited to travel and to embark on a new pioneering settlement. Often owners felt they had no option but to break up slave families.

Once settled on new land, planters had to buy new slaves from the old communities. They scoured the towns of the border states, advertising for slaves in local newspapers, announcing their interest in slave families, and claiming that they did not intend to sell on prospective purchases. They were, in their own promotional tactics, good slave owners, respectful of their slaves. Increasingly, however, they were forced to rely on the thuggish slave traders: men whose reputation for financial gouging and hard-hearted treatment of the slaves became the stuff of popular memory. It also fed the rising anger of early US abolitionism.*

Claims by potential buyers that they were solicitous for slave families' welfare had a hollow ring. What about the extended slave families? What about the old, the grandparents, the uncles and aunts and cousins – not to mention friends and other loved ones – and the broader community from which a departing family was being wrested? In practice, such self-proclaiming altruism was a smokescreen for a host of brutal realities. The transit was long and arduous. Even before they set off, slaves were corralled into local jails or warehouses. But the journey itself was the greatest problem for slave owners (as it was, of course, for the enslaved). The miserable history of family break-up is perhaps best known in the USA, but it was common throughout the Americas and involved perhaps more people in South America.

***

In Brazil and the USA, new enforced migrations of enslaved people developed in the course of the nineteenth century to provide the labour required by developing plantation economies in newly opened regions of the country. In Brazil, the prime mover was the rapidly expanding coffee industry; in the USA, it was the cotton industry. Both involved *domestic* slave trades which forcibly moved huge numbers of people from one part of the country to another. Once again, the lives of millions were blighted by uprooting and resale.

* Robert H. Gudmestad, *A Troublesome Commerce: The Transformation of the Interstate Slave Trade*, Baton Rouge, 2004, Ch.1.

8

Brazil's Internal Slave Trade

BRAZIL ABSORBED MORE enslaved Africans than any other region of the Americas. It was the first to adopt African slavery on a major scale and it was the last to end it. Brazil was effectively settled, developed and thrived on the back of Africans (with plenty of help, initially, from indigenous Indian slave labour). And in Brazil, as elsewhere in the Americas, the enslaved were moved around, shuffled here and there, bought and sold locally or across great distances, depending on the pressing needs of their owners, of slave traders and of the changing labour market of the country's different regions and economies. The country's major slave-importing regions absorbed huge numbers of Africans. Some 142,000 went to Amazonia, 854,000 to Pernambuco, more than one and half million to Bahia – and an astonishing 2,264,000 to the south-east of Brazil, mainly in and around Rio de Janeiro. Almost four million of these African victims came from West Central Africa (largely modern Angola).* The major engine behind most of these African arrivals, from the sixteenth century

* David Eltis and David Richardson, *Atlas*, p.257.

onwards, was the Brazilian sugar industry: at Recife (in Pernambuco), Salvador (Bahia) and Rio.

From an early date, Brazil developed patterns of transferring the enslaved huge distances within its own (ill-defined) borders. Tens of thousands of Indian slaves were forcibly moved – by sea – to the expanding sugar frontier of north-eastern Brazil from the early seventeenth century.* The arrival of increasing numbers of Africans effectively put an end to that early long-distance internal slave trade, though Indian slavery itself survived in Brazil well into the nineteenth century. The port of Salvador, on the beautiful St Ann's Bay, became the country's 'great entrepôt', receiving enormous numbers of Africans before dispatching them north to the states of Maranhao and Para. Merchants there sold them on again, along the Amazon and its vast tributaries, and even as far west as the mines of Mato Grosso. With each new mineral discovery, and with each new settlement in the interior, planters, prospectors and their slaves moved in, for example to Minas Gerais from the late seventeenth century onwards (for gold and diamonds – by 1735, for instance, Minas Gerais was home to ninety-six thousand African slaves, most of them working in mines). The enslaved were marched hundreds of miles to these new frontiers.

Until the nineteenth century, enslaved African labour had been cheap, but the effective ending of Brazil's 'legal' Atlantic slave trade in 1850 and the rising cost of illicitly imported slaves, led to the rapid emergence of a domestic, internal Brazilian slave trade. It fed the voracious labour demands of new Brazilian industries in freshly opened regions of the

* Richard Graham, 'Another Middle Passage', in *The Chattel Principle: Internal Slave Trades in the Americas*, Walter Johnson, ed., Ch.11.

country, but the major market for this domestic trade was the massive expansion of Brazilian coffee cultivation.

It is true that an 'illicit' Atlantic slave trade continued, with Africans landed at numerous locations close to Rio, but equally striking was the major enforced migration of slaves from older established regions to new, developing areas of the Brazilian economy. Slaves were moved south by ship, from Brazil's old sugar regions in the north-east, to the ports of Rio and Santos. For the Africans involved it was a seaborne trade which must have revived memories of the horrors of their Atlantic crossing.

Though the data for this domestic trade continues to be debated among historians, it was clearly much smaller than the Atlantic slave trade. The annual movement of slaves from one region to another stood at five to six thousand in the 1850s, rising to ten thousand per year in the 1870s. The total, of about 225,000, needs to be added to the numbers of slaves who were moved *within* a province. Something like four hundred thousand slaves travelled along these domestic slave routes, though the numbers may well have been higher. They endured protracted overland routes by foot, and some went by train to the new coffee plantations, but large numbers were shipped south from the ports of the old sugar regions – notably Salvador – to Brazil's southern ports, closer to coffee cultivation. Again, the personal stories are startling.

In August 1873, a boy of six – we know only his name, Victorino – boarded a steam ship at Salvador, bound for Rio along with fifty-four other slaves. All were sold to Manuel Veridiano de Pinto. A year earlier, another slave, Miguel – in the north-east province of Alagoas – had been emancipated, only to be enslaved again and sold to an Italian, who sold him yet again to a slave trading company in Rio in July 1872. They in turn, sold him, once more . . . and by 1881, the police were still trying to locate him – to explain the mistake: all along, he had been a free man.*

These and many more equally distressing stories took place in public view. Brazil's domestic slave trade was highly visible. As late as 1880, an outraged Member of the Chamber of deputies described slaves being moved in his own province of Bahia:

> Suddenly I heard a confused clamor of approaching voices. It was an immense caravan of slaves destined for the fields of Sao Paulo. Among men with chains about their necks walked as many women, carrying on their shoulders their children, among whom were youngsters of all ages, the whole march being on foot, bloodying the hot sand of the roads.†

Throughout the period from the 1850s to the 1870s the numbers involved in this domestic trade fluctuated according to the expansion or decline of Brazil's slave-based industries. But above all, coffee was the main driving force behind Brazil's domestic slave trade. Coffee had been introduced to Brazil in the early eighteenth century, though its cultivation (around Rio from 1760) was largely for local consumption. With the collapse of the Haitian coffee industry after the revolution, Brazil's valley of the Paraiba do Sul River proved an ideal location for the expansion of coffee cultivation. Later it was cultivated widely in Sao Paulo province. Efforts to grow coffee with

* Kim D. Butler, 'Slavery in the Age of Emancipation', *Journal of British Studies*, vol. 42, No. 6, 2011, pp.968–992.

† In Robert Edgar Conrad, *Children of God's Fire*, pp.354–355.

free labour were quickly discarded as unprofitable and cultivators turned to slave labour. By the mid-nineteenth century, Brazil's domestic slave trade, and the illicit Atlantic trade, had turned Brazil's coffee-growing regions into the country's most important centre of slave labour. The land was cheap (or free – thanks to the strong-armed tactics of new planters in ejecting existing tenants) and the labour required for opening up the new coffee lands was enslaved. Soon, the commonly used phrase was 'Brazil is coffee and coffee is the negro.'*

Ships with their human cargoes from Africa, from Bahia and Pernambuco, converged on the coastline close to Rio, and after landing, the Africans were marched on, yet again, to new coffee plantations. Before 1791, the French colony of St. Domingue had been *the* major coffee producer in the Americas, but that ended with the slave revolt and the collapse of that colony's economy. Brazil found itself ideally placed to fill the gap in the coffee market. Equally important, the rapidly expanding population of the USA began to consume coffee in prodigious volumes. By 1830, Americans were drinking six times as much coffee as tea: nine times as much by 1860. Coffee imports into the USA rocketed: the one million pounds imported in 1791 had grown to sixty-two million pounds by the end of that century. Consumption soared following the removal of the tax on coffee in 1832 and by 1844, 150 million pounds were imported into the USA with each American now consuming more than six pounds of coffee annually. World coffee production (in Brazil, Java and Sumatra) expanded rapidly to cope

* William Sullivan, 'Brazil is Coffee and Coffee is the Negro: Coffee and its Role in Changing the Brazilian Labor Force during the 19th Century', *Historian*, 2014.

with global demand, and as the price of coffee dropped, the USA was established as a nation of coffee drinkers. Above all, Americans drank Brazilian coffee, bought in return for a range of US imports. By 1852, New York had its own coffee exchange, just as Liverpool had a cotton exchange, and in both cases, a substantial proportion of those commodities was cultivated by slaves: coffee in Brazil, cotton in the US South. US cotton and Brazilian coffee planters relied for their labour on the massive internal trade in slaves.

By the time Brazilian slavery ended in 1888, coffee was generating 60 per cent of the nation's export earnings. None of this could have happened without slave labour, most of which had been acquired *within* Brazil itself.*

Brazil's domestic slave trade had the effect of gradually shifting the nation's slave population from its old (largely sugar) regions to new (largely coffee) regions: from Bahia and Pernambuco in the north-east, to the centre and south of the country (to Minas Gerais and Sao Paulo). In 1819, there were 606,251 slaves in the sugar region; by 1872 that had declined to 508,846. By contrast, the slave populations of the central and southern regions, which had stood at 375,855 and 125,283 respectively in 1819, had increased substantially – to 752,013 and 249,947 by 1872.†

The clear evidence that Brazil continued to thrive both on illicit African arrivals, and on a major domestic slave trade, greatly troubled local and foreign abolitionists (led by the aggressively abolitionist British). Whatever economic benefits accrued to Brazil and the USA from their slave economies, they

* James Walvin, *Sugar*, pp.84–85.

† Christopher Schmidt-Nowara, *Slavery, Freedom and Abolition in Latin America and the Atlantic World* , Albuquerque, 2007, p.217.

caused immense damage to their enslaved victims. Families were destroyed, lives were wrecked and social misery was spread across Black communities – all at a time of rising national prosperity which was derived in large part from slave labour.

The Brazilian domestic slave trade spelled upheaval and personal and family trauma in the lives of everyone involved: for those who were forcibly removed and those left behind. One former slave, interviewed in 1880, told how he had been bought by a trader in Miranhao, taken to Sao Luiz, sold to another merchant and shipped on again to Rio. There he a was kept in a slave warehouse until bought by a coffee planter who moved him on, yet again – this time by train to a coffee plantation. Some slaves passed through even more hands than this, sold from one trader/merchant/agent to another, in a bewildering confusion of short-term ownerships. Many were shifted in small groups, by ship. Merchant vessels offered to carry a 'small cargo of slaves' to the next port of call. Some ships carried large numbers of slaves – to the disapproval of other passengers:

> One cannot travel on the packets of the Brazilian Company except in in the company of this human cargo destined for sale in the South.

This was a trade which inevitably involved the nightmare of family separations. One observer was horrified to see:

> Children yanked from their mothers, husbands separated from wives, parents from children.

Visit the slave market, he continued, 'and you will be indignant and stricken with the spectacle of so much misery.' Some merchants, 'warehousing' the enslaved in Rio, were notorious for the wretched condition in which they kept them housed, awaiting sale and movement onwards. One slave trader, though claiming that he took care of his slaves, lost twenty-two out of thirty-eight in his care in 1879.*

Some of the most revealing, and heart-rending, evidence from this Brazilian internal trade is not the general, overall data, but simple personal examples: glimpses of faces in the crowd. Corina, a twenty-year-old woman sold into prostitution in Bahia in 1867, was bought by a dealer in Rio who sold her to a female brothel owner. Corina had a child – who was taken from her to enable her to return to work as a prostitute – but by then she was in a diseased condition, struggling to save money to buy her own freedom. †

Children too were sold on their own, without regard to their parents. Luis Gama, sold at the age of eight in Salvador, was taken to Rio, then to Santos, later by foot to Sao Paulo City (80 km away). He worked as a domestic servant in a boarding house, learned to read and write, joined the army – but ran away and was discharged dishonourably. He then began to write poetry and political articles, eventually becoming an editor and prominent Brazilian lawyer and abolitionist. Yet throughout his ordeal as a slave, he *should* have been free: his initial sale had been illegal, because he had been born free and, late in life, was able to prove it.‡ His was an exceptional story:

* Q. in Richard Graham, 'Another Middle Passage: The Internal Slave Trade in Brazil', in *The Chattel Principle*, p.304.

† Richard Graham, 'Another Middle Passage', p.307.

‡ Richard Graham, 'Another Middle Passage', p.306; Christopher Schmidt-Nowara, *Slavery, Freedom and Abolition*, pp.152–153; Robert Edgar Conrad, *Children of God's Fire*, pp.229, 467–469.

many other free Blacks were seized and sold as slaves but experienced much less happy endings.

Such stories of personal misery could be repeated thousands of times and lie scattered in the paperwork of slavery, notably in legal documents which are replete with painful personal accounts. Yet this evidence is merely the visible, formal tip of a vast history of slave family separations, physical and sexual abuse, enforced long-distance travel, escapes, violence and punishments. Equally, it is evidence which underlines the unflagging determination of the enslaved to escape: to get home, to return to the point of Brazilian origin, back to loved ones, to familiar faces and places. This often involved endless perseverance. Often too, it ended in heartbreak and failure. Some people were able to save money, some managed to travel huge distances to find a way back to their loved ones – sometimes *decades* after separation and loss. One widowed mother placed an advertisement in a Pernambuco newspaper, searching for a daughter who had been sold away *thirty years earlier.*[*]

Like slave owners everywhere, Brazilian slave owners were permanently troubled by slaves seeking an alternative to their lives. Most troublesome of all were young males who devised their own ways of dealing with such upheavals. Widely regarded as 'turbulent' men, they were easily provoked, liable to run away or strike back, and not easily controlled. They were a cause of endless trouble: some slave holders regarded them as not worth the effort. Slave owners preferred more biddable, more pliant slave labourers.

Slavery in Brazil, like slavery across the Americas, was a heartless system which hinged on the enslaved's status as

* Richard Graham, 'Another Middle Passage', p.309.

property. They were things – *chattel* – and treated as such. The ties of affection and friendship, the invaluable bonds of kinship and family, all meant little to slave owners intent on securing the best material return from their human property. Everywhere, this created a toxic and volatile human brew: a volatility that we find in all corners of the enslaved Americas. The wonder is that slave owners were able to maintain their control. How did they manage, for centuries, to keep the lid on this explosive social system?

9

The Domestic US Slave Trade

As we have seen, the internal sale and removal of slaves across huge distances was a widespread feature of slavery throughout the Americas from the first. We see it in a huge variety of sources from the nineteenth century – including some spectacular graphic images of the enslaved being force marched away from home and families. And we can see it in early colonial newspapers which are littered with advertisements for slave sales. Once sold, the enslaved were removed and dispatched to their new owners who, even when local, would invariably be distant from a slave's relatives and friends. The North American colonies saw regular movement of slaves from one corner of a colony to another – and between the various colonies. What, for example, happened to the 'middle aged negro woman with her two male children the oldest four years of age' – offered for sale in February 1799 in Fredericksburg, Virginia? And what was the fate of the twenty-five slaves 'the property of James Dunlop, Jnr of Great Britain' when they were offered for sale? When Reuben Thornton died, his debts were paid by the sale of:

> Two good sawyers and a girl of about 12 years old (together with two working horses).*

There were many thousands of such sales, with people sold individually or in groups, *but rarely* as families. Their qualities and their value were determined by age, their skills and their physical condition, and though efforts were sometimes made to keep a slave family together, a slave owner's debts, death and economic misfortune generally led to family break-ups. Slaves were sold and bought *as assets*, and were parcelled out just like all other assets.

Such slave sales, and the resulting upheaval for the people involved, were common throughout the colonial Americas. But in both the USA and Brazil, the transformation of local economies in the nineteenth century created a totally new phenomenon of slave migrations; new in scale and consequences for the country and in the profound damage caused to its victims. It was driven by the rise of new major industries – tobacco, coffee and cotton – each with a voracious appetite for slave labour, and all serving to transform the older, relatively small-scale upheavals into massive migrations which became industries in their own right. Both in the USA and Brazil, internal, domestic slave trades developed which in many respects mirrored the Atlantic trade in their traumatic impact on the people involved.

Settlers on new lands in the US South needed labour for their new properties, and from c. 1790 onwards the number of

* Frederic Bancroft, *Slave Trading in the Old South*, New York, 1931, pp.19–20 This book, though very dated, is filled with rich material about enforced slave migrations.

slaves grew dramatically in Tennessee, Kentucky, then in Alabama, Mississippi, Louisiana and Texas. Across those states there was a veritable explosion of demand for enslaved labour of all kinds, skilled and unskilled. Settlers unable to travel back to the old slave states to buy enslaved labour, turned to a new breed of slave traders: brutal, callous men with a reputation for the ruthless handling of slaves. In the early nineteenth century, the enslaved populations of the old slave states – Virginia, Maryland and North Carolina – were growing fast and became a major exporter of enslaved labour. They offered rich pickings for slave traders, who set up shop in border towns, dangling money before local slave owners, crowding their human purchases into local warehouses and pens, before heading out, the slaves chained 'as though they had committed some heinous offence against our laws.' Nothing was able to stop the enslaved 'being wrested from their offspring and children from their parents, without respect to the ties of nature.'*

These were of course the years when the US South provided the textiles industries of Massachusetts, Lancashire and Germany with enormous volumes of raw cotton. It was also the period when, in the words of Michael Tadman, 'American slavery broke loose from the eastern seaboard and rapidly established its domain over vast regions extending as far west as Texas.'† These migrations were driven by planters moving on to new cotton lands and by slave traders buying slaves and driving them for resale to the new cotton frontier.

The numbers of people involved were huge. Each decade between 1810 and 1850 saw an average of two hundred

* Frederic Bancroft, *Slave Trading in the Old South*, pp.23–24.

† Michael Tadman, *Speculators and Slaves*, p.7.

thousand people uprooted and moved to the US South. Upwards of one million people were forced elsewhere, creating heartache and misery among those who moved and those left behind. Armies of people saw loved ones and friends disappear over the horizon. It was, after a fashion, a repeat of what had happened to the Africans torn from their communities and who vanished into the belly of the slave ships. This time, however, the slave trade involved people who overwhelmingly had been born in the USA. Though there was a migration of slaves from ports in the Chesapeake region to New Orleans, the main migrations were overland and by river. Though the miseries of those treks did not reach the levels of inhumanity we find on the Atlantic slave ships, they too were characterised by privations, sufferings and brutality. As on the slave ships, the domestic trade involved gangs of people shackled together: they became a common sight on their way to the South in the years before 1860 across the USA. Gangs of thirty to forty were common – sometimes as many as a hundred clanking their enslaved way to the cotton fields.

These streams of humanity consisted largely of young people. Slaves over the age of thirty were much less at risk of being sold south. Most common of all were slaves uprooted from their families in their teens and twenties, In addition, the children of slave marriages were also greatly at risk of being torn from their families and sold onwards to the cotton plantations. The literature created by those journeys groans with sorrow. Black and white commentators were united in their accounts: of weeping slaves, strained faces and bowed backs as coffles of slaves departed for the new world of the southern cotton plantations. Men walked ahead – shackled 'two-and-two together', followed by 'quiet slaves' (those whose spirits had already been crushed), followed by women – and then the children – with mothers with babes in arms bringing up the rear. When survivors of these migrations looked back they remembered the pervading misery:

> The poor man to whom I was ironed wept like an infant when the blacksmith, with his heavy hammer, fastened the ends of the bolts that kept the staples from slipping from our arms.*

They shuffled on, whatever the weather, sometimes managing twenty miles a day, resting at night in tents, in wretched public houses – or simply by the roadside. For many, trains offered easier transport, though usually on longer journeys and normally in a 'nigger car'.

Visitors to Washington provided graphic accounts of miserable groups of slaves loaded into railway carriages – all chained – and all supervised by brutal men wielding canes.†

Many others moved away along the country's mighty rivers, from St Louis, down the Mississippi to New Orleans, or down the Ohio and Mississippi to Natchez. Time and again, observers noted the way the slaves were shackled to each other. Perhaps the most haunting journeys (reminders of the Atlantic crossing) were experienced by those who were shipped from the Chesapeake along the Atlantic coast, south into the Gulf, usually destined for New Orleans. The ships involved were fitted out specially – again not unlike the Atlantic slave ships – for the specific loading and transport of slaves. Many seaborne troubles flared on those vessels: physical distress, sickness, slave

* Michael Tadman, *Speculators and Slaves*, p.73.

† Michael Tadman, *Speculators and Slaves*, p.7.

rebellions – and a lingering fear among the crew (and passengers). It could take twenty to twenty-five days to sail from Norfolk to New Orleans: though not as protracted as an Atlantic crossing, it was horribly reminiscent of the distress endured by the slaves' African forebears. Here was the latest phase in the apparently unending saga of slave upheavals and despair. And once again, what accentuated the misery was the related destruction of family life.*

The foremost historian of this domestic slave trade makes the point simply – but forcefully. In each decade before the Civil War, that trade:

> Carried hundreds of thousands of slaves, mostly children and slaves of marriageable age, and yet virtually no child was traded with its father, nor wife sold with her husband.

It was, in Michael Tadman's words, 'a process of destruction.' The US domestic slave trade was driven by the stark economic imperatives of slave owners and of the US market. Large numbers of children and adolescents were sold, locally and long-distance, not on the grounds of planned or carefully thought-out human relations; not according to a sense of humane decency or a need to protect and preserve slave family happiness. It was yet another vivid illustration of the 'scientific management' of the slave system which appears in the paperwork and accountancy of slavery. It was a system driven by the cold scrutiny of dollars and cents.

Every slave had a value – especially the young and healthy, with their potential of many years of future labour. Each person

* Michael Tadman, *Speculators and Slaves*, Ch.6.

had an individual value – but it was an individual, personal value, unrelated to a family of community. For all the debate about slave owners recognising the importance and value of slave families, the overriding consideration was simple economic value. Hence, most slaves were sold individually and their value was decided by the needs of owners and purchasers. 'The logic of the market pervaded.'* Moreover, when slaves *were* sold as a family group, that naturally included old and sometimes disabled family members: the very people who would have been difficult to sell individually. At first glance, the sale of family groups might seem to be reflect a policy influenced by a humane decision of not breaking up that group. It was, on the contrary, economic self-interest. The old, the sick, the infirm could be got rid of on the back of their younger and healthier relatives. Again, it was market forces, not sentiment, that drove the domestic slave trade. It is true that sometimes it was obviously in the slave owners' interests to preserve the slave family as a unit, but that rarely had anything to do with sentiment. It was driven essentially by self-interest. Thus, a hand bill from a Charleston auctioneer in1833:

> A valuable negro woman, accustomed to all kinds of house work. Is a good plain cook, an excellent dairy maid, washes and irons. She had four children, one a girl of 11 years of age, another 7, a boy about 5, and an infant 11 months old. Two of the children will be sold with the mother, the others separately, if it best suits the purchaser.†

* Michael Tadman, *Speculators and Slaves*, pp.133–137.

† Michael Tadman, *Speculators and Slaves*, p.139.

Throughout the history of US slavery in the era of King Cotton, abolitionists attacked slave owners and slave traders for continuing to break up slave families. Even when sold in-state, the distances travelled were sometimes enormous. For the victims involved, being relocated from one corner of a state to another was to vanish off the face of the earth. Moreover, no one knew *where* they had gone or what had happened to lost relatives. Such family destruction caused personal and family heartache that lasted decades. When former slaves, in deep old age, tried to locate long-lost relatives their pleas echo with misery. Their searches were often simple requests for information from anyone who might recall a name, an owner or a location. Those seeking loved ones, torn away decades before, often had only the vaguest of information to go by:

> Kansas Lee wished to learn the whereabouts of her children, four girls and one boy, who were, when last heard from, living in Baltimore, Md . . .
>
> My children were owned by the mother of Benjamin Keene. Address KANSAS LEE, Box 507, St Joseph, Mo.*

It is 1,000 miles from Baltimore to St Joseph.

As late as 1911, the Mayor of Baltimore received a letter from Ann Whaley, a woman (who thought she was 101) in New Orleans, begging him to:

* Heather Andrea Williams, *Help me to find my people: The African American Search for Family Lost in Slavery*, Chapel Hill, 2012, p.158.

> kindly inform me if you can of the whereabouts of my relatives living in your city. My mother's name was Minta Whaley. She was owned by Capt. Peter Whaley . . . There are relatives of mine living in your city or some of their posterity.*

Forlorn (and largely unsuccessful) pleas for help speak both to the longing and ignorance of the people who had been abandoned and those who had been removed. Loved ones had effectively disappeared, just as their forebears had vanished from African families: cast to the far side of the Atlantic and . . . who knows where to?

The long-distance domestic US slave trade (what historians have labelled 'inter-regional') was a highly selective business. In their advertisements, slave traders sought out particular age groups and physical types of slaves before corralling them into groups for the journey to the cotton kingdom. They wanted healthy young boys and girls for field work and, in the case of girls, for their future children. These were the slaves with the greatest economic potential to planters and slave traders assembled their groups with this in mind. But at every point, these groups of enslaved struck at the heart of the slave family. Children, adolescents, and young adults were plucked from their parents and siblings simply to satisfy the specific needs of southern planters. There was a raw and unpalatable truth behind this: people in the border states who *sold* their slaves to the slave traders, and the slave traders who bought them, were driven not by any respect for the slave family, but by what was

* This, and hundreds more, similar advertisements are being collected on the invaluable website LAST SEEN: Finding Family After Slavery: informationwanted.org

best suited to the economic interests of slave owners and traders.*

Slave owners were themselves acutely aware of the distress caused by such separations. They tried to hide an impending removal of people from their relatives. They told lies, made pretences and hid decisions to the very last minute. They would send slaves away on an errand for example, before removing their relatives in their absence. Slaves would return home to find that their children/wife/husband had vanished and their family had been destroyed. Some men became unmanageable when they lost their wives and children and they too had to be sold. Such outbursts and grievances subsided in time but the heartache never disappeared. Moreover, the very real *fear* of separation lingered over *all* the enslaved – even those who had been traded great distances. They could never be sure that they would not be traded again. They never knew what changes in an owner's personal or economic fortunes might bring about.

We know of the slaves' continuing outrage and distress through the abundance of personal testimony, especially in slave narratives – evidence which echoes with inescapable fear of a repetition of upheaval and removal. The cries of slaves' distress offer us the most widespread and eloquent evidence of their love and attachment to lost family members. Through all the manifold tribulations of the enslaved experience – from African arrivals through to the miseries of the nineteenth-century domestic slave trades, the family had become the bedrock of slave life. Yet for untold legions of people, their families were assaulted, damaged and often simply destroyed by the changing economic needs of US slave owners and slave

* Michael Tadman, *Speculators and Slaves*, pp.146–154.

traders. For years, historians have argued about the very existence of the slave family. Yet the most telling evidence about the history of family lies in the anguish of people whose families were destroyed. It was as if slaves could never escape the reality and the threat of upheaval and family trauma. They were, in the eyes of their masters, mere beast of the field – and were sold and moved around accordingly.

The evidence is irrefutable. One in five slave marriages in the Upper South were destroyed by these enforced removals, but if we add *local* upheavals to the long-distance migrations the figures are much worse: upwards of one in four marriages were wrecked by such enforced removals. Add to this, removals we cannot count (i.e., when slaves moved alongside their owners, or were given away as gifts, normally to relatives) and family upheavals become even more widespread. Although it is hard to be precise, scholars now think that one third of first marriages among the enslaved in the Upper South were destroyed and only a small proportion (perhaps 4 per cent) were ended by the slaves themselves. The threat to their marriages came from their owners.*

In all this tumult, what happened to slave children is another bleak chapter in this wretched account. The very young were rarely sold on their own – for obvious reasons. The risk, however, increased from the age of five, and especially between the ages of twelve and fourteen. What made these figures worse is the fact that children often lost their fathers when they were sold along with their mothers. The end result was that at least one third of children in the Upper South were forcibly removed from one of their parents – or both – in the years before the Civil War. It

* Michael Tadman, *Speculators and Slaves*, pp.169–171.

may even have been higher. It is true that most slave children spent about ten years with their parents – with all the benefits that brought – but how do we weigh those benefits against the lasting distress and damage caused by removal and separation? Equally, how can we assess the worry – the nagging and unavoidable concern – that they might, in the blink of an eye, face enforced separation from parents? Every young slave lived with this inescapable threat: it was as unavoidable a feature of slave life as the unrelenting toil. The enslaved knew that the sudden and unexplained disappearance of loved ones (not to mention friends) was a ubiquitous threat. It cast a shadow across the lives even of those who remained personally unaffected.

Slaves were in no doubt about who caused such anxiety and sorrow. It all stemmed directly from their owners, especially from the planters whose harsh decisions paid little attention to the slaves' happiness. They duped slave mothers and spouses when they conducted these enforced sales and removals. Domestic slaves regularly *witnessed* the owners actually counting the hard cash after the sale of their relatives and friends into the brutal maws of a slave trader. The victims were never in any doubt about who caused their pain. The person at the centre of their miseries, the root cause of their inescapable worries, was the slave owner. He or she held the slave family's fate in the palm of their hand.

Slaves born in the US South – the region which imported slaves from the Upper South – were much less at risk of being forcibly removed and sold away, though certain regions of the South *did* export slaves. Equally unsettling, those areas of the South which absorbed large numbers of slaves via the domestic slave trade became the home for people who had been torn away from spouses, parents and siblings. How did the consequent personal bitterness and unhappiness feed into the slave community? At its simplest we know that it became part of southern slave folklore and memory, among men and women who remarried, formed new families – but who told their families of what had happened to them, and who was responsible. Here was family life which had unhappiness and betrayal blended into it. This was the essence of family life among US slaves before 1860.*

***

For the generations of Africans shipped into the Americas the sagas of upheavals and seaborne transportation had been the stuff of folk memory and of slave storytelling. As long as ships continued to unload Africans in North America, African voices added their own accounts to the slave memory of upheaval. African languages, accents, deflected via local interpreters and via patois versions, kept alive the slaves' knowledge and awareness of Africa and the Atlantic crossing. Theirs was an acute nightmarish vision: of violence, of enslavement and of dangerous travel by land and water, and culminating in the terrors of the Atlantic slave ship. The intensity of these memories may have faded as Africans died out and as new generations of people born in the Americas came to dominate the slave communities in North America. But then, almost as if to revive the bleakest memories of the enslaved past, domestic slave trades evolved to weave their own cruel web of dislocation for the enslaved people of the USA.

***

* Michael Tadman, *Speculators and Slaves,* pp.175–177.

If we consider the broad sweep of enslaved history in North America before the Civil War, what stands out are the continuities and the common, shared experiences of enslaved people. There were, of course, enormous differences among the slaves: differences between men and women, from one kind of work to another, between African and local-born. But their *shared* experiences were more striking than all these variations. In the eyes of the law and in economic practice, they were all chattel – things – objects. They were bought and sold, inherited and bequeathed: they were items of trade in a slave owner's wider commercial portfolio. And as such, they were scattered here and there, in Africa, across the Atlantic, between and within European colonies and national states in the Americas. Wherever slavery thrived, slaves understood the cause of their manifold woes: the people who owned them and who traded them, in shackles, from one place to another. Theirs was a life which was debilitated and humiliated in equal measure. Yet it was also a life which yielded great profit from their labours. Slaves knew who made that profit: the people who, quite literally, held the whip hand. And that knowledge nurtured a brooding resentment and defiance which was greatly feared by slave owners and which flared, in moments of greatest tension, to challenge slavery itself.

In the last half century of slavery in the USA, 60 per cent of the country's domestic slave trade took place not because slave owners were obliged to sell their slaves but because they intended to profit from them. It was an enforced migration of people driven by financial speculation. In the process, it destroyed slave families on a huge scale. But the slave owners attempted to justify their actions. In the US South, planters and their supporters (in pulpits and political assemblies) argued in public and in print that slaves were lazy, promiscuous and incapable of sustaining regular family life. Only the compulsion and restraints of slavery, so the argument went, could secure the necessary social and labouring discipline from the enslaved labour force. Both in practice and in print, slave owners regularly told of their despair and failure in trying to bring slaves together in domestic and productive harmony. Yet these were the very people who orchestrated and financed the widespread break-up of slave families. Time and again, proslavery writers dismissed the slaves' attachment to family, citing instead their preference for casual and promiscuous sexual relations. The reality was not only utterly different, it was, in fact, the polar opposite. The claims promoted by generations of planters and their friends were a classic illustration of blaming the victims. It was to become part of the ideological and political stream that flowed into the development of modern racist attitudes. It was one element of the tendency to strip Black humanity of all social qualities held dear by Western culture, more especially the unwavering attachment to family life. It was a slave owner's belief which morphed into a deeply entrenched social assumption about Black inferiority. All this of course had complex historical roots, but the intimate story of the slave family – both in reality and mythology – lay at the heart of that assumption. Even more alarming, it was an assumption which became essential to a school of historical interpretation. Southern historians were important in propagating the mythology about the enslaved family. Today, the contrary reality is there for all to see.

North American slavery was not merely an institution of grotesque exploitation, but it spawned a deeply racist ideology which rode roughshod over the social and historical realities.

The people who owned, bought and sold slaves in vast numbers did so with little or no regard for the slave family. Yet they clearly knew how much the slaves valued their families: they saw them weeping, and begging, heard their night-time wailing, and coped with their entreaties to be reunited with loved ones. For most of the uprooted, reunions were not to be. Many lived out their lives, in slavery, then in freedom, in the lingering hope that they would, one day, be reunited with loved ones. Theirs was a heartache which echoes down the years and was heard, time and again, well into the twentieth century. It survives to the present day, in the drive to reconstruct lost family ties.

Part Four

MANAGING SLAVERY

10

A World of Paper: Accounting for Slavery

SLAVERY LEFT BEHIND an astonishing paper trail all round the world. We can only guess at the volume involved, but it is to be measured by mile upon mile of shelving. It forms a substantial part of national archives of all the major slaving powers, and of the nations which evolved from Europe's settlements in the Americas. Slave papers – broadly defined – crowd the shelves of civic and local archives and libraries, and slave-related literature fills the legislative records of Parliaments, Congresses, Assemblies and churches, of international organisations and conventions. Alongside this wealth of information, there are incalculable (and often unknown) private collections of material left by merchants, planters, agents, sailors, landowners – on both sides of the Atlantic. Today, all this – and much more besides – forms an archival treasure trove for anyone wanting to study the history of slavery.

When I began my own research on slavery, I spent much of the summer of 1967 poring over eighteenth-century plantation ledgers, in a hot airless building in the rural heart of Jamaica. Those papers – with their detailed record of Worthy Park, a Jamaican sugar plantation – had been salvaged from an attic where they had lain hidden and unknown for perhaps two centuries. (They now rest in the island's National Archives.) More documents for that project were subsequently located in Kingston and Spanish Town, in London and Washington D.C.* In the years that followed, my research on slavery took me to archival collections across the Caribbean, Britain, North America and Australia. But in the summer of 1967, I could not have imagined that those crumbling ledgers, many of their pages eaten away by tropical termites, were just the start of what became a global paperchase. Yet it ought to have been clear from the start, because Worthy Park was just one small aspect of a remarkable system scattered across a vast physical geography. The slaves at Worthy Park came from Africa, their owners originated from England (and eventually returned to Cornwall), plantation supplies were shipped from Ireland, England and North America, and the sugar and rum produced there was shipped to Britain.

The history of Worthy Park is merely one illustration of the variety, richness and ubiquity of the paperwork of slavery. Though much remains untapped, it has spawned a remarkable scholarship which grows year on year. This raises a simple, but deeply puzzling question, however. In the face of this archival abundance, why was slavery ignored (at worst) and marginalised (at best) until relatively recently? Equally curious – why has slavery quite recently become a topic of widespread curiosity and importance? Why now?

Although it is hard to prove definitively, there is a strong case to be made that the enslaved people of the Americas were better

* See, Michael Craton and James Walvin, *A Jamaican Plantation*, Manuscript Material, pp.332–333.

documented than any other comparable historical group. We have parochial detail about early modern communities, rich sources about military personnel, and we possess huge volumes of material about modern populations thanks to the rise of modern census data. But there is nothing comparable to the documentation about the twelve million-plus Africans embarked on the Atlantic slave ships. Despite this simple but essential fact, the formal study of those people lay neglected, ignored – and even unremarked – effectively until the mid-twentieth century. Thereafter, however, there has been a veritable tsunami of slave-based scholarship.

***

Bookkeeping

Slavery – in the Americas and the Atlantic slave trade – was a form of commerce. As such it was recorded and documented in the account books of everyone involved. From the quaysides of the Atlantic's major port cities, to trading houses in India and China, to the plantations perched precariously on the very edge of the frontiers across the Americas, the data of slavery was entered in appropriate paperwork. It was, however, a widely fragmented and *dispersed* economy which left its documentary evidence – just like its African victims – scattered to the four corners of the world. This may, in part, explain why slavery was neglected for so long: its paperwork was dispersed and forgotten. Even so, the evidence is there – in the account books. Everything – and everyone – involved in Atlantic slavery was accounted for.

The crude reality of slavery was the reduction of Africans to items of trade, and we know so much about them *for that very reason* and because of the remorseless accountancy of slavery. The origins of double-entry accountancy are to be found in the major Italian city states of the fifteenth century. It was a system that required literacy and numeracy, the existence of private property, a money economy and the role of credit. Italian merchants developed intricate dealings throughout the Mediterranean and beyond, and needed a system of keeping track of their increasingly complex commercial dealings. The method they adopted – double-entry bookkeeping – quickly became the standard method of recording commercial activity and was eagerly adopted by merchants and bankers throughout Europe. The system was codified and published by a Franciscan monk, Luca Paccioli, in his book *Suma de Arithmetica* in 1494, which sought to codify 'the system used in Venice', whereby a merchant:

> must always put down on a sheet of paper or in a separate book whatever he has in this world.*

Within fifty years, other books on accountancy, each refining and improving on the original, had been published in Italian, later in Dutch (1543), French and English in 1543 and 1547, German in 1547 and Spanish in 1590. In 1567, John Weddington published his account of 'howe to keep merchants bokes' and explained how accountancy should work. It was 'a breff order or instruction as the trewe manner, to keep merchant Bokes' and was, he claimed, 'daily practized by many notable

* A. C. Littleton, *Accounting Evolution to 1900*, New York, 1933, pp.12, 23, Ch.V.

marchntis of Italie'.* Though Scotland did not have its own edition until 1683, that heralded what has been called 'the Scottish ascendancy' of the eighteenth century with a flurry of accountancy books published there.†

The upsurge in Scottish accountancy coincided with (and greatly assisted) the remarkable flowering of Scottish commercial prosperity, and the rise of that nation's learned culture. Educated Scots scattered to all parts of British imperial trade and settlement and were to be found poring over their papers in the captains' cabins of Britain's massive maritime fleet, in the counting houses of Bengal, and on the plantations of the Americas. By the mid-eighteenth century, there were various Scottish publications on accountancy. Scottish printers manufactured ledgers specifically for plantations, with sections devoted to keeping a daily record of sugar and rum production. Others listed produce imported and exported, with space provided for 'the numbers of free and slave people on the property.'‡ This rise of professional accountancy in Britain was of course a reflection of the emergence of British economic power, and by the late eighteenth century the names of professional accountants appeared regularly in trade directories (though some continued to double as 'writing masters').§

***

* M. F. Bywater and B. S. Yarney, *Historic Accounting Literature: a Companion Guide,* London and Tokyo, 1982, p.58.

† M. F. Bywater and B. S. Yarney, *Historic Accounting Literature*, p.9.

‡ B. W. Higman, *Plantation Jamaica, 1750–1850: Capital and Control in a Colonial Economy*, Kingston, 2005, p.97.

§ Wendy Habgood, *Chartered Accountants in England and Wales*, Manchester, 1994, pp.3–4.

From its early days, the transatlantic slave trade was a highly bureaucratic and regulated system which left behind a mountainous trove of documentation. At every stage it was a business shaped by written instructions and by carefully recorded transactions. Unlike the piracy of the initial slave voyages (and of popular memory) it became a finely tuned and finely recorded enterprise.

The template for the bureaucracy of the Atlantic slave trade was established by Spain. Its *Asiento* system was, by design and management, an astonishingly intrusive bureaucracy. Licences were issued (for a fee) from a central office in Seville to a variety of traders, but increasingly to Portuguese merchants who had access to essential finance and to the main areas of the African coast where trading had already been established. The *Asiento* was not simply a general permit to trade in African slaves, for each specified the number of Africans to be carried, and the ratio of male to female slaves. Sometimes the *Asiento* specified exactly which destination the Africans should be taken to. In 1615, for example, the *Asiento* granted to Antonio Fernandes d'Elvas was for the annual delivery of five thousand Africans to Cartagena or Veracruz.*

The *Asiento* system gave birth to a remarkable administration, with offices in Lisbon, Seville and Madrid which supervised each phase of slave trading between Europe, Africa and the Americas. Licences were granted to networks of businessmen, often consisting of relatives and close friends, many with existing trading links to Africa, India and the Americas. Once the licence had been paid (or guarantees provided in lieu) the ship faced three inspections, first to ensure its seaworthiness

* Linda A. Newson and Susie A. Michin, *From Capture to Sale,* Ch.1.

and that it was suitably manned. Any shortcomings were checked on a second inspection. Finally, the ship was inspected for a third time on the eve of departure – with particular attention paid to food. If the inspectors were satisfied, the vessel could then leave for Africa. The complex *Asiento* bureaucracy left a detailed paper trail. It was also the prototype of the literate and numerate system what would characterise slavery in the Americas. Both at sea and on land, slavery generated unprecedented volumes of paperwork.

The early Portuguese slave traders operating under *Asiento* licence kept detailed account books, listing the goods acquired and how much they cost. In their trade in Africa and the Americas, transactions often took the form of barter, with enslaved Africans exchanged for an equivalent value in specified goods. An African might, for example, be purchased for a given length of textile, a number of iron bars, guns, or a volume of cowrie shells and alcohol. In the same mode, the provisions acquired to feed the enslaved Africans were calculated by the equivalency in other goods.

Just as Europeans and Americans developed a keen awareness of the market needs and fashions of trade on the African coast, so too did African traders develop a sharp appreciation of what they could demand from the seaborne traders. They learned what was available and what they preferred from the arriving ships. Traders thus had to scour global markets to please the demands of Africans traders and hence the remarkably mixed cargoes of goods imported to West Africa from widely scattered places on earth.

In all this, there was, inevitably, a degree of uncertainty. Despite the mastery which the trading data provided, African markets were often unpredictable. There was always an element of risk and the danger that a vessel might arrive at the wrong spot, with the wrong goods at the wrong time. The Atlantic trade was commercially and physically hazardous, though in time, some of the uncertainties were reduced or minimised, especially in matters of navigation and sailing. Nonetheless, the physical dangers of oceanic travel in tropical waters never disappeared. Equally, the commercial risks remained. As the Atlantic trade evolved, the commercial risks were reduced largely through trial and error: the simple experience of buying and selling Africans. The slave trade became increasingly well-managed. What had started as a small-scale business rooted in networks of relatives and trusted friends evolved into a complex global industry with state backing and major financial support. As it did so, it changed from transporting relatively small numbers of African victims into a truly colossal international enterprise which fed huge numbers of victims to the American slave markets. Throughout, it thrived on careful accountancy which absorbed and analysed all the commercial data involved.

***

A great deal of responsibility rested on the shoulders of the masters of the slave ships. They too were expected to keep a detailed account of their commercial transactions. Ships' masters were in charge of a major investment: in the vessel, its crew and cargo and, as the ship crossed the Atlantic, for the lives and survival of hundreds of Africans. A master's wide-ranging duties were spelled out in bold simplicity by the master of the *Arthur* in 1677–78, who noted the he was responsible for 'All the actions and transactions from Gravesend to New Callabar and from thence to the Island of Barbados our port of

Discharge.'* A century later, a Liverpool merchant warned his captain, in 1782, that:

> It behoves you to be very circumspect in
> all your proceedings, and very attentive
> to the minutest part of yr Conduct

The reason was simple: you had 'a large Capital under you'. A slave ship might be worth £12,000 and the master was charged with every aspect of the voyage. He hired the crew, bought the provisions, haggled for slaves, sailed the ship and sold the Africans in the Americas. In the words of Marcus Rediker, he was 'the monarch of his wooden world.'†

It was a demanding position. By turns, the captain had to be master-mariner, stern manager of an often-difficult crew, chief negotiator in the unusual routines of slave trading, and head jailor of a floating prison. Although each master had a degree of freedom in how he managed a ship and the voyage, each sailed with strict instructions from the ship's owners. In October 1717, the Royal African Company planned for a cargo of four hundred Africans to be collected from the Guinea Coast – even specifying the age groups of the Africans to be bought: men aged twenty to twenty-five, women aged sixteen to twenty, boys from the age of ten to fifteen, and girls from twelve to fifteen: 'The Women as Near as possible to be all Virgins.'‡

* 'Journal of the *Arthur*', Dec 5th 1677–May 25 1678, Elizabeth Donnan, *Documents,* I, pp.226–234.

† Marcus Rediker, *The Slave Ship,* pp.191, 57–58.

‡ The outbound cargo was worth £1,330: 'we hope twill purchase you 240'. Minutes of Correspondence, 10 October 1717, Elizabeth Donnan, *Documents,* II, p.15.

Company orders sometimes specified how much should be spent on each slave. In 1702, one master was told 'if possible do not give above Ten Iron Barrs for Men Slaves and Seven or Eight for Women and five or six for Boys and Girls.'* But even the most attentive merchant recognised the need for masters to use their discretion – but:

> on no Account bring any old Men or fallen-breasted Women. It is better to return without Slaves than to crowd the Ship with such.†

In time, and as merchants acquired detailed knowledge about navigation in African waters, they even issued sailing and navigational instructions. When the Bristol ship the *Dispatch* sailed for Adony in the Bight of Biafra in 1725, Captain Barry was ordered not to 'proceed over the Barr, but rather that you Anchor as usual in the bests and Convenients place for safety.' He was ordered to:

> let your knetting be fix'd breast high
> fore and aft and so keep 'em shackled and hand Bolted
> fearing their rising or leaping Overboard

With his ship fully loaded, Barry was ordered to head to Antigua where further instructions would be waiting for him. If the new orders had not arrived, he was to hasten to Nevis, or,

* Invoice of goods, Captain James Westmore, 1702, Elizabeth Donnan, *Documents*, IV, p.79.

† 'Letter of Instruction to the Master', Charleston, 24 July 1807, Elizabeth Donnan, *Documents*, IV, p.568.

if not possible, to South Carolina – and sell the Africans to a Mr Joseph Wagg. The master and senior officers were allowed to buy two slaves each – from their own money – to sell as a bonus on the voyage.*

This detailed account of the planning and financing of a single slave voyage might stand as a blueprint for thousands of others. By then – 1725 – the Atlantic trade had become a massive commercial concern which had delivered something like five hundred thousand Africans to Jamaica and to Barbados, and more than two and a half million to Brazil. It had become a well-oiled machine, and the men who ran it – living in Europe and Brazil – knew how to make it work as efficiently as possible. Nonetheless there were inescapable dangers and difficulties. The perils of oceanic travel and navigation were fixtures. So too was the threat posed by the enslaved Africans. Yet despite all this, a quite remarkable commercial system had emerged. The group of businessmen in Bristol who owned the *Dispatch* were able to micromanage a complex global venture which ranged from Africa, to the Caribbean and North America. They drafted detailed instructions for every aspect of Capt. Barry's undertaking, right down to warnings of specific navigational dangers in the Atlantic. Barry sailed with exact instructions about the kind of Africans he should buy – and for how much – how to manage the prisoners on board, where to stop for provisions and how to feed the Africans. He was told exactly where to deliver the Africans – with alternative destinations if circumstances had changed. At each point in this widely scattered geography, the Bristol merchants had contacts able to

* 'Instructions to Captain Wm Barry October', 7 October 1725, Elizabeth Donnan, *Documents*, II, pp.327–329.

accept the slaves, or revise Capt. Barry's instructions. Finally, they recommended the captain 'to the Good God Almighty's protection . . .' In reply, Capt. Barry acknowledged his orders, 'which I promise to perform (God willing) to the utmost of my power.'

The ship's owners, and their captain, felt no inconsistency in calling on the help of the Almighty in what, today, seems a godless enterprise. In both the Bristol office, and the captain's cabin, no one troubled themselves about the ethics of their venture: all threw themselves on the Lord's mercy. Though modern readers might find this troubling, few contemporaries felt the slightest twinge of religious or ethical doubt – still less of guilt. This was to change – and quickly – with the rise of abolition in the late eighteenth century.

For the time being, however, we are left with a stark reality. To many, perhaps most people, this vast complicated trade in African humanity remained a morally neutral territory. It was a world of enormous and everyday dangers, which yielded profit to its backers and planners, but it was a matter which afforded little space for moral or religious doubt to those same men. In the port cities of Europe and the Americas, in Africa, on the high seas, the men in charge were masters of a complex operation, and they had, at their fingertips (in ledgers, order books, letters, memoranda, invoices and receipts) an accumulation of data which explained how to make profitable trade in African humanity.

***

As slave trading expanded, it prompted changes in the way business was conducted in major port cities. Merchant houses grew bigger, squeezing out smaller, local competitors. In Bristol and Glasgow, and to a lesser extent in Liverpool and London, larger merchant houses came to dominate the local slaving industry. In Bristol in 1702, more than two hundred companies imported slave-grown tobacco. Fifty years later that had dropped to thirty. Similarly, Bristol's sugar importers – more than five hundred strong in the 1720s – had shrunk to eighty-five by the end of the century. A similar concentration took place in London and Liverpool. By the last years of the eighteenth century, 40 per cent of Bristol's slave trade was dealt with by only two merchants. Trade was concentrated into fewer hands: a 'revolution of scale' in Atlantic slaving helped by the 'availability of marine insurance and credit to large, seemingly secure firms.' It also illustrated 'the greater economic efficiency in the conduct of business, with large turnovers of goods speeded up by the concentration of resources.'* The slave trade, alongside its ancillary trades in the production of slave-grown commodities, had developed into a recognisably modern economic system which was closely monitored and moderated by detailed accountancy.

The development of the Atlantic slave trade was part of a much broader transformation in the way the Western world conducted its commercial affairs. Global trade generated remarkable waves of information about how business was conducted everywhere. In the case of the slave ships, each discrete area of commercial activity developed via letters, instructions, logs and legal documents. All this took place in a Western world which was itself being changed by the impact of

* Kenneth Morgan, *Slavery, Atlantic Trade and the British Economy, 1660–1800*, Cambridge, 2000, pp.81–82.

widening literacy and printed material. Those changes were on display in what might seem, at first glance, to be the most unlikely of places: the proliferation of coffee shops. From the mid-seventeenth century onwards, those 'penny universities' became venues for masculine sociability, but also acted as centres for business activities. In the City of London, banks and insurance companies emerged from coffee houses. Coffee shops also became centres of up-to-date commercial information (and gossip). In major port cities, many of them were close to the water's edge and established themselves as the crossroads of news from the far-flung corners of global trade. London's *Jamaica* and *Virginia* coffee houses explain themselves: places where people bound for, or arriving from, those distant colonies could meet, pass on information and exchange news. In June 1757, the *General Advertiser* contained the following advertisement:

> To be SOLD
> (At a reasonable Price)
> A negro boy, about eleven Years old,
> Strong and healthy, without a blemish . . .
> Whoever wants such, applying at the Jamaica
> Coffee-house will be further informed.

Eight years later, 'A likely Negro Boy, About ten Years old' was available via the same coffee house.* People went to coffee shops to read newspapers, which published the latest shipping news

* *Runaway Slaves in Britain: bondage, freedom and race in the eighteenth century.* University of Glasgow, https://www.runaways.gla.ac.uk/, accessed 18 October 2020.

and recent information from inbound ships. Newspapers in Britain and North America proliferated, thanks to the income from the commercial information and advertisements they carried. The great bulk of the *content* of newspapers was overwhelmingly commercial.

Newspapers also had global reach and impact. British newspapers, with all the latest political and international news, were eagerly awaited in the Caribbean colonies. Jamaican newspapers were similarly filled with commercial information: news of the arrival of ships and their cargoes (the most important being those from Africa). Barbados was the first British colony to have a twice-weekly newspaper, in 1738. By then, newspapers were also a major source of information in New York, Philadelphia and Boston. By contrast no newspapers were published in French and Spanish colonies before 1776. In the British case, the flow of commercial information both within Britain and within the Atlantic economy, was also greatly helped by a relatively swift postal service, launched during the reign of Queen Anne.*

In port cities, newspapers became established as the bulletin board for the myriad details about shipping: vessels arriving, leaving – or lost, alongside news, culled from arriving vessels, of sister ships, their whereabouts and fortunes, in Africa and the Americas. Colonial newspapers recorded the arrival of important cargoes. The *Virginia Gazette* (first published in 1736) listed mahogany landed in Virginia from the Caribbean, Africans just in from a slave ship, alongside manufactured goods being unloaded from ships fresh from Europe. This information was wedged between shoals of advertisements and news of tobacco in

* B. W. Higman, *Plantation Jamaica*, pp.116–117.

Glasgow, sugar in Liverpool and London, Africans in Jamaica and South Carolina. Ships arriving in Rio, having rounded the Cape of Good Hope en route home to Europe from India, carried goods and people from distant corners of Portuguese and Dutch trade in Asia: from India and islands in the Indian Ocean, from Japan and from Batavia. Rio (and Lisbon) were the most socially and commercially complex of urban centres.

Colonial newspapers were also littered with advertisements for runaway slaves and provide us with some of the most important and revealing data we have about the lives of enslaved people in the Americas. At times, the detailed descriptions are astonishing. A slave owner in Rio in 1845 sought a runaway blacksmith, named Jose Antonio, aged twenty-five to thirty, originally from Benguela:

> Short in stature, thin, well-made body, dark
> color, face rather long, pale jaw, almost no
> beard, lips rather full, round head, and is in
> the habit of going about with long hair, small
> eyes, long eyelashes, good teeth, nose medium large,
> speaks in a refined, humble, and insincere way, may have
> some old and small marks of punishment on his buttocks.*

He was carrying spare clothes, sometimes changed his name ('whenever he runs away'), usually claims to be free – and had a firearm.† Many such descriptions provide telling detail about the precise origins of the slave. Domingos Sabaru, a twenty-year-old in Brazil in 1752, not only had smallpox marks but also:

* Robert Edgar Conrad, *Children of God's Fire*, pp.362–363.
† Robert Edgar Conrad, *Children of God's Fire*, pp.111–115.

> . . . four small spears on top of his right eyebrow, two circles on the top of the left eyebrow, a small grid in the middle of the eyebrows, a star at the temple.

We know from these details that the man originated in Savalou, Benin.*

Newspapers became an important means of recovering lost or runaway slaves, and were a major noticeboard for buying and selling the enslaved. It was here, in print, that slave owners could offer slaves by advertising their skills, strengths, personal qualities and all-round suitability. A clutch of various Brazilian advertisements from 1821 reveals how owners emphasised such skills and personal qualities. They included 'a skilfull shoemaker . . . with no vices or bad habits' and an Angolan who was 'a very good maker of combs, both tortoise shell and animal horns.' Three Angolan women were advertised for their domestic skills: 'all with very good figures and the ability to do every kind of work in the house.' We learn that another female domestic slave was 'still young and without vices.' Another was ideal for wet-nursing ('a black woman with milk'). Children were regularly sold on their own, though some, barely into adolescence, were pitched into the most arduous or adult labours. Other slaves were sold when their owner was leaving Brazil, while some were purchased to accompany an owner on overseas travel.†

Thousands of such advertisements litter newspapers throughout the Americas in the era of slavery: they were also common

* Adair Rodriquez, 'How African markings were used to construct the idea of race in colonial Brazil', *The Conversation*, 21 January 2021.
† Robert Edgar Conrad, *Children of God's Fire*, pp.111–115.

in Europe. The habit of acquiring Black domestics (both enslaved and free) became a marked feature of polite fashionable European societies in the seventeenth and eighteenth centuries, and can be seen in any number of contemporary portraits, in graphic satire and in newspaper advertisements. Indeed it was the *existence* of such sales, in England, that contributed to the early unease about the very institution of slavery itself. In 1744, London's *Daily Advertiser* published this notice:

> To be sold. A pretty little Negro Boy, about nine Years old, and well limb'd. If not dispos'd of, is to be sent to the West Indies . . . He is to be seen at the Dolphin Tavern in Tower Street.

A few years later, the same newspaper offered 'a Negro boy age about fourteen years old, warranted free from any distemper . . . [who] has been used two years to all kinds of household work, and to wait at table; his price is £25.' He could be purchased at the George Coffee House in Chancery Lane.*

The most important role of newspapers, however, was the access they provided to commercial news and information. This was especially important in the major ports of the Atlantic trading system. The men who financed and insured the shipping and cargoes in the Atlantic required prompt and accurate information about shipping, and though newspapers were invaluable, the insurance syndicates especially required something more specific and organised. In 1734, *Lloyd's List* was launched to deal with the huge growth of maritime insurance.

* David Olusoga, *Black and British: A Forgotten History*, London, 2016, p.82.

Lloyd's Register of Shipping (1760) provided further help for insurers. Shippers and merchants could now monitor their global trading investments more closely.

Lloyd's List was a crucial indicator of the ups and downs of Britain's slaving fleet. It was available in a host of places, initially in coffee houses but later in the formal exchanges which emerged in major port cities. The publication became an important source of information in trading houses and quayside offices from Falmouth (often the first and last port of call for ships in the Atlantic trade) to Glasgow. Moreover, the information contained in *Lloyd's List* – the departures, arrivals and the losses – became a feature in newspapers from London to Philadelphia and Kingston. Provincial and colonial newspapers recycled the news culled from London newspapers, cutting and pasting, splicing everything with an array of local news and a multitude of advertisements. Readers were kept informed, at a great distance and time lag, about what was happening in other parts of the empire (notably the capital) and throughout the vast global network where the maritime fleets plied their trade.

The massive expansion of maritime trade from the seventeenth century onwards, and particularly the emergence of specialised trade, stimulated the rise of maritime insurance. Few trades were as specialised as the slave ships, and the insurance which evolved to cover them had its own byzantine complexity which few could fully understand or master. By the mid-eighteenth century, insuring African slaves as cargo was an accepted feature of maritime insurance. As grotesque as it sounds to us, the Africans were classified as 'perishable goods', that is goods which had to have their value specified in the insurance policy. The insured Africans had prices on their heads. They could not be insured for 'natural wastage', i.e. when they died naturally. Brazilian slavers in the nineteenth century resolved this matter by killing Africans on board who showed signs of contagious illness. A slave who simply died ('natural wastage') was non-recoverable on insurance, but dying via 'perils of the sea' or when killed in revolt, *was*. Legal authorities in all of Europe's major slaving nations struggled with this issue, both in court cases and in legal treatises, and they have left us with the delicate problem of seeking to untangle their decisions and concepts. John Weskett's English digest of insurance laws (1781) classified slaves alongside cattle. Portuguese insurance law likewise classified the insurance of slaves at sea as they did beasts. The French regarded them as 'moveable stock' and the Dutch classified a slave as 'a head' just as they did cattle. The enslaved Africans were, at sea, as they were to be in the Americas – chattel, mere things.*

One man who mastered the complexity of British maritime insurance was Lord Mansfield, and it fell to him to pronounce on the murder of 132 Africans on board the *Zong* in 1781, as described in Chapter 6. The case, heard in 1783, went straight to the heart of the Atlantic slaving system, exposing the pretence that Africans lost their humanity by falling into the maws of the slave traders. The case was paraded, with full legal jargon and courtroom posturing, before England's most eminent judge. Was it merely an insurance matter? Or was it – as early abolitionist claimed – a question of mass murder, for which the men responsible should be brought to justice? Today, it is clear that the *Zong* case was a tipping point in the history of the Atlantic slave trade. Thereafter critics of the slave trade (and

* Robin Pearson and David Richardson, 'Insuring the Transatlantic Slave Trade', *Journal of Economic History*, vol. 79, Issue 2, June 2019, pp.417–446.

slavery) were galvanised into political action. Within a mere four years a national and far-reaching abolition campaign had sprung up across Britain, with its sight firmly set on the abolition of the Atlantic slave trade.

By the time of the *Zong* case, maritime insurance had generated a massive corpus of literature of its own, the most obvious (and mundane) format being the various *Lloyd's Lists*, and the proliferation of data about shipping in newspapers on both sides of the Atlantic. It is a literature that also exposed the immense dangers involved in slave trading. Between 1741 and 1807, *Lloyd's List* recorded no fewer than 188 wrecks 'lost on the coast of Africa.' For all that, the trade continued to thrive and as it did, the centre of maritime insurance shifted from its original home in Amsterdam and Rouen, and by the mid-eighteenth century London had become the most important centre for European maritime insurance.* Right down to the present day, insurance remains a major factor in the prosperity of the City of London, though the roots of that financial history often go unnoticed. Some of them lay in the remarkable expansion of Britain's global maritime trade – in which the Atlantic slave trade was a major element.

The ebb and flow of factual data about the business of the slave ships has enabled scholars to reconstruct the enforced movement of Africans across the Atlantic with astonishing accuracy. Such evidence – the accountancy of slave trading – was just the first phase of a much broader – and dispersed – recording and assessing of slavery. Africans landing from the slave ships, and their children born in the Americas, were henceforth recorded and tabulated by yet another system of accountancy: by

* Joseph E. Inikori, *Africans and the Industrial Revolution*, p.340.

the people who owned them and who expected a return for their investment. Henceforth, the enslaved were assessed for their labour value and output.

***

Although historians have recently become especially interested in the way plantation slavery (notably in the USA) was micro-managed via a modern accountancy system, the Atlantic slave system was carefully accounted for *long before* the enslaved landed in the Americas. Though it is true, as we shall see, new systems of accounting were applied to slave labour on US sugar and cotton plantations in the nineteenth century, Atlantic slavery had been shaped by close accountancy. The purchase, transportation and labouring lives of enslaved Africans had been directed, from the first, by a unique blend of brutal control harnessed to close commercial scrutiny and management. Of course, it is also true that *all* forms of overseas trade were managed by a literate and numerate culture. The first European commercial expeditions and settlements – to Africa, Asia and the Americas – all relied on accurate bookkeeping. European monarchs and states, the Papacy and ad hoc private speculators – all required penmanship and numerate assessors to order, regulate and calibrate their ventures. Clerks in Spain, Portugal and Italy kept a careful tally of the trade in African humanity first on the coast of Africa and, later, to and from the Atlantic islands. All this took place *before* the leap to repeat those human and commercial experiments in the Americas. That move across the Atlantic constituted a quantum leap which involved even greater risks and uncertainties for the European merchants, mariners and for the colonial settlers and their offspring. It also created seaborne horror of an unprecedented nature for millions of Africans. Even the sufferings of the Africans involved were carefully documented. The fact that we know so much about them, in such astonishing detail, is testimony to the way they were recorded by literate and numerate clerks.

It is no accident that that Africans entered the paperwork *as numbers*. They were added and subtracted as mere figures in an account book. Africans were *the* central and pivotal element in this whole Atlantic system, linking the continents of Europe, Africa and the Americas: numbered, documented and loaded into the belly of the slave ship much like the cargoes of textiles, ironware and cowrie shells shipped to Africa to pay for them. This complex and highly documented commercial system blended commercial sophistication with the most brutal forms of inhumanity.

Company instructions

The men (and they were overwhelmingly men) in charge of this global system were the merchants and backers who organised, financed, filled and insured the slave ships in their home ports in Europe and the Americas: from Rhode Island to Rio, from Glasgow to Lisbon. They methodically sifted through the paperwork accumulated from all corners of the Atlantic system to plan and implement their next maritime investment. They then placed their vessel and its cargo (on a voyage that might last two years) in the hands of their chosen ship's master. They had to trust him, but they also gave him precise instructions about how to go about his business.

Though a slave ship captain cast off with very clear instructions for the voyage, many voyages did not go to plan. Supplies were critical, and each ship needed to load food and water in Africa to sustain the growing numbers of Africans acquired on the coast. It was difficult to know how much food was required, not least because the ships lingered on the coast for months until they had gathered a sufficiently large group of Africans – usually bought in ones and twos or small groups. Throughout, the prisoners had to be fed and watered. Storing food for the African prisoners posed its own problems. A ship with five hundred slaves 'must provide a hundred thousand yams' but that was difficult 'because it is hard to stow them, by reason they take up so much room.'*

When the *Swallow*, owned by the Royal African Company, headed to Calabar in 1678, she carried 'fine spirits', beans, flour, peas, tobacco, vinegar, salt, fish and beef – all described as 'Negro provisions.'† The same company's ship *Arminian Merchant* departed for the River Volta in 1689 carrying trade goods valued at £925/6/2 alongside provisions for the Africans valued at £161/5/9. These were merely the *initial* provisions required, because as the ship traded for Africans, more food had to be purchased on the African coast. Each item, every transaction, was accounted for, down to the nearest penny, in returns submitted to the Company in London. The *Arminian Merchant* bought potatoes, limes, fish and plantain for the Africans – and had to hire local boats to ferry the food back to the mother ship.‡ The

* 'The Slave Trade at Calabar, 1700–1705', Elizabeth Donnan, *Documents*, I, p.15.

† Accounts of the *Swallow*, 1679–81, Elizabeth Donnan, *Documents*, I, pp.256–257; *The Mary*, 1680–81, Elizabeth Donnan, *Documents*, I, pp.262–263.

‡ Accounts of the *Arminian Merchant*, 1689–91, Elizabeth Donnan, *Documents*, I, pp.371–373.

Hannibal, packed with seven hundred Africans, left Ouidah for Barbados in July 1694, provisioning en route at São Tomé, where it took on Indian corn, kidney beans, plantain, yams, potatoes, cocoa-nuts, limes and oranges 'for the use and refreshment of our negroes.' Each purchase was explained and itemised: kidney beans cost $3 for four bushels, plantains $2.50 for a thousand, yams fetched $25 per thousand. Lime, oranges, lemons and bananas 'for little or nothing.' In that case, the provisions did not prevent a disaster. A week after leaving São Tomé, the ship was hit by 'the white flux' (a form of dysentery). The *Hannibal* lost fourteen crewmen and a catastrophic 320 Africans – almost one half of the original complement.* Sometimes, provisions were hard to come by on the coast, and ships' captains complained that African traders drove a hard bargain. Still, in order to feed their enslaved Africans, they had to pay the going rate. Whatever the cost, the ships' owners expected to receive a detailed account.

In time slave traders were able to estimate in advance, and with some degree of accuracy, what was needed to sustain a ship filled with Africans as it crossed the Atlantic. The Royal African Company calculated, in 1713, that 'Provisions for 100 negroes to be taken in at Guinea' would require 80 chests of corn, 4 bushels of salt, 20 gallons of palm oil and a quantity of Malagetta pepper. The company also knew how much each of those items cost, both in local African currency and its sterling equivalent.†

Behind the minutiae of these transactions (listed in their tens of thousands) lurks a major historical point. The trade in

* Voyage of the *Hannibal*, 1693–94, Elizabeth Donnan, *Documents*, I, pp.408–410.

† Account, 13 August 1713, Elizabeth Donnan, *Documents*, II, p.157.

African humanity was carefully tabulated and accounted for, down to the smallest detail. Notwithstanding all the unpredictable accidents of bad weather, warfare and unexpected circumstances in Africa and on the high seas, and despite the impact of sickness, drought, slave revolt and violence, the Atlantic slave trade was managed in precise detail. Failings had to be explained, shortcomings justified. Each voyage was carefully managed at each point of its vast geographic span: from a ship's home base (be it Rio or Liverpool), on the African coast, through established local agents in secure forts, or via transient sea captains and their African counterparts, through to company agents or traders at the myriad landing points in the Americas. It was an exacting accountancy that generated copious literary and numerate details, creating a paper trail which leads us to all parts of the Atlantic trading system – and beyond.

At each location of this widely scattered commercial system, men put pen to paper to describe what they did, explain their commercial decisions, compute the profit and loss of the transactions they were responsible for. Each voyage was designed to make a profit for the individuals and syndicates who had financed the voyage, and for that, they required an accurate account. Well before enslaved Africans entered the ledger books of slave traders and plantation owners in the Americas, and long before the productivity of their labour was analysed, their value to the people who bought and transported them had been laid bare in the heartless arithmetic of Atlantic slave traders.

Accounting for Africans

In the relatively short period when the English slave trade was in the hands of the Royal African Company, the accounting

HQ of that trade was London. Paperwork flowed back and forth between offices in London, the masters of their ships, the Company employees on the African coast and their agents in the Americas. The Company operated a remarkable international accountancy system. In 1710, a detailed analysis of the Company's assets in the African slave forts presented a forensic evaluation of company resources. It listed and evaluated every building, every room in those buildings and all the essential contents – to a total value of £279,555.* The details were entered into the Company's papers by clerks living in the African forts themselves. The clerks were contracted to 'keep a true and particular of all the proceedings' and to:

> daily, duly and truly enter the Account of
> all and every particular Buying, Selling,
> Receipts, Payments, and all other Transactions.†

Of all the details logged by these men, the most valuable were those of the enslaved Africans locked in the fort's cells awaiting onward movement to the slave ships anchored offshore.

We learn how much was paid for each African. On 3 September 1728, the *Judith* (which had departed from Gravesend two months earlier) was collecting Africans at the Junk River on the Grain Coast. The master numbered them, and listed their price. His first purchase, 'a boye, No. 1', was in return for two guns and four brass pans. Another boy,

* Valuation of the African Forts, 1709/10, Elizabeth Donnan, *Documents,* II, pp.109–113.

† Contract of Francis Moore with the Royal African Company, 23 July 1730, Elizabeth Donnan, *Documents*, II, pp.388–393.

'No. 2', for two guns and two basins. A man, bought the following day ('No. 3') cost four guns, some powder and two basins. Three days later the ship acquired a boy and a girl ('No. 5') in exchange for guns, basins, powder, some spirits and some textiles.

Day after day through September 1728 this process continued: individual Africans acquired in exchange for a variety of items shipped from London. At the end of the month, they purchased an African ('No. 38') in return for guns, powder and textiles. The bookkeeping was punctuated by the inevitable African deaths, but by the end of April, the vessel had delivered forty-one Africans to the designated agent in Barbados. Two weeks later, the surviving 173 Africans were handed over to the agents in Jamaica: seventy-eight men, thirty-three women, 'Fifty two boys Large and Small. Ten girls.'*

Throughout the entire voyage, the African victims were mere numbers. They left the ship as they entered it, nameless: a mere number, though sometimes with a simple mention of their size or condition, their gender and whether adult or child. Each person had a value measured by the volume and price of the commodities traded in exchange. They even died as numbers, their very existence removed from a ship's log book by the deletion of their number from a list.

Ships' logs

All ships' captains were obliged to record daily events in the ship's logbook. Each ship had a logbook, but the logs of slave ships were different: they become a litany of African

* Account, 1728–29, Elizabeth Donnan, *Documents*, II, pp.366–380.

suffering. As they crossed the Atlantic, the logs became what the master of the *Arthur* in 1678 described as an 'Acctt of what Negroes Dyed every day.' The paperwork was dutifully reported back to the London HQ.* In August 1675 Capt. Peter Blake, master of the *James*, began trading for Africans – and gold – along the Gold Coast. The following May he anchored at Barbados and began to sell his human cargo, but he had trouble disposing of what he, and everyone else involved, called his 'refuse slaves'. Instructions waiting for him in Barbados ordered him to Jamaica if the Africans did not reach a certain price.

Blake considered it a profitable voyage – his tally of the losses incurred between September 1675 and June 1676 showed that twenty-eight men, nineteen women and four boys had died. A separate column in his account listed each cause of death. Three centuries later, it still makes mournful reading, though it could be replicated thousands of times. Ten died on the African coast, eleven after arriving in Barbados – the rest on the Atlantic crossing. Sometimes death came suddenly and unexpectedly.

'Departed this Life suddenly.'

'Departed this life of Convulsive and Fitts.'

'Departed this life of a feaver.'

Some were clearly sick from the first: 'thin and consumed to nothing and so dyed.'

'Very thin and wasted to Nothing and soe dyed.'

'Departed this life of a Consumption and Worms.'

'Miscarryed and the Child dead within her and Rotten and dyed 2 days after delivery.'

* Journal of the Arthur, 1677–1678, Elizabeth Donnan, *Documents*, I, pp.226–234.

'Very sick and fell overboard in the night and was lost.'

' . . . dyed of a Great Swelling of his face and head.'

'Sickened and would not eat nor take anything.'

Africans died of the flux, of consumption, by suicide, by dropsy. One woman:

> Being very fond of her Child Carrying her up and downe wore her to nothing by which means fell into a feavour and dyed.

For all its horror – culled from one single voyage – this grievous account is not unusual. Indeed, it was typical of thousands of Atlantic crossings. The details and the numbers vary from ship to ship – fewer or more deaths, slower or swifter crossings, peaceful or rebellious voyages, good or ferocious weather. But *all* slave voyages were reduced to this stark tabulation: a listing of sickness and death on board. Often too, it was drawn up alongside similar casualty rates among the crew.

Here then is not merely the story of one Atlantic crossing, but the raw human evidence required by the ship's owners to analyse and scrutinise the voyage. Today, what leaps from the page, and strikes the modern reader as a catalogue of human suffering was, for the ship owners, a *commercial* account – a table of profit and loss. A ship's log presented its own brutal system of accounting fashioned around the survival and the deaths of its African victims.*

***

* An Account of the Mortality of Slaves aboard the Shipp *James*, Elizabeth Donnan, *Documents*, I, pp.20–208.

There is nothing unusual about the manner of listing the outbound cargoes destined for Africa. What *is* striking, however, is that the same ships' human cargoes were documented in the same fashion. When the Royal African Company dispatched the *Sarah Bonaventure* to the Gold Coast in 1676, every item of outbound cargo was listed: the number of iron bars, various textiles – from Britain and from India – the exact volume of tallow, the number of muskets and barrels of knives. Each item was numbered in one column, described in the next and all entered alongside their value. When the master began the protracted process of exchanging those good for Africans (and for gold) he again logged each transaction in the smallest detail. Hence we know how much he paid for each African (man, woman, boy or girl) in terms of the imported commodities. He completed his task by disembarking 475 Africans in Jamaica.*

Transforming Africans into numbers did not end when Africans were sold from the slave ships. When Africans entered the slave auctions and plantations of the Americas they were logged, yet again, by armies of clerks whose job it was to chronicle their lives in even greater detail than before, adding to the profusion of evidence about the enslaved. All this is familiar to any student of the slave trade, but it is rarely viewed as an aspect of complex international accountancy. Everyone involved in the management of slave ships, from the docksides of the Atlantic's major ports through to ships' masters and the traders in Africa, was busy adding their own data to the complex commercial equation. Atlantic slavery was a global system which relied on the literate and numerate abilities of many

* Accounts of the *Sarah Bonaventure*, 1676–77, Elizabeth Donnan, *Documents*, I. pp.217–221.

thousands of people. Moreover, it was so successful a business, over so many centuries *because* of the careful measurement and economic assessment involved. This accountancy of slavery, as we shall see, is best known on the plantations of the Americas. But accounting for slavery was a well-oiled commercial machine long before then. It was as old as the Atlantic slave trade.

11

Managing Slavery

As the slave economies matured, landowners learned how to get the best from their properties: how best to divide and organise the land, how many hands were required to work each piece of land, how many labourers were required for each specific task. They learned how much a single labourer could achieve, and how much time was required. What evolved was a carefully calibrated assessment of land and labour. Where factories were part of the process (notably in sugar) slave owners also developed an expertise in the management of time and production. A finely tuned work discipline evolved in the hands of slave owners long before it came to characterise the modern industrial world.*

At first this was most striking in the world of sugar cultivation where planters learned what to expect from each area of sugar cane cultivation, and how many slaves were required to cut the cane. They knew when it was time to harvest the cane, and how long it took to get the cane to the nearest factory

* See the classic essay, E. P. Thompson, 'Time, Work-Discipline and Industrial Capitalism', *Past and Present*, No. 38, 1967, pp.56–97.

(cane rotted quickly if left on the ground too long). In this, and in all other crops – rice, tobacco, cotton and coffee – they also depended on the experience of enslaved workers. Men and women with years of know-how in the fields had important advice to offer on every step of the process. Across the enslaved Americas, there evolved carefully orchestrated and monitored agricultural systems. But this leaves us with a puzzle. Men who were calculating and precise in managing their business were, at the same time, often brutal and sometimes tyrannical to the workforce. Slavery developed as a complex system which blended close agronomic management – and crude physical brutality.

Thomas Thistlewood is, today, perhaps the most notorious of Jamaica's slave owners, his reputation sealed by the detailed diary he kept of his persistent violence and rape of his slaves. He was also a meticulous recorder of the smallest detail of economic life on his properties, cataloguing the work and the productivity of each of his slaves. He logged the weather and its impact on local agriculture in the same meticulous fashion that he recorded his sexual assaults on dozens of women. Yet from the moment he landed in Jamaica from England – a Lincolnshire man with no experience of enslaved labour – he was in no doubt that the system could not function without the lubricant of violence. He doled out whippings or a regular basis, and most of his slaves could expect an assault at some point in the year. Women faced a more gruesome ordeal. Like sugar men elsewhere, Thistlewood also rewarded good work and behaviour: extra food and drink, clothing and free time.*

* Trevor Burnard, *Mastery, Tyranny and Desire: Thomas Thistlewood and his Slaves in the Anglo-Jamaican World*, Chapel Hill, 2004.

Plantations varied enormously in size and importance, and the properties Thistlewood managed were relatively small, though Jamaica was unusual in having large numbers of big plantations, which were home to more than two hundred slaves. In the USA by contrast there were only 312 plantations with more than two hundred slaves in 1860: Jamaica (much smaller of course – and with a smaller slave population) had 393 such plantations in 1832. Yet whatever a plantation's size, owners managed them as highly regimented and carefully regulated units. And the labour force everywhere was subject to a tight labouring discipline. How they worked, what they produced or managed, how much time was required for each and every task – even how they spent their free time – all this was recorded and documented in plantation ledgers.

The pioneering settlers of land in the Americas set about converting the best areas of wilderness into cultivable fields. That required water and access, by road or river, to enable produce to be transported to ships destined for Europe and Africa, and for the import of the goods and people required by the new settlements: tools, timber, animals, seeds, foodstuffs – and, of course, Africans. Though we tend to think of plantations as places that produced great volumes of commodities for Western consumption, they were also major consumers, devouring an enormous range of imported goods – and human beings – from widely scattered societies: from Europe, India and Africa. They imported enslaved labour from Africa and clothed that labour in Indian and European textiles, feeding them with fish from North Atlantic fisheries. They bought tools used in the fields and factories from Europe. Plantations also imported great volumes of paper, notably the ledgers in which they recorded the property's daily routines. This huge array of imported goods, most of it shipped thousands of miles, formed a major strand in the complex economic links between slavery and the global economy.

Unlike towns and cities, with their higgledy-piggledy development, plantations tended to evolve in an orderly and organised manner. Slave housing was located close to the workplaces in fields or factory. In the words of William Beckford in 1790, ideally slave dwellings should be close to the workplace:

> some distance from the works, but not so far removed as to be beyond the sight of the overseer.

Even in their homes, the labourers remained under the watchful eye of an overseer, whose task it was to ensure that the labour force was up to its various tasks and not too troublesome or restless at home. Factories needed to be close to water or wind power, and with easy access to the harvested crops from the fields. Around this central focus of cultivable land, water, roads and labour, there emerged a simple collection of buildings: homes, offices and workplaces – a nucleus of buildings which formed the heart of the plantation life.*

There were of course enormous variations in this pattern; differences dictated by topography and by changes brought about by the physical growth of the plantation. Yet if we look at surviving visual images of plantations, we can grasp the philosophy behind them. They were designed to function as rational and disciplined units which brought together land, labour and management into an efficient unit of production. The trial and error, and guesswork, in the early days of

* B. W. Higman, *Jamaica Surveyed,* p.81.

settlement, gave way to an orderly management of land and labour. Ideally, the whole process (in the words of a Jamaican *Planters Guide* in 1823) would be:

> Laid out on a piece of paper, of a size sufficient to have the whole delineated upon it.*

This process of plotting and surveying the land generated many hundreds of maps and mounds of surveyors' paperwork which, alongside plantation papers, provide the documentary basis for so much modern research.

Examining the physical layout of plantations also allows us to enter the mental world of the slaveholders themselves. They organised their land, their communication routes, water supplies and processing systems in an economically rational fashion. They aimed to create working plantations – whatever their size – as well-ordered, profitable places, eliminating as far as possible haphazard factors. Landowners made strenuous efforts to squeeze the maximum returns from their land – and that meant extracting the most from the enslaved labour force. Slave owners organised their land and their business dealings with the outside world as efficiently as possible, using huge numbers of clerks – bookkeepers – to record and monitor all transactions. They also imposed a labouring discipline on the enslaved labour force, which, for all the foresight and planning, remained a system which was driven by brute force and violence.

Time was valuable to slave owners, and they saw to it that their slave labour force made the most of their waking hours.

* B. W. Higman, *Jamaica Surveyed*, p.8.

This involved long hours in the fields – as long as natural daylight allowed ('From sun-up to sun-down') with time, after dark, at other chores (especially if there was a local factory). But the cycles of crops had their own rhythms and timescales, and there were periods of the year when slaves were less pressed at work. It was then that owners turned the labourers onto other tasks around the property – or loaned them out as labourers to other people and other work. Even 'free time' was important, and even the most brutal and ignorant of slave owners came to recognise the benefit of granting free time to the labour force. It was hoped that a refreshed labour force would return to their labours revitalised. Slaves also needed a regular break to tend their own needs in and around their homes, or in their plots of land and gardens, to grow their own foodstuffs or tend to their animals. Archaeologists have recently confirmed that slaves provided a substantial part of their own diet. They became self-reliant in cultivating foodstuff, in rearing animals, and trapping or fishing for their own food supplies. And of course, they brought their own African culinary traditions (and ingredients) to the way they cooked and fed themselves.* Even a labour gangs' free time was used by management for their benefit.

Plantations became highly organised labour camps where discipline was the driving force. We are familiar with the way tight work discipline became a feature of industries in the nineteenth century, but similar – though much more brutal – labour disciplines had been perfected on the plantations of the Americas many years earlier. An attachment to labour discipline was the core philosophy of slave owners everywhere:

* Kenneth G. Kelly and Diane Wallman, 'Foodways of Enslaved Laborers on French West Indian Plantations', *Afriques*, 05, 2014.

regulated, intrusive – and always and everywhere oiled by the application of violence.

***

Successful planters learned how to change and to adapt their labouring systems. At Worthy Park, a Jamaican plantation founded in 1670, the early division of slaves into broadly based labouring gangs changed in the late eighteenth century. In the 1780s, the owner, freshly arrived from Britain and perhaps guided by manuals on how best to manage a sugar plantation, was determined to make his slaves more efficient. He changed how the labour force worked by carefully selecting gangs, each chosen by age and strength. The slave elite (drivers and head slaves, and skilled artisans) all received more favourable treatment, in housing, food, clothing and free time. Beneath them, the rank-and-file field hands, were slotted into various subdivisions, their tasks dictated again by age and strength.

Females undertook the most demanding of field work: if slave owners had preconceived ideas of what females could not do, their ideas faded in the face of the demography of slavery. For confirmation we need only look at the numerous contemporary pictures – sketches, drawing and caricatures – of field workers on plantations. All reveal women working alongside men, wielding axes and machetes in the heaviest of labour, harvesting and carrying the various crops. Gender clearly did not count: what mattered to the planter was strength and durability. There were as many women as men capable of picking the cotton or cutting the cane (or carrying heavy baskets of manure to the fields). Strength was all important. Those with no strength at all – people reduced by old age, sickness or harsh treatment (more likely, a combination of all those things) had no place in the scheme of things.

As we have already noted, this wealth of information is available because every aspect of plantation life was recorded by another crucial group of workers on plantations: the clerks and bookkeepers. They, however, were free, not enslaved. Planters employed bookkeepers to keep a daily tally of life and labour on their properties. Like the captains of the slave ships and the daily log entries, bookkeepers were in effect the diarists of plantation life. These educated men were lured to slave colonies by the prospects of a better life, and spent their days toiling over large ledgers in which they entered every aspect of life, death and of daily labour. They tabulated which slaves worked on which piece of land: how much time they took to weed, to plant, to fertilise, how long it took to cut the cane and how long it took to bring in the harvest or crop: how long it took to get sugar cane to the nearest factory. There, other bookkeepers logged the process of converting sugar cane to raw sugar and molasses. The accumulation of data made it possible to assess which group of slaves worked efficiently – and even which individuals were not pulling their weight – or couldn't. To add to this daily data in plantation ledgers, there were the parallel observations of overseers. Men on horseback roamed the fields, communicating with the slave driver (himself a slave) about the day's progress (or lack of it). On smaller properties, the owner – or local manager – would combine all these varied functions. But whatever the size, and whoever was ultimately in charge, the field work was managed as efficiently as possible. A slackening of pace, not enough land planted or cleared, not enough cane, cotton, tobacco, coffee harvested – all and more would bring down the heavy hand of a planter's retribution.

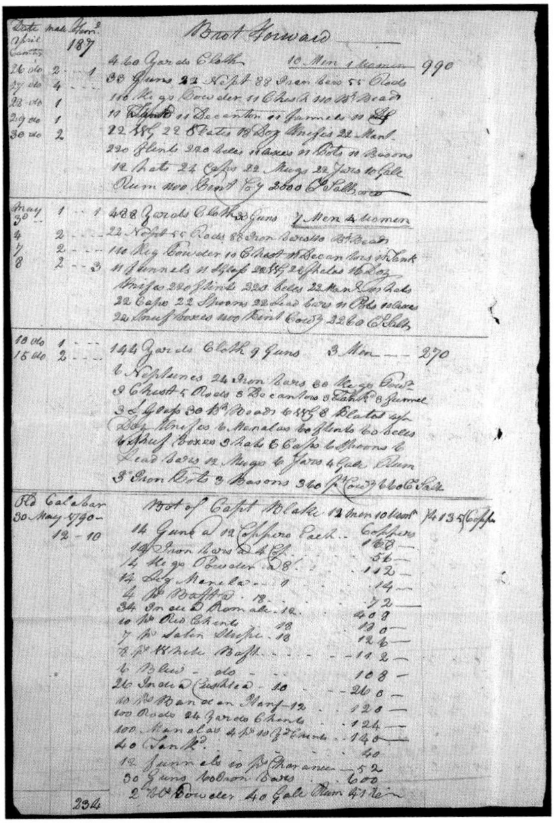

Brot Forward

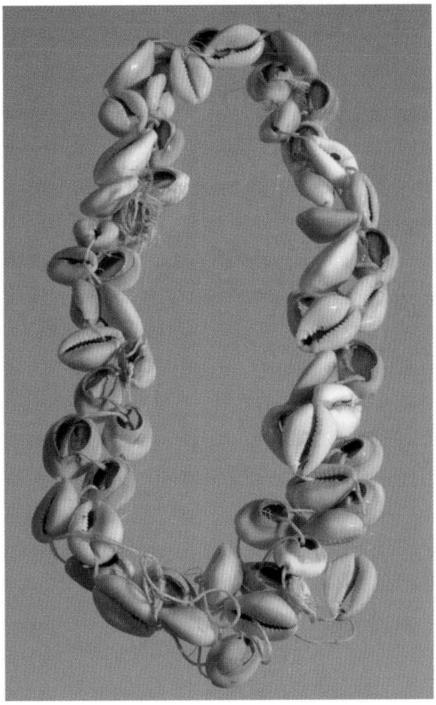

Cowrie shells from the Indian Ocean, exchanged in their millions for enslaved Africans. *(Heritage Art/Heritage Images/Topfoto)*

(above) Slave trader's trade book, 1789, listing items used in exchange for Africans. *(Mary Evans/The National Archives, London)*

(right) The sale of forty-five slaves by a Bristol trader, 1771–1793. *(Mary Evans/The National Archives, London)*

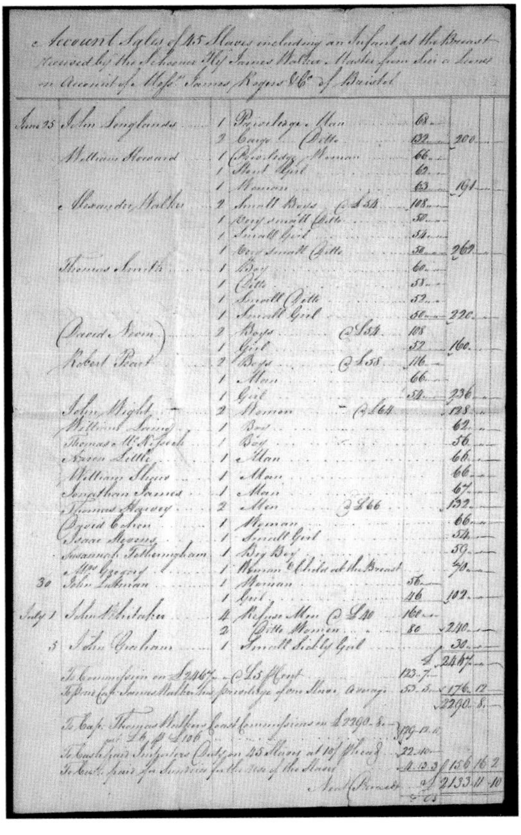

Account Sales of 45 Slaves including an Infant at the Breast

Sailors and enslaved Africans on the deck of a French slave ship, 1800s.
(Lithograph by Pretexat Oursel, 1800s/Slavery Images)

Africans on slave ship *Albaroz*, seized by the Royal Navy in 1846.
(National Maritime Museum, London/Slavery Images)

Africans overcoming the crew on the *Amistad*, 1839 – later the cause of a famous US legal battle.
(Granger Collection/Topfoto)

Africans seized on board the ship *Wildfire* and brought to Key West by the US Navy, 1860.
(Mary Evans/Everett Collection)

Enslaved workers, male and female, in the boiling house of an Antiguan sugar plantation, 1823.
(British Library/Science Source/Mary Evans)

Men and women cutting sugar cane, Antigua, 1823, with smoke from the factory in the background.
(The Stapleton Collection/Bridgeman Images)

Incendie du Cap.
Révolte générale des Nègres. Massacre des Blancs.

A gory image of the violence during the slave rebellion in St. Domingue/Haiti after 1791.
(Library Company of Philadelphia/Slavery Images)

A common sight in Brazil: slaves carrying a white mistress. *(Slavery Images)*

Urban slavery in Brazil, 1819–1820. *(Slavery Images)*

Brazilian skilled slaves – shoemakers – and punishment for making a mistake.
(Mary Evans/BeBa/Iberfoto)

Brazilian street scene – of urban slaves carrying heavy loads, 1853.
(Thomas Ewbank/Special Collections Department, University of Virginia Library/Slavery Images)

US slaves picking cotton – destined for the textile industries of Massachusetts, Britain and Germany.
(Special Collections Department, University of Virginia Library/Slavery Images)

Arise! Arise! and weep no more
dry up your tears, we Shall part
no more. Come rose we go to
Tennessee,
that happy Shore, to old virginia
never — never — return. —

(above) The US domestic slave trade: the enslaved being marched to a new location in Tennessee, 1853. *(Rockefeller Folk Art Museum, Williamsburg Foundation/Slavery Images)*

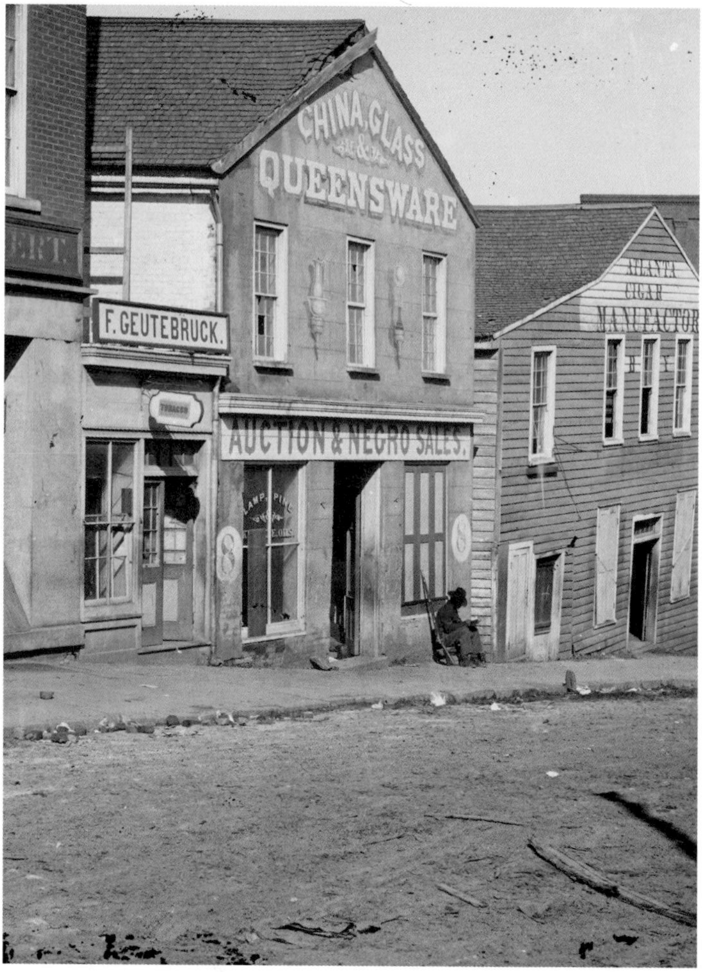
CHINA, GLASS
&
QUEENSWARE
F. GEUTEBRUCK.
AUCTION & NEGRO SALES.
CIGAR
MANUFACTOR

(right) A slave auction house in Atlanta, 1864. *(Mary Evans/ Library of Congress)*

Field work was punishing, especially for Africans fresh from the slave ships who were vulnerable to a host of dangers: new ailments, the new environment and new forms of strenuous labour in addition to the illnesses many had acquired on the Atlantic crossing. If Africans were thrown into the most strenuous of labour soon after arrival, there was usually an increase in death rates and sickness. Most slave owners learned the importance of allowing Africans to adapt and acclimatise to the new environment and regime after the ordeal of the crossing. They also needed to learn new tasks. However physically strong, all were now confronted with unfamiliar patterns of work, with strange tools and an alien pace and rhythm. In effect, Africans had to learn the new discipline of slave labour. Some were given less robust work around the property but eventually – usually after three years – their owners were able to gauge which men and women were suited for the most demanding of labour. By then, however, some had not survived the transition from Africa to the Americas. They joined the long list of victims of enslavement and transportation.

Management at a distance

The careful and detailed management of slave properties is sometimes caught most clearly in the correspondence between owners and their agents. Many planters (large or small) hoped – and planned – to leave their remote slave properties and return 'home' to Europe or to a distant city. Many – perhaps most – never made it, spending a lifetime in what they clearly regarded as a lonely exile – but ever hopeful their fortunes would improve and allow them to leave. Those who departed left their lands and slaves in the hands of agents and attorneys, hoping that their investment in land and labour would continue to keep them in comfort – but far removed from slavery. By the end of the eighteenth century, the British Isles and France were dotted with slave owners: people who had quit the slave colonies and settled (sometimes in places they had never even seen). Some returned 'home' to create a lavish lifestyle, building stately homes that rivalled and even surpassed their aristocratic rivals and neighbours. Others enjoyed more modest returns, but *all* of them became part of a returnee slave-owning culture that was a striking feature, particularly of Britain in the eighteenth and nineteenth centuries. The correspondence between such absentees and their managers provides a treasure trove for historical researchers.

***

Letters and reports criss-crossed the Atlantic commenting not only on the state of a property's material and economic condition, but also issuing orders – about how the slaves should be worked and treated, ordering their movement from one job to another, or from place to place, to improve their performance. What evolved was an astonishing transatlantic management of people and land. Men and women living in, say, Bath or London, Galloway or Yorkshire, dictated the labouring lives of Africans and their children in the Caribbean.

The more successful absentee planters kept a careful tally of their distant properties via a number of agents, some in London, others on the ground in the islands. If the commercial returns did not meet expectations, they might order a thorough investigation, even studying the commercial progress of comparable properties in the islands. The first Lord Harewood held 'repeated conferences' with merchants and planters to uncover why his investment in land and slaves was so disappointing in the 1790s. Scrutiny of his twelve slave properties reveals a struggling commercial concern in the twenty years to 1795. Harewood was able to gain a clearer understanding of his investments by a change of attorneys in Barbados and Jamaica and a consequent firmer control over the day-to-day management of the slave properties. By then, of course, Harewood was firmly ensconced in the splendours of Harewood House.*

Much less grand, but nonetheless prosperous, the Elletson family owned Hope plantation, perched in the hills above Kingston, Jamaica, but by the 1770s, they had returned to England where they received regular letters from their attorney (and from their friends). The letters, entrusted to the captain of the ship carrying the sugar from Hope to England, spelled out how Hope was managed: which slaves had died, who had given birth and who was sick. They were even informed that 'The house Negroes desire to be remembered in the most respectful manner to you.'†

Friendly neighbours added their own observations – not all of them encouraging – to the absentee owners. The Rev. Poole, for example, told Mr Elletson in London that the changes to the slaves' working week on Hope ('having their Saturday Afternoon taken away') meant that 'Your negroes have been greatly dissatisfied.' Mrs Elletson was outraged to learn of 'Acts

* S. D. Smith, *Slavery, Family and Gentry Capitalism in the British Atlantic: The World of the Lascelles, 1648–1834*, Cambridge, 2006.

† The following discussion draws on the Elletson family correspondence in the Huntington Library, San Marino. Stowe Collection, (Grenville Papers) ST14.

of Inhumanity' resulting in slave deaths. Plans to expand the sugar lands – 5,000 miles away – were thwarted by a shortage of slave labour at Hope. There were also persistent problems about feeding the slaves adequately, though the Elletsons were reassured about repairs to the slaves' houses and about the care of slave children.[*]

Letters from the Elletsons in London to their Jamaican attorneys gave instructions about a host of management details: about buying more land, more slaves, paying bills, making repairs:

> For God's sake direct the Overseer to be
> particularly attentive to the Negro provision grounds . . .[†]

When Mr Elletson, the owner, died, his widow continued this transatlantic management of her Jamaican assets, sometimes offering detailed suggestions for improvement: why not enhance productivity by introducing a plough?[‡]

She ordered items to be shipped to Jamaica (and queried some items) and made suggestions about how the labour gangs should be organised:

> I would wish to have a succession of acute Boys
> put to different Trades, so that there may be a plenty of
> Tradesmen of all sorts upon the Estate.[§]

* Letter from Joseph Stewart, 1769. Letters from Rev. Poole, 30 November and 20 December 1769, Grenville Papers.

† Letters, 18 and 19 May 1772, 25 June 1770, Grenville Papers.

‡ Letter, 17 January 1776. Grenville Papers.

§ Letter, 28 September 1770. Grenville Papers.

Those slaves 'not Necessary about the House nor can be useful to the Estate' should be hired out to other people.*

Mrs Elletson expected to receive a detailed headcount of the enslaved labour force every six months and was especially concerned about the welfare of the children and what she considered the 'casualness of the midwifery of the mothers.'† She had plans for the future of Hope estate by buying 'as many men boys as possible' before buying 'ten or twelve able Men payable in sugar and rum.'‡ Even when Mrs Elletson left London to travel to Europe, she kept in contact with Hope's manager. She wrote from Aix in France that the slaves' health was 'the foundation of our prosperity at Hope.'§

Throughout this correspondence, Mrs Elletson was acutely aware of the critical importance of Hope's enslaved labour force. In 1772, she instructed a new overseer to be 'careful to avoid all unnecessary and severe punishment.' She wanted the slaves to 'perform as much as may be with content and cheerfulness not in fear and misery.'¶ She monitored each young slave as they grew to maturity, ordering them to be instructed in whatever skill or trade seemed appropriate.**

Like Thomas Thistlewood, who kept a meticulous account of the weather on his property in the west of Jamaica at much the same time, Mrs Elletson, living in Curzon St, London,

* Letter, 3 November 1770. Grenville Papers.

† Letter, 26 May 1771. Grenville Papers.

‡ Letters, 17 January 1776, 28 September 1770, 3 November 1770, 26 May 1771, 15 September 1771. Grenville Papers.

§ Letter from Aix, November 1771. Grenville Papers.

¶ Letter, 16 May 1772. Grenville Papers.

** Letter from Aix, November 1771; Letters, 16 May 1772, 4 September 1773. Grenville Papers.

demanded a diary of the weather at Hope to be sent to her 'by every vessel that sails from Kingston.' Unlike Thomas Thistlewood, however, Mrs Elletson was acutely aware of the need *not* to brutalise the slaves, but rather to avoid 'all severe (take notice of the word) I say severe punishments.'* She was furious to learn that, when 'Mulatto Boy Billy' had escaped, he had been shipped off the island without her knowledge. This close slave management – from Britain – extended to ordering the inoculation of all Hope's slaves against smallpox in 1775.†

Through this welter of transatlantic correspondence – each letter taking months to arrive in Jamaica, with replies equally slow in return, Mrs Elletson insisted on detailed reports on every aspect of the management of her Jamaican property. She expected to be told about the exact condition of her slaves: their health, their eating and working habits – with equally detailed reports on the weather. In crop time, she expected a regular flow of information about the progress of the sugar, right through to the factory processing. Nor was this merely a generalised demand; she wanted *exact* details about the quality of the sugar cane from each of the cane pieces.

This remarkable example of a woman micromanaging her slave property from a distance of 5,000 miles was far from unique. She received *all* the data required for the careful management of land and labour on the far side of the Atlantic. Mrs Elletson was but one example of what was a widespread feature of slave and plantation management. Whether resident on a slave property, or domiciled thousands of miles away,

* Letter, 5 September 1773. Grenville Papers.

† Letters, 3 March 1774, 2 Febraury 1775. Grenville Papers.

plantation owners handled their land and labour by careful scrutiny of all the available data. Sometimes, they were led astray by devious, self-serving or cruel overseers and managers. But even then, they had other helpers on hand: neighbours, friends or local attorneys who kept an eye on an absentee property and, when necessary, were willing to bring the absent owner up to date. Associates told owners of the impact of drought, the hunger, health (or ill-health) of the enslaved, the productivity and yield from various corners of an estate, and the progress of developing young slaves – and the decline of the old. This profusion of paperwork, moving slowly east and west across the vastness of the Atlantic, enabled slave owners to manage slaves and land. It was a form of management which required more than mere brutality. The Elletsons, like others, tried to weed out those overseers and managers whose random and capricious violence was damaging both to the slaves and to the profitable running of a slave property.

And yet for all that, no slave owner we know of totally abandoned the most severe of physical punishment and discipline.

Despite the inescapable and intrusive nature of management, and despite the violence that hovered over slaves everywhere, many slave owners imagined that their slaves held them in fond regard. There was an element of self-delusion in all this. Mrs Elletson, for example, shortly after giving birth to a son, instructed the manager at Hope to tell the slaves that she would shortly send a picture of herself and the baby for the slaves to see.* This bizarre story offers a glimpse into the self-delusions and warped paternalism that prevailed among many slave owners. Today, the idea that slaves might have held their owners

* Letter, February 1777. Grenville Papers.

in high regard and even feel affection for them, seems fantastic. Not least because, at heart, slavery – for all the careful, intrusive and finely regulated management – was lubricated by brute violence.

12

Brute Force

MANAGING AFRICANS ON board the slave ships was a matter of brute force and intimidation. But how did slave owners in the Americas manage and control their enslaved labour? In particular, how did large slave properties handle the deeply resentful labourers (who sometimes greatly outnumbered their masters)? Slave owning came in a variety of forms. At one extreme, there were people who owned only one or two (notably in towns) using them as domestics or as day labourers rented out for income. At the other extreme – and perhaps the most familiar – were major planters who owned large gangs working their plantations. Every slave owner faced problems of control – at its most basic, how to stop enslaved people running away – and all faced the challenge of getting them to work. How did slave owners make the most of their enslaved labourers while, at the same time, keeping the lid on so volatile and dangerous a human brew?

***

Enslaved Africans were turned over to a multitude of occupations. Their prime task, of exploiting the untapped riches of the

Americas, was achieved through brutal systems of slave labour that had not been seen, on such a scale, since classical antiquity. Millions of African workers, and their children born in the Americas, were marshalled, cajoled and disciplined into routines of labour that were utterly alien and new. Though it is true that brute force – best-known by the sound of the lash – was vital in coercing slave labour, violence alone does not explain the commercial success of slavery over so many centuries.

From the first days of settlement, slave owners faced the basic problem of how to *control* large numbers of disaffected Africans. Across swathes of the tropical and semi-tropical Americas, the enslaved greatly outnumbered their owners and managers. On large plantations, slaves might outnumber their masters by ten to one. Such numerical predominance had also been true on the slave ships. But there, Africans were kept as brutalised prisoners, not as workers. In many regions of the Americas, not only were the enslaved overwhelmingly in the ascendancy but they were universally disaffected, sullen and resistant, and slave owners had to devise complex systems for maintaining their dominance and control while making them work. Their simplest and universal tool was brute force.

***

From childhood to old age and physical decline, enslaved Africans and their children were valued for their labour and their labouring skills. Sickness and age robbed them of their value to their owners. The old, the sick, the infirm and feeble were simply dismissed, in the brutal accountancy of slavery as 'useless' or 'worthless.' How to extract value from a reluctant and defiant army of slaves was a problem that taxed slave owners everywhere, and owners spent their lives calculating how to secure the best returns from their labour force. It was never simple, not least because no one wanted to be enslaved, and the work involved some of the most strenuous and arduous forms of labour: logging in the jungle, working in rice paddy fields, hacking away at sugar cane, picking cotton in the blistering Mississippi heat, mining for gold and silver – all physically taxing – and all under the beady eye of slave drivers and taskmasters (some of them slaves themselves). And yet despite the difficulties, slavery not only survived for centuries, but was profitable.

In large measure, its durability derived from its adaptability. Africans were first used in the days of crude and precarious settlement, when crossing the Atlantic, and settling on new land, was itself a dangerous undertaking (for everyone), and it was still functioning profitably in the age of steam. By the mid-nineteenth century, slave-grown Brazilian coffee, and sugar cultivated by Cuban slaves, were transported from plantations by train, thence loaded onto steam ships destined for the USA. There, both were processed in modern industrial refineries and factories in Baltimore and New York. Slavery was durable, adaptable and profitable.

***

The most basic and universal means of getting slaves to work – and the one we are perhaps most familiar with – was by force and by violence, though this had its limits. Many slave owners recognised that violence could be self-defeating: too much, too indiscriminate, too excessive, and it could prompt non-compliance and even violent reaction. Despite this, wherever we study slavery, there we find someone – wild, uncontrollable, mad or sadistic – whose violence was grotesquely extreme and whose behaviour outraged and worried neighbouring slave owners. Sadistic slave owners were frowned on as much as weak ones by other slave owners, because they posed a danger.

If any popular image survives today of slaves at work it must surely be an image of slaves being brutalised, and nothing captures that impression better than the whip. Graphic pictures of the whip – especially when used against female victims – became a powerful tool in the armoury of abolitionists in the nineteenth century. Crude woodcut images of slaves being flogged pepper abolitionist literature, and accounts of slaves being whipped or beaten became a major trope in accounts of travellers visiting slave societies. Darwin in Brazil and Dickens in the USA were only two of an army of writers offended by what they saw and heard on their travels in the Americas. Indeed, accounts of violence towards slaves form a vast literature in all European languages and span four centuries of American slavery. Violence was endemic to the entire history of slavery. A Jesuit remarked of Brazilian sugar planters in 1711 that some owners:

> sometimes give more care and attention to a single horse than they do to half a dozen slaves.*

The whip was an inescapable feature of slavery across the Americas. We need to recall, however, that corporal punishment – including floggings – was also an unquestioned aspect of many other social and penal forms of behaviour. Husbands

* Robert Edgar Conrad, *Children of God's Fire*, p.58.

beat wives, parents beat children, masters beat apprentices, officers beat (and flogged) lower ranks, and jailors flogged prisoners. What seems grotesque today, passed unremarked and unchallenged in societies which had not yet turned against cruelty. Flogging was not merely tolerated but it was widely thought to be essential. Flogging of the most savage kind was a common feature of military life. The British army did not abolish flogging men until 1868 (in peacetime) and 1888 (in wartime). Captains and officers on merchant and naval ships, flogged their men for a host of reasons, usually in front of the assembled crew. Exemplary floggings were intended to punish the victim and warn and subdue the rest. A sailor in the Royal Navy who stole a ring belonging to the wife of a shipmate, received 'twenty-nine lashes with a cat-o'-nine tails, and was then washed with saltwater.'* A whip was a basic piece of equipment in any shipmaster's locker and no captain would leave port without one. It was not outlawed in the Royal Navy until the major reforms of 1879. When the US had banned naval flogging in 1850 it was against the wishes of many of its serving officers. For all that, slave punishments belonged in a category all their own. They were widespread, extreme and largely unchallenged. Not surprisingly, alongside guns and the chains, the whip was an essential tool on the slave ships: a vital weapon for the small handful of sailors charged with the transport of hundreds of angry and defiant Africans. Long before enslaved Africans stepped ashore in the Americas, they had been confronted by the sound and the power of the whip.

***

* N. A. M. Rodger, *The Command of the Sea*, London, 2004, p.13.

It was an article of faith that physical punishment was essential to successful slave management. No slave owner we know of totally abandoned the smack of severe control. Most felt, at heart, that slavery could not function without the lubricant of violence: for backsliders and for the defiant. Even a liberal Catholic priest, writing of Brazil in 1758, accepted that 'There is no doubt that the owners of slaves ought to punish them and correct their mistakes when they know through experience that their words alone are not effective.' He thought that punishment, however, 'should not go beyond the *palmatoria,* the switch, the whip and shackles.'* A Brazilian agricultural handbook of 1839 spelled out the issue in precise detail. Supervision of slaves 'would be a mere waste of effort without punishment.' It should be moderate and thoughtful, and administered 'in full view of all the other slaves.' For the most serious of offences 'and for the run-of-the-mill slaves, fifty lashes will be sufficient.'†

The enslaved were expected to work at tasks and at a rhythm not of their making and they could – and did – slow down and hinder the demands made of them (though always at great risk to themselves). They dragged their feet, wilfully misunderstood instructions, made deliberate errors – though always running the risk of punishment. Slave drivers and owners knew what they could expect from a slave's time at work: how much work and productivity was to be had. Sloppiness, bad timekeeping, lack of effort – all would prompt an array of punishments which were familiar to slaves everywhere. In the words of a

* 'This Rustic Theology' (1758), in Robert Edgar Conrad, *Children of God's Fire*, pp.292–297.

† 'Advice on Plantation Punishment . . .' (1839), in Robert Edgar Conrad, *Children of God's Fire*, pp.297–301.

Brazilian plantation manual, 'Fear . . . is the only way to force slaves to meet the responsibilities that their condition imposes upon them.'*

The whip accompanied the lives of the enslaved from the moment they entered an Atlantic slave ship to their dying days in slavery. Memories of whippings lingered on in Black communities, and were recalled by former slaves in deep old age, to be repeated by their descendants as a horrible recollection of slave sufferings. Whips were used to corral Africans into line when they were captured, to maintain order and punishment on board the slave ship, and to discourage slacking at work in the field. Whips were used for any number of reasons – for the most serious acts of defiance through to petty offences. In the grip of cruel handlers, the whip doled out pain simply for the hell of it. Those slave owners who lived far from their properties had to be vigilant about the damage caused by rogue drivers. Mrs Elletson, who as we have seen owned a Jamaican estate, but was living in London in 1774, was outraged to learn of the 'Villainous Conduct and behaviour of Rutland [the overseer] towards my Negroes.' She was especially concerned about 'his severe punishments and Cruelties to those poor wretches' for failing to deliver the expected amount of hay for the horses.†

At much the same time Thomas Thistlewood regularly inflicted savage punishments on his Jamaican slaves, sometimes of an extreme and grotesque nature. Sadistic owners, drunken overseers or men crazed by the dangerous isolation that shaped their lives (virtually alone in a sea of hostile Africans) punished,

* 'Advice on Plantation Punishment . . .' (1839), in Robert Edgar Conrad, *Children of God's Fire*, p.298.

† Letter, 3 March 1774. Grenville Papers.

tortured and damaged their slaves whenever the mood took them. Off-hand violent cruelties and beatings were part and parcel of the everyday dangers of slavery. Nor was this restricted to slaves in the fields. Domestic slaves faced the casual anger of a mistress and the predatory sexual advances of the men of the house. The smallest of domestic failings – in cleaning, cooking and childcare – might bring a blow or a physical assault. However, slaves usually regarded domestic service as the best work on a property. The ultimate punishment handed down to house slaves was demotion to fieldwork, and field hands liked to secure a better position for their children – in domestic service.

Like much else in the history of slavery, Brazilian slave masters were among the first to establish the widespread use of the whip on their slaves. A seventeenth century remark captured the habit:

> Whoever wants to reap benefit from his negroes must maintain them, make them work well, and beat them even better: without this there will be no service nor any profit.*

Few slave owners resisted the temptation to whip slaves. One slave owner in Paraiba, commenting on Angolan slaves, noted that their work was 'always maintained with many whippings.' Some slaves suffered even worse torments than whippings, because, thought one master, the slaves were 'like devils.' A Brazilian law of 1688 sought to protect slaves from extreme punishments, and allowed them to report a master's cruelty to

* James H. Sweet, *Recreating Africa: Culture, Kinship, and Religion in the African-Portuguese World, 1441–1770*, Chapel Hill, 2005, p.74.

state or church officials. Slave owners found guilty could be obliged to sell their slaves. But such laws had little practical effect, especially in remote regions where most plantation slaves lived and where formal authority, of church or state, was distant and inaccessible. When Pedro Pais Machado killed a freeman and slaves for injuring one of his cattle (he hanged one slave by his testicles) he was later released because he was 'a noble person with family obligations.' Even clerics were guilty of violence. Father Salvador dos Santos, Abbott of the Benedictine monastery in Olinda from 1746 to 1749, beat his slaves so badly that many ran away. One was left so long in chains that his foot was 'mutilated'. Another, terrified of being put in the stocks, tried to cut his own throat. Though a doctor managed to save the man's life, the monks complained that the treatment 'cost a great deal.'*

Throughout its long history, Brazilian slavery was characterised by brutality towards the enslaved. Visitors were regularly shocked by the apparent lack of restraint in the savagery meted out to local slaves. They were burned or scorched with hot wax:

> branded on face and chest, tortured with hot irons, had their ears or noses lopped off, or suffered sexually related barbarities as a result of jealousy.†

Eventually, opinion in all the slave nations moved slowly against such violence towards slaves – even in Brazil, where regulations of 1839 specified how many blows should be administered for

* James Sweet, *Recreating Africa*, pp.74–75.

† David Brion Davis, *Inhuman Bondage: The Rise and Fall of Slavery in the New World*, New York, 2008, p.118.

specific offences (though accepting that whipping itself was essential). Fifty lashes were thought to be the maximum:

> Anything above this number is more likely to arouse anger and revenge.*

***

Perhaps the most vivid and best remembered accounts (in English) of the enslaved being whipped belong to US slavery in the nineteenth century. As that century advanced, accounts of brutality proliferated not perhaps because such violence increased, but because of the rapidly changing social and political context. There was, of course, a massive increase in the number of slaves in the US, Brazil and Cuba in the nineteenth century, but this ran parallel with ever-more strident (and well-organised) attacks on slavery in both Europe and the Americas. Slavery was scrutinised as never before by a growing army of abolitionists, and their findings were reported to an expanding readership eager to learn about the appalling violence done to the enslaved. To put it simply, there was a huge audience waiting to learn more about slavery, and to add to the denunciations of slavery. Slavery had *always* been brutal, had *always* used violence to control and punish. What changed, in the nineteenth century, was the massive increase of information in circulation *about* that violence. Cheap print, mass literacy, large crowds at lectures and anti-slavery meetings – all and more created a vast and unprecedented audience and readership for

* 'Advice on Plantation Punishment . . .' (1839), in Robert Edgar Conrad, *Children of God's Fire*, p.299.

the accounts of violence done to the enslaved.

As ever more people read and heard about the essential violent nature of slavery, public revulsion grew. Accounts of slave floggings helped to strengthen a public feeling that slavery was morally rotten and should be ended. It was increasingly difficult for slave owners to hide their violence towards slaves. The reality of their habits began to seep into broader public awareness. Countless examples were paraded before the reading public. Bennet H. Barrow, a slave owner in Louisiana, occasionally ordered *all* his field slaves to be whipped – alongside specific tortures to be handed out to particular slaves. Though it is true that he also doled out incentives and benefits, his enslaved labour force knew that his power ultimately lay in his whip.*

Supporters of whipping continued to argue that slaves would not work, nor would they accept their place, without the threat of the whip. In the words of Benjamin Franklin, the slave, by definition:

> is subject to severe Punishment for small Offences, to enormous Whippings, and even Death, for absconding from his Service, or for Disobedience to Orders.†

Such punishments were not merely commonplace but formed the warp and weft of slavery history. Turn the pages of any number of letters, diaries, and comments by slave owners, and slave punishments leap off the page. They sometimes accompany comments that startle the modern reader. On 22 May 1712, the

* David Brion Davis, *Inhuman Bondage*, p.196.

† Quoted in Andrew Delbanco, *The War Before the War*, New York, 2019, p.50.

Virginian planter William Byrd recorded in his diary:

> My wife caused Prue to be whipped violently notwithstanding I desired not, which provoked me to have Anaka whipped likewise who had deserved it much more, on which my wife flew into such a passion that she hoped she would be revenged of me.*

As a child, Alexander Hamilton had witnessed slaves being lashed in the street to quicken their pace. Slave runaways in North America were so commonplace that laws were passed ordering whippings for slaves caught out of doors after local curfew times. Even on the US west coast, in 1844, whippings were prescribed for slaves who did not leave the Oregon when they were emancipated. As US abolition gathered pace after the 1820s, abolitionists regularly published examples of slaves being whipped (and lynched) – most famously the 'Black List' of recent outrages against the enslaved, published by Benjamin Lundy and William Garrison.†

Famous visitors to slave societies were repelled by the incidents of violence towards slaves which they encountered. Alexis de Tocqueville was appalled to see a slave beaten with a walking stick – to the apparent indifference of a crowd of spectators. The USA was no different from other slave societies, with violence common for slave wrongdoing and an inescapable threat of everyday slave life. In the words of a former slave, writing in 1836:

* Quoted in Andrew Delbanco, *The War Before the War*, p.55.

† Andrew Delbanco, *The War Before the War,* pp.76, 128, 144, 218.

> Any white man who meets a slave off the plantation without a pass, has a right to take him up, and flog him at his discretion.*

Although this is a story that is easily caricatured, it is also easy to minimise its harsh reality. Violence towards slaves was *not* the exception but rather an inescapable threat and aspect of their lives, though it was most visible, widespread – and audible – when they laboured in the fields.

The crack of the whip, long familiar in the sugar fields of Brazil and the Caribbean, could be heard in Louisiana once sugar took root there as a major industry in the nineteenth century. Here too, the slave drivers became infamous for their violence ('prowling sullenly about, watching every motion of the bondsmen.') One planter, who believed in the value of a 'good flogging', regularly set about the task with relish, whipping his slaves 'until there is no place to whip.' His enthusiasm for violence gave him palpitations: 'damn their skins I wish they were all in Africa.' Some inevitably went too far. John Palfrey had to dismiss an overseer who was 'a man of violent and unimaginable temper and of a jealous, suspicious and vindictive disposition.' Many others, however, continued with their violent behaviour unimpeded. William C. Riley assaulted a slave with a paddle, stripping the skin off the man's back. He assaulted slaves with a stick of sugar cane and beat them with his fists.†

Like so many thousands before them, the slaves in Louisiana's new sugar fields had to endure grotesque acts of violence: tied

* Andrew Delbanco, *The War Before the War*, pp. 30, 194.

† Richard Follett, *The Sugar Masters: Planters and Slaves in Louisiana's Cane World, 1820–1860*, Baton Rouge, 2007, pp.173–174.

to a bed of ants or similar excruciating tortures. Killing was unusual, but not unknown (despite the obvious economic loss involved). Above all though, it was the whip which was, again, the most common form of punishment.

Whips came in various forms, though some were more notoriously vicious than others. It was the slave driver's essential tool, his 'emblem of authority'. Of course whips were used widely on rural properties – to goad the horses, the oxen and cattle. On slave plantations, sometimes the very same whip sufficed for livestock and humans. More often though, the slave driver had his own favourite whip for handling the slaves. Some used bundles of switches. Others used 'cow-skins', a whip infamous because it would 'make the woods ring' with the shrieks of the slaves. US planters, like many before them, sometimes tried to restrict the disciplinary power of their drivers, laying down the numbers and nature of blows they might administer. Some even forbad the use of whips in the fields (a sure sign of the concern they felt about the abuses involved). As they watched the slaves at work – areas of land weeded, planted, harvested – and the volume of crops harvested – sugar, cotton, tobacco, rice – slave drivers assessed if the targets had been reached, or spotted who was failing to keep up. It was no slip of the tongue that one of the terms used to describe a slave driver in the US South was the 'whipping boss'.* Some used a whip of knotted rope, designed to lacerate a slave's back. More painful still was the use of a paddle, an item measuring 16 inches long, covered in leather and applied to a slave's buttocks. As one female victim recalled – seventy-five years after the beating:

* William L. Van Deburg, *The Slave Drivers*, Westport, Conn., 1979, p.3.

> Dey strip yo' down naked, an two men hold yo' down and whip yo' till de blood come – Creuel. Oh Lawd.

Planters knew exactly what a whip could achieve – and they instructed their drivers accordingly. William Minor, a Louisiana sugar planter, thought that whipping should be inflicted 'in a serious, firm, and gentlemanly manner' and the victim should realise that the punishment was 'for his bad conduct only and not for revenge or passion.'

At its simplest, the whip was just another tool in the slave owner's management system. But it had to be used sparingly if it was to have its desired effect. 'Indiscriminate, constant, and excessive use of the whip is altogether unnecessary and inexcusable.'

Some chose to put slaves in stocks or in fetters rather than whip them, but, like the whip, this involved public humiliation as much as private agony. It also reminded others what to expect if they stepped out of line. Despite many slave owners being aware that punishment needed to be moderate, it was often administered beyond their sight: far from their eyes, in distant fields. And even the most temperate of slave owners could lose patience – and reach for the whip.*

Yet for all this litany of violence, the management of slavery did not rely solely on brute force. However universal and inescapable, violence was used alongside other, highly effective methods of managing the enslaved. Slave owners worked their labour gangs via rewards and promises, threats and bonuses. They gave them more food or clothing, more free time or better accommodation. They granted them liberties and privileges

* Richard Follett, *Sugar Masters,* pp.173–179.

(especially for elite slaves). At times, the enslaved were even allowed to earn and keep money. Each slave owner – from the humblest to the mightiest – judged what was the best mix of measures: what was best suited to persuade their workers to toil to the owner's advantage. There were a few carrots. But the stick was ever present.

13

Working

THE MAJOR PORT cities of American slave colonies were teeming with enslaved Africans. Most of course were simply in transit – awaiting onward sale, but many lived there; local town residents plying their various trades or labouring at all the physical demands of urban life. Two cities stand out: Rio de Janeiro and Kingston, Jamaica.

By the late eighteenth century, some nine hundred thousand Africans had landed in Kingston – though most were destined for onwards movement. By then, more Black people lived in Kingston than in Boston, Philadelphia and New York combined. Kingston was the heart of Britain's slave empire and a majority of its residents were Black and the majority were women. Kingston's enslaved lived very different lives from their contemporaries scattered across the island's plantations. They were used in construction and roadworks, in the myriad quay-side jobs found at all busy international ports – loading, unloading, refitting and repairing (large numbers were skilled carpenters), or working as sailors both on local small craft or on major ocean-going vessels. The largest group of slaves living in Kingston, however, were domestic servants – mainly women

– serving all the domestic needs of the city's prosperous merchant, trading and plantocratic class. There, they lived cheek by jowl with local white people (and hence the large number of mixed-race people in Kingston, people born to slave women of white masters). Slavery in Kingston differed sharply from the slavery which dominated the rural economies of the Americas. Historians speak of it as 'public facing' – more visible and public, not out of sight, as it tended to be on remote, distant plantations.* Of course, Africans were to be found in all the major ports of the Atlantic world (small groups slowly came together in European towns and cities) concentrated inevitably in those ports which received the apparently endless waves of Africans stepping from the Atlantic ships.

Enslaved people in cities were much more independent (and therefore harder to control) than those on rural properties. For that reason alone, many slave owners distrusted them. They mixed with free Blacks, with free people of mixed race, they picked up a subversive attitude that was hard to handle. They moved around freely, mixing socially with friends, enjoyed urban pleasures – drinking, gambling, the free-and-easy life of port taverns which were awash with all the news from the far corners of trade and empire. They were also a conduit for the information that flowed from the ships and their sailors, fresh in from Europe and Africa – just like their counterparts in Europe. Frederick Douglass stated it simply:

* Trevor Burnard, 'Slaves and Slavery in Kingston 1770–1815', in *International Review of Social History*, vol. 65, April 2020. (*Special Issue on Urban Slavery in the Age of Abolition.)*

> A city slave is almost a freeman, compared with a slave on a plantation.*

Not surprisingly, rural slave owners were generally keen to keep their slaves away from towns. In the USA, with the rise of King Cotton in the nineteenth century, the proportion of slaves living in towns actually declined, but that was largely because the South was overwhelmingly rural: it had few major towns. With the notable exceptions of New Orleans, Mobile and Charleston, the South was 'almost totally rural'.† If we need to look at urban slavery at its most extreme – its most concentrated, important and intricate – we need to study Brazil, especially Rio de Janeiro.

That city was crowded with enslaved Africans, from the quaysides outwards. In the bustle of the busy docks, Africans were not only unloaded as human cargo and shifted to nearby yards and warehouses (to be kept there until ready for onward sale) but they were at work loading and unloading the ships. They were the human beasts of burden undertaking *all* the heavy work required in and around Atlantic (and local) shipping. Gangs of slaves carried enormous loads to and from the ships, in and out of warehouses. A North American visitor to Rio in 1846 caught the image perfectly. On the streets of Rio:

> Slaves are the beasts of draught as well as the beast of burden.‡

* Peter Kolchin, *American Slavery*, London, 1995 edn, p.179.

† Peter Kolchin, *American Slavery*, p.177.

‡ Robert Edgar Conrad, *Children of God's Fire*, p.121.

Slave labour gangs on the streets of Rio were often led by men who sang or beat out a working rhythm. The head of a gang of coffee-carriers (each load weighing upwards of 160lbs) 'shakes a rattle, to the music of which his associates behind him chant.' And all done at a trot. It was just one of those call-and-response songs that echo across the history of American slavery. Other gangs carried huge baskets of coal, of masonry or flanks of freshly slaughtered beasts still reeking with blood fresh from the slaughterhouse. Wherever you looked, there were gangs of enslaved Africans straining as they carried enormous loads great distances, with many suffering from a range of highly visible physical damage to their legs and bellies.

The major ports of the Americas (but most strikingly those in Brazil) were home to large numbers of enslaved people – women especially. Many were hired out by owners, others worked on their own during the day, returning to their owners, with their casual earnings, at the end of a day's work. The remarkable variety of work they did is captured in newspaper advertisements, with slaves offered for sale and for hire, or sought after, when they had escaped. Skills and trades of every description were on offer – shoemakers, comb-makers, females trained for domestic work, cooks, waiters, children (to be trained up in domestic service), bakers, wet nurses (to breast-feed their owners' babies), peddlers hawking water, fish or market produce, stonemasons, sailors. And everywhere there were prostitutes – often paraded flagrantly in a style which offended more sensitive souls.

In Rio there were huge numbers of enslaved washerwomen (one man thought upwards of two hundred) pummelling their soapy items in public fountains, the neighbouring field strewn with items drying and bleaching in the sun. Other domestic slaves queued at the same fountains to fill vessels for their household's domestic consumption – the queues sometimes guarded by police to keep order and prevent people jumping the queue.

Everywhere there was noisy confusion, with throngs of people, bales, boxes, crates and carts – all carried, lifted and pulled, not by animals, but by Africans. The shafts of heavy-duty wagons and carts were manned not by horses or oxen – but by slaves; some pulling, others pushing from behind. Some even worked while shackled. Visitors were taken aback by the common sight of the enslaved – men and women, young and old – struggling to cope with heavy duties while chained by the ankle or neck.

Newcomers to Rio were overwhelmed by the raucous turmoil of slave life on the streets. Of course, all major cities were noisy (dirty and smelly) and crowded with working people noisily hawking their labours and their wares in public, and knocking on residents' doors. But even by contemporary standards, Rio seemed extreme. 'The "cries" of London are bagatelles to those of the Brazilian capital,' one visitor noted.

To peer from the window of a Rio townhouse during the day was to witness an endless procession of slave-borne goods and services. All of life's essential foodstuffs were paraded alongside delicacies ('heavenly bacon'), household items from cutlery to china, women's clothing, shawls and handkerchiefs, shoes and children's toys and even 'works of devotion'. 'These things, and a thousand others, are hawked about daily.'*

Slaves carried their goods on their heads, in baskets and in tin chests (bearing their owner's name). Valuable items were

* Robert Edgar Conrad, *Children of God's Fire*, p.117.

covered in glass cases fixed to portable counters. Slave women with babies and small children strapped to their back, paraded their various wares in front of them. Householders did not even have to step outside to buy: they merely opened the door – snapping fingers, or calling out for a particular item – to have the appropriate item rushed to the door by the nearest slave hawker.

Most striking of all was the sight of slaves carrying *people* in sedan chairs and hammocks. It was a sign of Brazilian status to be carried by slaves: the more prosperous the slave owner, the more elaborate the sedan and the dress of the slaves carrying it. It was a Brazilian version of the European habit of being served by Black servants attired in costly and fashionable attire. The city of Salvador – with its steep climb from the port to the city centre – provided an excuse for the prosperous to be carried – by the enslaved. People being carried by slaves became a feature of Brazilian slavery at large.

There was, then, an astonishing panorama of slave labour on view in the major ports of the Americas, much of it backbreaking and brutish. Some slave labour – notably domestic work and street hawkers – would have been familiar to any inhabitant of Europe's major cities, though some was unique to the slave societies of the Americas. Yet for all its excesses and exploitation – for all its cruelty and harshness (so shocking to generations of visitors) – the slavery of urban life was not the beating heart of slavery. Africans were not shipped across the Atlantic in such vast numbers solely to service the varied demands of city dwellers: they arrived and passed through their first port of call to work elsewhere – destined overwhelmingly for life as agricultural labourers in distant and generally isolated locations. They were fated to live out the lives of enslaved labourers far removed from the bustle and turmoil they encountered when they first landed. Instead, they were to live and work in places that were as quiet as the ports were noisy. Most were heading for plantations, places where, for much of the time, the loudest of noises as they toiled in the fields was the crack of a whip.

***

The image of large numbers of slaves, working in field gangs, was used relentlessly by abolitionists in the nineteenth century, largely because it captured all the worst features and excesses of slavery. Understandably, it is an image which has lived on in the popular memory. More recently, however, historians have been at pains to stress the remarkable range and diversity of enslaved labour. Across swathes of the Americas, legions of slaves laboured in a wide range of crops for which gang labour was inappropriate or impossible: working in arrowroot, cocoa, coffee, long-staple cotton, hemp, naval stores, pimento, rice and timber.* Those crops, and others, used a task system of slave labour. Moreover, the nature of task work itself varied greatly from one crop to another. Nonetheless, task work involved its own form of discipline and though it may have lacked the eye-catching brutalities of gang labour, it was nonetheless arduous and alien – especially for newly arrived Africans.

Task work was the basis of slave labour in rice and long-staple cotton cultivation in South Carolina and Georgia, and in cotton cultivation in the Bahamas and in Grenada. By contrast, the

* See Philip D. Morgan, 'Task and Gang Systems' in Stephen Innes, ed., *Work and Labor*, Chapel Hill, 1988, Ch.5.

enslaved working in the forbidding and often dangerous rainforests of central America (felling mahogany and floating the huge logs to awaiting Atlantic ships) formed gangs which worked at their own labouring system. Whatever the industry, trial and error enabled slave masters to calculate what each slave, or group of slaves, could achieve in a particular time period, or area of land. Slaves on coffee plantations were allowed to complete particular tasks in a given time: with their task completed, they were released to work on their own plots or spend time as they wished. Much the same routines developed among skilled artisan slaves. Coopers were expected to complete making a barrel within a certain time, similarly with joiners making planks. Thereafter they could turn to their own work. Task work was essential across the Americas, but it looked – and felt – very different from the world of gang labour in the sugar and cotton fields, characterised, in the words of William Beckford, the Jamaican planter, by its 'regular discipline in the work.' This was the slave labour which became infamous both for its discipline and its violence – administered, in the field, by slave overseers and drivers. In the worlds of Solomon Northrup (now well-known for his memoir, subsequently made into a film, *Twelve Years a Slave*), 'The requisite qualification for an overseer are utter heartlessness, brutality and cruelty.' Such men ruled the vast lands of the US cotton South, and marshalling the 150,000 slaves of Louisiana's sugar fields. They had long ruled the enslaved who worked in the same crop across the Caribbean and Brazil. The work was harsh and was monitored and managed with an intensity that regularly provoked images of military discipline.

Organised into gangs, the first and the strongest people undertook the heaviest field labour. This gang was the key, remarked an admiring commentator in 1823. 'Nothing animates the planting system more than the well-being of this admirable effective force, composed of the flower of the field battalions.' It represented:

> the very essence of an estate, its support in all weathers and necessities, the proprietor's glory, the overseer' s favourite.

In sugar, after a heavy day in the fields, the first gang were sometimes moved to the factory. They were a *team*, advancing in a line, in unison, cutting the tall sugar cane (which was removed and loaded onto carts by other gangs bringing up their rear). Supervised by the driver or overseers, their output documented and checked by bookkeepers for the pace and timing of their work. Ideally, a cook should be on hand to provide food at the agreed time. Hard work was rewarded (with rum) and punishments only administered when 'absolutely necessary, and that with mercy.' That ideal usually disappeared in the remoteness of distant fields, and in any case always depended on the mood of the man carrying the whip.

Behind the battalion of field slaves, other gangs cleared the fields, tended the animals, undertook the plantation's necessary skilled work, while others guarded the property: even the old and very young would be assigned roles on a plantation.* Here was a schedule of labouring regimentation which embraced all but the decrepit, the very old, very young and sick. Everyone – all ages, both male and female – was allotted a role in the plantation's working regime.

* Thomas Roughley, 'The Jamaica Planter's Guide' (1823), in *Slavery, Abolition and Emancipation*, Michael Craton, James Walvin and David Wright, eds, London, 1976. p.82.

Life's basic essentials – food and drink, clothing and housing – were provided by the slave owners, and all could be improved or withdrawn as a sign of approval or punishment. Clearly, slave owners needed to maintain the physical well-being of their labour force, though planters in straitened circumstances, or under bad management, sometimes cut back on life's essentials. Drought, storms, poor harvests – all and more (plus the disruption of warfare) intervened to complicate slave management.

The details of this entire system were assiduously documented by professional bookkeepers whose job it was to record and monitor every aspect of life on a slave property. This bookkeeping system was always important, but, as we have seen, it became especially vital when the owners of slave properties left the estate in the hands of managers and attorneys. Meticulous bookkeeping was an important ingredient in the success of a slave property, and by the late eighteenth century it offered a clear blueprint about how to manage land and labour. When Edward Long – one of Jamaica's most famous planters, and historian of the island – wrote an account of how best to manage a sugar plantation, the evidence he used was compiled originally by the bookkeepers on his properties. Bookkeepers, after a fashion, were the researchers for Long's publications. Those clerks of the slave system were essential to the management of slavery everywhere and their written records enabled owners and managers to make slavery work effectively. Those records have also made possible the historical reconstruction of the entire story.

***

Slavery was revitalised across the Americas in the nineteenth century. In the USA, the revival was driven forward by cotton, in Brazil by coffee and in Cuba by sugar and tobacco. The rapid spread of slave-grown cotton across the US South was facilitated by the experience of older cotton regions in the Americas, and by the availability of large numbers of slave labourers. The impact of Eli Whitney's cotton gin transformed everything, and enslaved labourers were quickly force marched into the new cotton lands of the South. As with sugar in earlier centuries, slavery marched in step with cotton cultivation. The result was astonishing. Before Whitney, the US produced 15 million pounds of cotton. By 1820 that had grown to 167.5 million pounds. In the same period, one quarter of a million slaves were moved south. As settlers moved in, local Indian people were removed from the lands, mainly by force but also by treaties, and enslaved labour was dragooned across the face of the USA. Thus did the cotton fields fill with gangs of slaves. It was, after a fashion, a repeat of what had been seen in the Caribbean three centuries earlier: the land was violently cleared of its indigenous inhabitants who were replaced by Africans, who were themselves victims of a violent system of enslavement and transportation. Enslaved labour flowed into the US South – alongside massive investment from Europe and the north-eastern USA – and cotton flowed out, to feed the expanding textile industries of the USA and Europe. It became a commercial cornucopia that rested on labour gangs whose working days in the cotton fields were regulated and marshalled by men with a bullwhip.*

* Sven Beckert, *Empire of Cotton: A New History of Global Capitalism*, London, 2014, Ch.5.

Not unlike earlier sugar barons, the cotton planters were alert to the latest agronomic improvements, experimenting with different kinds of cotton, collecting or borrowing the relevant books and journals to study. In addition, again like their sugar forebears, they experimented with – and studied – how best to organise their labour gangs. Although this intrusive management of slave labour in cotton has been hailed as the first of its kind, it had already been pioneered with great success on the earlier sugar plantations. Successful cotton production was anchored in a brutal work regime, but the genesis of that regime was pioneered and perfected in the violent world of sugar cultivation. The argument that the cotton plantation was the birthplace of a new form of industrial discipline overlooks the well-established discipline first forged in the sugar fields. Whatever its labouring origins, the US cotton industry yielded astonishing returns. By 1802, US cotton dominated the British market: a mere generation later it dominated both European and American cotton markets. In the half century to 1860, 'more than half of all American exports . . . consisted of cotton.'* Work in the cotton fields quickly followed the pattern established in Brazil and the Caribbean in sugar, of physical hardship in a hostile climate. Slaves first converted forests into farmland, then toiled in the cotton fields, all to the accompaniment of threats and punishment. They worked longer hours than they had in the old slave colonies/states to the north, and cotton planters worked their gangs harder than ever.

The US cotton industry was greatly helped by technological changes, nowhere more obviously than in the massive fleet of steamboats that ferried enormous cargoes of cotton down the

* Sven Beckert, *Empire of Cotton*, p.119.

Mississippi to New Orleans. By the 1830s, more than two hundred steamships worked the economy of that mighty river. By mid-century the numbers had increased to 1,500 and they were capable of carrying two million tons of cotton. At major ports of the US South, cotton was transferred to steam-powered ships for the voyage to New York and Boston or to Europe – notably to Liverpool.*

Lancashire's cotton industry – the engine of Britain's industrial revolution – acquired its raw cotton overwhelmingly from the slave economy of the US South. The port of Liverpool, which had risen to prominence on the back of the Atlantic slave trade, now thrived on importing slave-grown cotton – and exporting finished textile materials. The city's docksides, once crowded with sailing ships, were increasingly dominated from 1830 onwards, by steamships. Steam power – in the textile mills, on boats on the Mississippi, and on the ships in the Atlantic – played a major role in the revival and commercial success of slavery in the nineteenth century.

***

Simple machines had long been a feature of slavery in the tropical Americas. Converting sugar cane into crude sugar and molasses had traditionally involved simple industrial processes. Indeed, bigger sugar plantations had their own factories. Their chimneys, belching steam and smoke into the tropical sky, could be seen from a distance, and regularly feature in paintings and drawings of plantation life. The machines at work in

* For steamboats, see Walter Johnson, *River of Dark Dreams: Slavery and Empire in the Cotton Kingdom*, Cambridge, Mass., 2013, Ch.3.

those plantation factories imposed their own distinctive work discipline on slave labourers – and not only on those within the factory. Once a sugar factory was running, it required a regular supply of sugar cane from the fields; thus the sugar factories partly dictated the broader system of slave labour at the height of the sugar harvest. Both in the fields, and in the rudimentary factories, enslaved labour in the Americas had been subject to forms of labour discipline long before the emergence of modern steam power.

Even so, the impact of nineteenth-century steam power transformed everything. Old industries were revitalised by the application of new mechanical systems powered by steam. The latest steam engines were shipped from Britain and the USA to the sugar plantations of the Caribbean and Brazil, modernising sugar-making alongside the labour gangs working as they always had in the fields. New railway lines were laid in Brazil and Cuba, to transport coffee and sugar to the nearest port. In the last phase of slavery in the Americas – from the mid-nineteenth century onwards – modern technology did not push slavery aside so much as give it an increasingly efficient appearance and competitiveness. Slavery and modern industrial practices worked hand-in-hand in US cotton and sugar, in Brazilian tobacco and coffee, and in Cuban tobacco and sugar. Moreover, *all* those slave-grown commodities were refined, processed and transformed in modern factories when they reached the major port cities of the north-east USA and Europe.

The incorporation of new industrial systems into traditional, slave-based industries was a remarkable twist in the history of slavery and it formed a dramatic illustration of the adaptability of slavery. It also illustrates why slavery survived for so long. Steam power modernised factory production and utterly changed the bulk transportation of slave-grown commodities and the refining, packaging and distribution of those same slave-cultivated goods was modernised in new Western industrial facilities at dockside on both sides of the Atlantic.

This process was at its most obvious in the cotton revolution in the US South. Powered by major US capitalist interests – notably the banks and financiers of the north-east – and by heavy investment in steam power, it thrived on the voracious demand for cotton from the factories of the USA, Britain and Germany. Yet all this would have been worthless without the forced labour of armies of field slaves on the cotton plantations of the US South. Their lives were supervised and managed in fine detail. Planters and managers logged all the details of their slaves' labour, the data entering their account books to become the very stuff of plantation management. The managerial awareness of what people and land were capable of, gave cotton planters the means to drive their enslaved labourers harder than ever before. They – like sugar planters in Louisiana and Cuba at the same time – were able to maximise the efforts and the returns of their slave labour force. Slavery had, in effect, been modernised. The old violent systems had been grafted onto the new.

The cotton industry of the US South also adopted the careful bookkeeping of older plantation economies but, again, brought it up to date by the adoption of more refined accountancy. US cotton planters used printed account books, manufactured by Thomas Affleck, a Scottish immigrant who had initially trained as a bookkeeper in the Bank of Scotland. Affleck now applied his bookkeeping experience to cotton management. His *Plantation Record and Account Book* allowed planters to keep a detailed account and tally of every slave and every plot of cotton production. The data which was accumulated, month after month, became the statistical basis for an ever closer and more harshly applied management of land and labour though in fact, sugar planters had been doing much the same for a century and more.*

Affleck's *Plantation Record* proved enormously successful, was reprinted in various formats many times, and was adapted for sugar as well as cotton cultivation. Others quickly followed Affleck's success, publishing cheaper versions. Such account books, however, did not reach or affect *most* cotton planters (most of whom were smallholders). Twenty thousand planters owned only small numbers of slaves, but the account books were vital to the cotton barons who produced the great bulk of US cotton. With up-to-date data to hand, cotton planters (and even wheat farmers) could make important decisions about how to get the best from their land and their slaves. Quantification thus became vital both to an understanding of how well (or badly) a property was functioning and itself offered a statistical pathway to greater efficiency and profitability. The real curiosity here is that though historians claim this as a breakthrough, a similar accountancy of slavery, and the use of the resulting data to force the slaves to even more strenuous and productive efforts, had long been in use on the sugar plantations of the Caribbean. And there too, the army of scribes, like Affleck, had been educated in Scotland.

Scotland, the Caribbean, Brazil, the US South; sugar, coffee, tobacco, and cotton – all were pieces in an extraordinary global industry. At the heart of everything lay the lives and labours of millions of Africans.

* Caitlin Rosenthal, *Accounting for Slavery: Masters and Management*, Cambridge, MA, 2018.

Part Five

DEMANDING FREEDOM

14

Finding a Voice

THROUGHOUT THE LONG years of slavery in the Americas, and in all the unprecedented volumes of information we possess about the enslaved, where do we turn to hear the slaves' own voices?

They had their own, manifold ways of protesting, of asserting themselves, and of resisting the violations done to them. But for years, slave voices remained noises off stage: distant and scarcely audible, few and far between – and largely ignored. That is no longer the case. Their voices are now central to how we understand slavery.

We know that all the enslaved people of the Americas wanted something different – for themselves, for their families and loved ones, and for those around them. Above all they wished to be free, and they said so, time and again, throughout the history of slavery in the Americas. They made demands, some of them wrote about visions for a different life, many took steps (often dangerous steps) to bring it about it. Moreover, the people who owned them, the people who denied their freedom – on the slave ships and in the Americas – were all too aware that the enslaved wanted freedom: they were the front line – the people who had to remain vigilant knowing that the enslaved would seize any opportunity to claim that freedom. At critical moments, especially when the enslaved were being moved in large numbers, at sea and on land, they were shackled to prevent them fleeing.

One way of assessing the slaves' desire for freedom is to examine their owners' universal and unflagging efforts to *deny* that freedom. Slave owners were permanently aware that without a complexity of restraints – social as well as physical – without ferocious punishments and without tight discipline and control, the enslaved would seize their freedom. At one level, all this may seem glaringly obvious, but it still begs the question: how do we gauge the aspirations of millions of people whose voices were largely mute and whose lives were recorded merely as the transient possessions of their owners? What sort of hopes and visions did they have? Though the great majority of slaves remained silent, their voices muted by the brutality of slavery, there is an abundance of evidence which, if we look closely, allows us to speak with some confidence about slave aspirations. Not surprisingly those hopes ranged from simply making everyday life more tolerable, through to ambitious schemes to bring slavery to an end, and to secure a very different kind of existence, i.e. a life of freedom and equality.

***

The millions of Africans transported to the Americas *had* known something different: they had led a different life. All of them had experienced a life *before* enslavement, and in societies that were utterly different from their lives in the Americas. All carried with them their own distinctive African backgrounds and features – not merely physical appearances and facial markings – but the cultural attributes shaped by a particular African past: language, religions and beliefs, culinary traditions – and of course their memories of an African life. Despite the physical distance, and despite the passage of time, Africa continued to loom large in their lives, and shaped much of the culture they created in the Americas. Many, perhaps most, yearned to return home but those dreams faded with time and with the emergence of new families and communities in the slave quarters. A tiny few did indeed return, though they tended to be high-ranking Africans, or literate Muslims whose rank and status seemed so out of place among the labouring gangs of the Americas. Most famously, Ayuba Suleiman Diallo (better known as Job Ben Solomon) and the two princes of Calabar (Ancona Robin Robin John, and Little Ephraim Robin John from Calabar) returned home after enslavement and transportation to the Americas, thence to freedom in Europe, before the final leg back to Africa.*

Others returned, from the late eighteenth century onwards, via ill-fated schemes to repatriate the 'Black poor' from London and Nova Scotia, and, later, Africans freed by abolitionist navies – though rarely to their home regions of Africa. Other North American colonisation schemes encouraged freed US slaves to return to Africa in the nineteenth and twentieth centuries. But the obstacles to such schemes were enormous, most notably the grip of slavery itself, and the family and social roots which Africans put down in the Americas.

* Douglas Grant, *The Fortunate Slave: an illustration of African slavery in the early eighteenth century*, Oxford, 1968; Randy Sparks, *The Two Princes of Calabar*, Cambridge, MA, 2009.

A new vision for Africa

Outsiders had long been aware of Africa's natural resources. Overland caravan routes, and later the armada of trading ships, had exposed a continent which teemed with many sought-after commodities and products. Though gold remained the lodestar of course, the slave system diverted commercial (and national) interests towards African humanity. By the late seventeenth century, the prosperity yielded by the Americas seemed utterly dependent on African labour, and Europeans and their American settlements came to regard the African as vital to their well-being and to their economic future. It was, however, an unusual economic relationship. Africa provided raw muscle which was channelled through the discipline of slave labour, and seemed essential for the prosperity of the Americas. By the early eighteenth century Africa meant slaves, and slaves meant prosperity for the West. Here was a continent able to deliver apparently limitless supplies of humanity to the slave traders on the coast. Many of the other forms of trade with Africa – important, useful and profitable – seemed almost incidental to the main purpose which Africa fulfilled: of satisfying the demand for enslaved humanity in the Americas.

But did it *have* to be like that? Was Africa simply *doomed* to a perpetual subservience, disgorging its peoples at the whim and pleasure of outsiders? Were there not other ways of doing business? Might it be possible for example (as indeed it had been in the early years of trade between maritime Europe and West Africa) for Africans and Europeans to trade as 'normal' trading partners, free of the defining (and crippling) demand for African slaves?

When a small handful of critics began to promote this idea of a more normal trade with West Africa, it was no accident that Africans were prominent among them. People who had passed through the blistering experience of slavery, and who had emerged as pioneering voices of Black freedom by the mid-eighteenth century, were among the first to attack slavery by advocating 'normal' trade with Africa.

***

There was a long European tradition of criticising slavery, but it had been largely overshadowed by the benefits which spilled forth from the slave system. Criticisms of slavery took on a much greater force when they came from people who had endured it at first hand. It became even more persuasive when Africans began to *publish* their memoirs of slavery, not least because few people expected to read the published thoughts of Africans. All the major Atlantic slaving nations, and their colonial satellites in the Americas, were literate cultures, and all, to a degree, *defined* themselves through the written and printed word. There were of course many other cultural attributes they could point to as gauges to their culture: the arts, architecture – and perhaps above all, their religion. The millions of African victims were taken from very different kinds of societies: communities which Europeans and Americans regarded as uncivilised and brute. Of course, it was in the interests of outsiders to ignore or deny the full nature and sophistication of African societies, preferring instead to fall back on what soon became crude caricatures of African life. By doing so, Western slave-trading nations were able to elevate and distance themselves from the Africans they enslaved. Europeans (and Americans) were civilised, Africans were not. This crude distinction (which came in various shapes and sizes) also enabled those involved in slaving to justify and condone African slavery. Though it was a complicated historical process which changed enormously over time, at its core was the belief that white people were justified to treat millions of Black people as slaves – to view them as their personal items of property, to be bought and sold as white people saw fit. And all that hinged on the belief that Africans and their descendants were uncivilised, pagan – and deeply inferior.

In the eighteenth century, however, new voices – Black voices – began to challenge this idea. Africans had, throughout, made their views known. They did not need the written or printed word to make clear their feelings about slavery: it was writ large in their behaviour and especially in their persistent defiance. But the eighteenth century saw the effective start of an utterly new (and ultimately revolutionary) dimension to these objections. The simple fact that slaves and freed slaves began to write and to publish their own views was in itself a major blow against the old stereotypes of the slave lobby. It was a literate refutation of one of the basic principles underpinning the slave system.

In the course of the eighteenth century, the printed word emerged in a new, widespread and more popular format. Reading, writing and printed material became everyday features of Western life. Men in coffee shops, women in their salons and libraries, common folk in taverns – all had access to a great variety of printed materials. It was a world that also gave birth to a new genre of writers – Black writers, and in the process, enslaved Africans found a new kind of voice.

Today, the most prominent of eighteenth-century Black writers are familiar, because they have been used, quoted, anthologised, and repeated, in a great variety of formats, from scholarly publications to the popular media. Yet they were people who were *not* expected to be literate. Atlantic slavery did not, at first, require literate workers, though it is true, as societies in the Americas became more complex, slave literacy did indeed become more useful. But *Black* literacy created a tension in the fabric of slavery itself: it was proof that Black people were not what the slave system claimed they were. They were not merely intended to be brute labourers for their masters, destined by their African origins solely to a life of harsh physical labour. This was the context for the emergence of Black writers from the mid-eighteenth century. Africans had discovered a voice which their masters recognised and heeded.

***

In the turbulent flow of people across the Atlantic, growing numbers of Africans found themselves cast ashore in Europe.* Lisbon had long had a Black community; by the mid-eighteenth century so too had London. Most had been shipped to Britain as enslaved servants, and as fashionable curiosities in a society generally unaccustomed to the presence of Blacks. By the late eighteenth century, this Black presence had become an inescapable fact, and is still visible in contemporary portraits, in local parish records, in criminal proceedings and in everyday records of contemporary social life. More uncommon, but much more revealing, were the writings of Africans published in Britain.

In 1772, James Albert Ukawsa Gronniosaw (c. 1710–1772) published a memoir in the fashionable English spa town of Bath. His was a story which could have been replicated a million times: of capture in Africa, transatlantic transportation and settlement in American bondage (in his case as a house

* Olivette Otele, *African Europeans: An Untold Story*, London, 2020.

slave) before freedom and a new life at sea. Gronniosaw later settled in Europe, married a local woman, and they raised a family, though enduring great poverty.*

Gronniosaw's memoir seems to have been prompted by Lord Mansfield's critical legal decision in the famous Somerset case earlier that same year. Though Mansfield's specific point of law was that slave owners could *not* remove slaves from England against their wishes, his judgement had the effect of ending slavery in England itself. The case also focused attention on Britain's Black community, and Gronniosaw's memoir formed another contribution to the arguments in print and in politics which swirled around that famous court case, and which had consequences far beyond the fate of James Somerset, who was at the centre of it.

Gronniosaw's book yields rich evidence for historians of the period. He wrote of Africa, of slavery in the Americas, of its brutalities, of his conversion to Christianity (a classic theme in slave narratives), of his unhappy life in England, and of the hardship of his family life with a growing band of children. He frequently despaired – poor, homeless and hungry – moving from place to place (Norwich, Colchester, Kidderminster) in search of work, and was often saved only by the generosity of friends and acquaintances. 'I did not mind for myself at all, but to see my dear wife and children in want, pierc'd me to the heart.' It was also the account of a Christian soul:

* The best anthology of the following Black writers is to be found in Vincent Carretta, ed., *Unchained Voices: An Anthology of Black Authors in the English-Speaking World of the Eighteenth Century*, University of Kentucky, 1996. See James Albert Ukawsaw Gronniosaw, *A Narrative of the Most Remarkable Particulars: in the Life of James Albert Ukawsaw Gronniosaw, an African Prince, as related by Himself*, London, 2017 edn.

> As Pilgrims, and very poor Pilgrims, we are travelling through many difficulties towards our HEAVENLY HOME.

At the heart of Gronniosaw's account lies a simple aspiration shared by millions of his fellow Africans: he wanted to enjoy family life on his own terms. This apparently unexceptional point is a reminder that Africans were shipped across the Atlantic, and settled into the enslaved Americas *not* in families but as individuals. As we have seen, one of the most important and remarkable achievements of slave life across the Americas was the creation of family life from the unyielding environment of slavery. In Europe and the Americas, the enslaved and freed people found partners with whom they shared their lives, and from those partnerships and marriages there emerged new forms of communities which became integral features of society on both sides of the Atlantic.

Though Gronniosaw was clearly an exceptional man, his words speak to the vision shared by many others: of the determination, despite the miseries of slavery and despite the poverty-stricken world of Black freedom, to shape a family and personal life of one's own choosing. It was an achievement which can easily go unnoticed.

A year after Gronniosaw's memoir was published in Bath, a nineteen-year-old enslaved woman from Boston published a very different kind of book in London. Born in Africa, she had been enslaved as a child of seven or eight and shipped to North America. Wearing little more than a piece of filthy carpet, she was bought in a market in Boston and was given her mistress's name – Wheatley. She was also named Phillis after the slave ship that had carried her across the Atlantic.*

* Phillis Wheatley, *Complete Writings*, London, 2002, Vincent Carretta, ed.

The young woman soon picked up an interest in reading and writing, and, thanks to English aristocratic patronage, had her poetry published in London in 1773, again in the wake of the Somerset case. In common with so many, later, Black writers the Bible was critical. She was, by any standard, a child prodigy, writing her first poems at the age of thirteen, impressing visitors to her Boston home by her studious and quiet presence. In 1773, her owner's son took her to England, where she was fêted by fashionable and aristocratic society. When her poems were published in that year, London reviewers were astonished, both by her youth but even more by the fact that she was a slave. One advertisement for her poems noted that:

> While in England a few weeks since, was conversed with by many of the principal Nobility and Gentry of this Country . . . and Others who unanimously expressed their approbation of her genius, and their amazement at the gifts with which infinite Wisdom has furnished her.*

Whatever the shortcomings of Wheatley's poetry, her work forms an important statement about Black potential and attainment. After all, here was a young person, barely out of adolescence, adopting a classic expression of that age of sensibility, yet doing so from a position of debased enslavement. What might she have achieved had she been free to enjoy very different opportunities? Such questions were of course prompted by the work of *all* the Black writers of the eighteenth century. If they could make such important contributions from a position of

* G. J. Barker-Benfield, *Phillis Wheatley Chooses Freedom*, New York, 2018, pp.104–105.

enslavement, what greater potential lay untapped among the armies of slaves on the far side of the Atlantic?

The brief fame enjoyed by Phillis Wheatley in London in 1773 stood in harsh contrast to her fate when she returned to Boston – as a slave. Within a year, though now a free woman, the death of her mistress left her destitute, and she scratched a living by selling her writing from door to door. She married a poor free Black, worked as a maid, lost two children, and died in poverty in 1784 aged thirty-one; her surviving child died a few hours later. It was a wretched, anonymous end for a woman whose fame and talent had flared briefly only a decade earlier. Her work survives, however, and though it may not perhaps find a place in the archive of major contemporary verse, it remains essential as a precocious Black voice which suggests the potential of many others around her.

To be heard, to be listened to, to express a view, to command a hearing – *to be in print* – all of these were denied to the millions of Africans trapped in the world of Atlantic slavery. Wheatley, and others, gave voice to the need to be heard: to register an opinion. It was an affirmation too of a vision of a different life. Wheatley's plea was for Black freedom – and she made it directly to George III.

> To the King's Most Excellent Majesty. 1768.
> Great God, direct, and guard him from on high,
> And from his head let ev'ry evil fly!
> And may each clime with equal gladness see
> A monarch's smile can set his subjects free!

Unlike Wheatley, one of her contemporaries, Julius Soubise, led a charmed life largely because of the patronage of aristocratic supporters. Born to a slave mother in St. Kitts, Soubise was purchased by a naval officer and brought to England in 1764, originally under the name Othello. Given to the Duchess of Queensberry, and renamed Soubise, he was immersed in the world of privilege and high fashion, and was regularly ridiculed in print for his foppish behaviour. He became a riding and fencing instructor and freely mixed in aristocratic society. But he attracted scandalous gossip because of his closeness to the Duchess. It was even reported that he had once been caught in her boudoir when she was partly dressed. Soubise revelled in being a dandy, and his reputation for womanising was parodied in the press and in contemporary cartoons. The long-suffering Duchess finally lost patience when he seduced her maidservant, and in 1777 he was disowned and dispatched to India – to a riding school in Madras, where he died in a fall from a horse.

For all his undoubted flamboyant foolishness, Soubise was not without important friends. (Ignatius Sancho, for example, spoke warmly of him.) But he remained a figure of fun in the press, perhaps because his antics were so outrageous. Soubise seems to have been a self-styled jester, yet even here, there was an important dimension to Soubise. He behaved like so many other young men around him, adopting the tone and style, the extravagant posturing of a love-struck *gallant*, anxious to win over his chosen woman. Though Soubise's behaviour now seems pretentious, it was not unlike the antics of many other young men of fashion. The difference, in this case, was that the *poseur* was an African and a former slave.*

***

* For details see Vincent Carretta, 'Julius Soubise (formerly Othello)' 1754–98, *Oxford Dictionary of National Biography*.

Before 1789, the most important, best-known and admired African voice in London was that of Ignatius Sancho, a friend of Soubise but more important as a man with a remarkable network of friends and acquaintances in high society. Sancho, like all other African writers of the period, was in great need of *acceptance*: they needed to reach beyond the image of slavishness. For that, to appeal to their British readership and to make potentially useful friends, they had to adopt the language and literary conventions of the day. Today the literary style adopted by most of the Black British writers seems hard to appreciate. To modern tastes it seems ingratiating and sometimes too humble; too flattering of their white readers, and far too deferential. We need, however, to recognise their enormous problem: they were writers who, if they wished to be taken seriously, had to conform to contemporary literary styles and conventions. The outcome is an African voice with a tone which might grate with many modern readers. Modern students might find it incongruous, nowhere more so than in the writing of Ignatius Sancho.

His extensive correspondence published in 1782, two years after his death, reveals a highly effective and well-placed African spokesman writing in a style, partly subservient, partly self-parody, which might seem so alien to modern readers. For all that, Sancho's was an important voice which offered a vision of African potential. Born about 1729 in Africa, or on a slave ship, he was taken to England as a child and raised by three sisters in Greenwich. His early passion for learning and self-improvement was spotted and encouraged by the Duke of Montagu. He married, had seven children, worked as a valet, was painted by Gainsborough and emerged as a man of refinement, an image he cultivated in a series of letters written to friends and prominent figures. Time and again, his letters returned to the question of slavery and the slave trade.

Sancho had a remarkable circle of friends and correspondents, whom he flattered, begged, cajoled and seduced. His letters were clearly designed to cultivate the image of a man of refinement and sensibility, able to hold his own among educated and privileged people. Yet there could be no steeper social rise than his. Now living in London, but born a slave, to an enslaved African mother, Sancho had risen from the abject squalor of a slave ship to being a friendly correspondent with the good and the great. Sancho had a vision for all Africans, demanding that *all* be accepted as equal, unhindered by barriers of race or social inferiority (the barriers so essential to the slave system). Today, Sancho's tone sounds faded, yet despite Sancho's apparent deference, his was an African voice speaking for millions of others. His introductory letter to Laurence Sterne in 1776 captures both his tone – and his aspirations.

TO MR STERNE.

July, 1776.

REVEREND SIR,

It would be an insult on your humanity (or perhaps look like it) to apologize for the liberty I am taking. – I am one of those people whom the vulgar and illiberal call '*Negurs.*' . . . A little reading and writing I got by unwearied application. – The latter part of my life has been – thro' God's blessing, truly fortunate, having spent it in the service of one of the best families in the kingdom. – My chief pleasure has been books. – . . . – Consider slavery – what it is – how bitter a draught – and how many millions are made to drink it!' . . . I am sure you will applaud me for beseeching you to give one

> half-hour's attention to slavery, as it is at this day practised in our West Indies. – . . . – Dear Sir, think in me you behold the uplifted hands of thousands of my brother Moors. – Grief (you pathetically observe) is eloquent; – figure to yourself their attitudes; – hear their supplicating addresses!*

A mere seven years after the posthumous publication of Sancho's letters, new voices were heard from within London's Black community. The first, Quobna Ottobah Cugoano, published a memoir *Thoughts and Sentiments*, in 1787. Cugoano had been born in present-day Ghana and was enslaved as a boy and shipped to Granada where he worked in a slave gang. Taken to England in late 1772 by his master, he was educated and later baptised as 'John Stuart'. Cugoano arrived in England shortly after the Somerset case, at a time of heightened interest in the wider issue of slavery, a time when pioneering abolitionists felt that they had made a breakthrough in their early attacks on the slave trade. Cugoano later wrote of his approval of Lord Mansfield's decision, believing, like many others, that the Somerset case had indeed been a serious blow against slavery and the slave trade.

That case focused attention on the problems facing all those people who, like Cugoano, had been brought to England as slaves, but who found their legal status uncertain. Paradoxically, they also discovered that life in England had a liberating potential. Though Britain was clearly the heart of a massive Atlantic slave empire, *slavery in England* itself was of dubious legality. (The situation differed in Scotland because of the separate legal system.) After 1772, the legal arguments about slavery in

* *Letters of the Late Ignatius Sancho, An African*, Vincent Carretta, ed., London, 1998 edn.

England prompted a much broader debate about the politics, morality and economics of slavery and Cugoano had arrived at the very moment when the issue of slavery was in the air.

Cugoano's *Thoughts and Sentiments* (1787) was the first English language abolitionist publication written by an African. In those first days of the abolition movement, the prime (indeed the sole) aim of the campaign was the abolition of the slave trade. Cugoano, however, wanted something altogether more sweeping. He demanded an end to the entire Atlantic slaving system. Though early abolitionists hoped, in time, to see the end of slavery, it was an African who thrust the case before the reading public. Cugoano's book offered a much more radical and far-reaching vision than anything argued by earlier abolitionists.

By the time Cugoano published his book, he was a free man, living in a fashionable part of London and was employed as a servant by the prominent painters Richard and Maria Cosway who portrayed him in paintings and sketches. Cugoano was, then, well placed to meet fashionable London society of the period and he managed to persuade a number of eminent figures to subscribe to his book (and thus make publication possible). Cugoano was clearly an articulate man of pronounced views, and was called upon by other Africans in London to join their protests on a number of issues (notably in letters to the press). He was also active in the problem of London's Black poor from 1787 to 1788.*

Early in 1787 the first committee for the abolition of the slave trade was formed in London: all but two of its members were Quakers. From that small beginning there swiftly developed a national, vociferous and highly effective campaign to end the slave trade. Though Cugoano's book was part of the

* David Olusoga, *Black and British*, pp.210–212.

early abolition campaign (which was launched, like his book, in 1787) there was a major distinction between Cugoano's vision and what the Abolition Committee wanted. Ending slavery was far too utopian, too extreme a demand, for abolitionists and they settled instead for the aim of ending the Atlantic slave trade (though hoping that abolition would eventually lead to full Black freedom at some unspecified point in the future). Cugoano by contrast demanded an end to slavery. His was a vision for the future which was much more radical than any other contemporary spokesman. What he wanted – demanded – was freedom for all slaves *and* an ending of the entire Atlantic slave system. At a time when even the most outspoken and aggressive of British and American abolitionists were content to argue simply for the end of the slave trade, Cugoano wanted to demolish the entire system. Cugoano's was more than a vision: it was a real *plan* for ending slavery.

Cugoano's book was a statement suffused with the devout Christianity of a convert: an African hoping to win over Africans and the enslaved in the American colonies, to the Christian cause. Cugoano's plea was as much the case of an evangelical as it was of a freed slave. (Doubtless too he was seeking to impress his readers by his devout Christianity.) For all that, his political and economic points are astonishingly radical. Slave traders, he proclaimed, 'are the servants of the devil.' He proposed an enquiry 'into the great and pre-eminent evil . . . of making merchandise of us' and demanded 'a total abolition of slavery [and] an universal emancipation of slaves.' A proclamation against slave trading and slavery should be sent 'to all the courts and nations in Europe' to secure their assistance. Emancipation should be imposed throughout the British Empire and slaves who have been in the colonies more than seven years would be instantly freed: others would be retained as labourers for a given period – but without enduring the normal vicious punishments of the slave system. Efforts should also be made to locate the lost African friends and relatives of the enslaved, and ships should be stationed off the African coast to intercept slavers. The slave forts ('dens of thieves') should become centres of Christian activity and thus become the entrée for 'a very considerable and profitable trade carried on with the Africans.' Cugoano hoped that these measures would 'bring more revenue in a righteous way to the British nation, than ten times its share in all the profits that slavery can produce.'*

This was a remarkably visionary statement – from a freed African slave – and was far more radical and far-reaching than any serious criticism of slavery up to that point. However heartfelt his case, even his friends must have viewed it as wildly optimistic. Yet within fifty years every single aspect of Cugoano's argument had come to pass. British slavery and the slave trade had been abolished, the Royal Navy and US navy had been converted into an abolitionist presence in the Atlantic, and major efforts were underway to bring the rest of maritime Europe into the abolitionist fold. Who else could claim such foresight, or to have had such grand ambitions fulfilled? Even today, Cugoano's importance is not fully recognised. It is surely a startling fact that the broad outlines of British emancipation and anti-slave trade policy after 1833 were effectively outlined and predicted by a former African slave half a century earlier.

Two years after Cugoano's book was published, he was joined by his friend and political associate Olaudah Equiano, whose memoir, published in 1789, has become perhaps *the* major slave

* Quobna Ottobah Cugoano, *Thoughts and sentiments on the Evil of Slavery*, Vincent Carretta, ed., London, 1989.

narrative of the slave era. Equiano's *Narrative* has been used, analysed and reissued for myriad purposes over the past forty years. Yet in 1960, Equiano was effectively unknown: today he has come to represent a host of key aspects of slave history. His face has even appeared on British stamps and his words have been repeated time and again to speak for millions silenced by slavery. Like his friend Cugoano, Equiano had a clear vision for Africa and for future dealings between Africa and the West. His argument was simple. He published his *Narrative* when the abolition of the slave trade was under active discussion in the British Parliament, and he seized the moment to argue for the development of normal trading relations between Britain and Africa. Instead of trading for humanity, why not trade for African produce and commodities, and, at the same time, cultivate African demand for British manufactures? After all, Africa was a vast continent (its immensity and potential not fully known or appreciated by outsiders in the late eighteenth century) which could become a massive market for British goods. Like Cugoano, he argued that trade would, in the process, help to 'civilise' Africa in the process by persuading millions of Africans of the benefits of Western ways while enhancing the commercial interests of the British. He was writing for a particular kind of readership and knew how best to appeal to them. With the slave trade abolished, he argued, the population of Africa would increase and that would encourage a growing demand for trade with Britain. Equiano was promoting a simple economic case: stop the slave trade and a normal trade would flourish.

When Equiano published his book, it was widely accepted that the African slave trade was vital for the wider Atlantic economy. Planters, traders, merchants – indeed everyone remotely associated with the Atlantic trade – simply assumed that ending the slave trade would spell economic doom. Equiano turned this argument on its head and asserted that an unfettered flow of business and trade between, in this case, Britain and Africa would actually bring great economic benefits – to both sides:

> If the blacks were permitted to remain in their own country, they would double themselves every fifteen years. In proportion to such increase will be the demand for manufactures.

Like Cugoano, what Equiano hoped for was an end, not simply of the slave trade, but of slavery itself:

> The abolition of slavery would be in reality an universal good.

Far from damaging British economic well-being, abolition of slavery would usher in a new and totally different form of commercial prosperity, one based on open trade with Africa.

This bold argument, advanced by an African, offering a new vision for the relationship between Africa and the outside world, was an idea which incorporated the demand for freedom from enslavement with the prospect of continuing material well-being for all concerned:

> I doubt not, if a system of commerce was established in Africa, the demand for manufactures would most rapidly augment, as the native inhabitants would insensibly adopt the British fashions, manners, customs, &c. In proportion to the civilization, so will be the consumption of British manufactures.

We now know that the ending of the slave trade, and the 'normalising' of trade between Africa and the outside world did *not*, in the event, bring about Equiano's vision. But in 1789

Equiano's concept was undimmed by subsequent disappointments. It was a vision of a continent freed from the damaging external demands for enslaved people:

> A commercial intercourse with Africa opens an inexhaustible source of wealth to the manufacturing interests of Great Britain, and to all which the slave-trade is an objection.*

Within the space of a mere two years, 1787 to 1789, two Africans, living in London – both of them freed slaves, both devout Christians, and both armed with a new-found and empowering literacy, offered a vision which struck at the heart of the Atlantic slave system. Both men were clearly influenced by the circles they moved in, most importantly the small group of Africans who had survived the tortuous passage form Atlantic slavery to freedom in London, and who proclaimed themselves to be the 'Sons of Africa' in letters to the press.† But they also enjoyed other important connections and links: with prominent evangelical Christians, with abolitionist Quakers and with other sympathisers who shaped their ideas, helped with their publications and steered them towards like-minded people in other parts of Britain. Whatever the editorial influence, and however consciously pitched towards a Christian and even evangelical readership, here was an African voice. It spoke in a manner, with an authority and from an experience which was unavailable to outsiders. It was a voice which laid down an African marker. It demanded freedom.

* Olaudah Equiano, *The Interesting Narrative and other Writings*, Vincent Carretta, ed., London, 1995 edn, pp.233–236.

† Kathleen Chater, 'Sons of Africa', Oxford African American Studies Center, 26 December 2020.

15

Demanding Freedom

THE LATE EIGHTEENTH century pioneering advocates of African freedom left a literary account which spoke for millions who lacked a formal political voice. But they had their own means of asserting their hopes. They too wanted something different, something better, for themselves and for others. For many enslaved people, physical escape seemed the only realistic route to freedom. It is true that a fortunate few were indeed emancipated by owners – for a variety of reasons: years of unwavering service sometimes brought freedom, though more likely that was granted when a slave was too old or infirm to work. Occasionally, masters freed people for personal, intimate reasons: slave lovers, partners and their children were sometimes freed on a master's death. One Brazilian slave, Candido, was promised freedom on his master's death, but on condition:

> during this entire period of my life he [should] not attempt to free himself by legal means, even if he possesses the money.*

* Robert Edgar Conrad, *Children of God's Fire*, p.320.

A few were freed by benefactors impressed by their industry or potential. Some masters promised freedom if the slave could save enough to buy their own freedom, i.e. effectively to emancipate themselves by raising their commercial value. Equiano was just one, paying £47 to his Quaker master in Montserrat in July 1766, money he had accumulated from his astute commercial dealings working as a sailor throughout the Caribbean, buying and selling goods as he stepped ashore from one place to another.

The enslaved placed enormous importance on freeing themselves and, when they could, other relatives, and went to remarkable lengths to secure a loved one's freedom. But freedom never came easily. Political freedom – formal emancipation – came many years after the pioneering African voices demanded it. It was *always* conceded with great reluctance and sometimes only after conflict and warfare, by one colonial power and one national state after the other. The process of emancipation spanned the century from the Haitian uprising of 1791 through to Brazilian emancipation in 1888. But wherever we study the drive for freedom, it was helped, hastened or even made possible by the actions of the slaves themselves. Many, however, were not prepared to wait, and throughout the entire history of slavery, found their own solution: many simply ran away.

From the first days of slavery in the Americas, slaves ran away (this had also been true of earlier slave societies). Though local Indian slaves who were familiar with the topography could escape more easily, Africans too ran away: they escaped from their captors in Africa, they tried to escape the horrific confines of the slave ships (even to the extent of throwing themselves overboard in mid-ocean) and they ran away in all the American slave colonies. Africans also fled when they were taken (as slaves) to Europe. Runaways fled for a multitude of reasons: to seek out a loved one (a child, a parent, a family, partner or friend), to escape the oppression of daily life and work, and some simply struck out to be on their own.

What were Africans to make of the world they escaped to in the Americas? They did not speak the main local language, the geography was unlike anything they knew from their homelands, and everywhere they were *hunted* by slave owners keen to secure their return. Some escaped for a short period before returning, chastened by the hardship of surviving in a hostile environment. Invariably too they were punished for their flight. In time, groups of runaways evolved their own free communities, notably *Maroons* in the Caribbean, and *quilombos* in Brazil. In North America, freedom beckoned in those colonies, later the northern states, where slavery had effectively died out or was abolished early. Here was the origin of what became an astonishing 'illicit' migration northwards, first from the border states, later via the well-organised abolitionist 'Underground Railroad' funnelling people north to freedom. The vast distances involved made it hugely difficult for slaves in the cotton region of the US to escape to northern freedom. In Brazil, however, geography often helped. The inaccessible frontier regions provided a temptation, though that too came with its own dangers and risks. Not surprisingly, most runaways were young, and more men (mainly young men) escaped than women, largely because women had children to care for. In the USA, when slave owners travelled north accompanied by a female slave, they made sure that the woman's children stayed behind as a guarantee – as hostages – against the mother escaping.

Runaways found it best to hide during the day and travel by night. In the words of one fugitive in the USA:

> I made it in the knight [*sic*] when the Moon was gon away and thar was no eyes To see but god.*

Runaways needed help en route, especially on long journeys: help from other slaves with shelter, food and advice. It was different in towns and cities with their own networks of slaves and freed Blacks, for protection and even work: scraping a living by selling foodstuff as a street vendor for instance. Jamaican newspapers were littered with rewards offered for runaways – people of all sorts and conditions, skills and strengths. And all too valuable to slave owners to lose. †

Recapture came with the risk of being sold on, to an even more punitive regime and with the consequent loss of loved-ones and friends – to say nothing of the physical punishments invariably involved. A range of local laws punished slave runaways – and anyone who assisted them – and slave owners organised patrols or licensed 'hunters' to track down and return runaways. In the USA, increasingly harsh (and politically contentious) 'Fugitive Slave Acts' became one of the critical factors in the drift to secession and eventually to Civil War in the 1840s and 1850s.

***

We know so much about slave runaways because slave owners, keen to get them back, sought their return through countless

* Herbert George Gutman, *The Black family in slavery and freedom, 1750–1925*, New York, 1977, p.267.

† *Runaway Slaves in Jamaica (1) The Eighteenth Century*, Douglas B. Chambers, ed., University of Southern Mississippi, February 2013.

newspaper advertisements and handbills. All are rich in information about the runaways: what they looked like, what they wore, what they did, where they might be hiding, who they were familiar with, and where, what they wanted – and how they might try to secure their freedom. Laws preventing and punishing runaways were passed in the early colonial period. A law of Virginia of 1691 authorised law officers 'to apprehend such negroes, mulattoes, and other slaves' and make it lawful 'to kill and destroy such negroes ... by gunn or otherwise whatsoever.'* Slaves needed a master's written authorisation to be off a property – to be 'abroad'. Anyone found without a pass, or letter of approval, was deemed to be a runaway. The need to prove their freedom created enormous difficulties for freed slaves who needed to keep paperwork with them to convince doubters that they were not enslaved. The odds were always against them. In colonial Brazil 'a black skin, combined with African origin, was strong evidence of slave status.' Although Brazil developed a strong tradition of slave manumission, with the subsequent growth of a large free Black community, free Black people had to *prove* their freedom in the face of widespread doubts and hostility. It is no surprise that large numbers were seized and re-enslaved either by simple kidnapping by brutal slave traders, or by their inability to produce the necessary documentation at the right moment. The same problem bedevilled free Blacks in the USA throughout the nineteenth century when slave traders developed a lucrative trade in seizing free Blacks and forcing them south to the cotton fields.

The law often conspired against freed slaves. By the mid-eighteenth century, Brazilian slaves with no obvious proof of

* Dorothy Schneider and Carl J. Schneider, *Slavery in America: From Colonial Times to the Civil War*, New York, 2001, p.157.

freedom, or without written instructions to be in public, could be categorised as, and rounded up alongside, stray animals. If they were not claimed by owners after notice had been given, they would be sold at auction. A letter from the King of Portugal in 1728 ordered that the income:

> derived from the slaves who are found without masters, like that from stray cattle, ought to be paid to my Royal Treasury.*

Local police published the names and descriptions of the slaves they held as 'strays' and subsequent advertisements gave notice of their impending auction – and the price expected.†

In their search for runaways, slave owners unintentionally left us with astonishing historical portraits of some remarkable people – alongside simple accounts of humble, ordinary individuals merely seeking an escape from bondage. Consider the search for this runaway in Jamaica in 1790:

> June 2nd 1790.
>
> Absconded
>
> A NEGRO SAILOR MAN of the
> Coromantee nation . . . is well acquainted in and
> with all the different islands to Windward;
> he has been on the Continent of America . . .
> he is artful, speaks the English, French,
> Dutch, Danish and Portuguese languages‡

* Robert Edgar Conrad, *Children of God's Fire,* p.323.
† Robert Edgar Conrad, *Children of God's Fire,* pp.326–327.
‡ *Daily Advertiser*, Kingston, 7 June 1790.

A few simple lines in contemporary newspapers hide a multitude of attainments and abilities, alongside the individual's hopes. They speak of personal and often intimate African lives thrown into the confused upheavals of travel and slavery in all corners of the Atlantic. John Cuffee, 'aged about Twenty-six years, has a blemish in the right eye' and his face heavily marked with facial scarring, was detained in a Pennsylvania jail in 1747, having worked as a sailor from Madeira to Maryland, but en route, his master had been shot by Spanish privateers. Another man, Cato, 'a short, well-set fellow, and speaks good English', had escaped in Philadelphia in 1748:

> When he went away he had irons on his
> legs, and about his neck, but probably has
> cut them off, as he has done several times
> before on the like occasion . . . he generally
> skulks about this City.

Sometimes, runaways were distinguished by an owner's initials branded on their body. Maria, a washerwoman in Jamaica, had been absent for months in 1782 – but was easily recognised by her owners' initials which 'she bears on one of her shoulders.'

Runaways sought to pass themselves off as free, adopting any number of guises – names, alibis, any elaborate story that suited their purpose. The Jamaican newspaper, *Cornwall Chronicle*, in March 1785 sought the return of 'a Negro man named HOMER . . . by trade a carpenter . . . As he is an artful, cunning fellow, and speaks good English, it is supposed he will endeavour to pass for a free man.'

Masters of nearby ships were warned against taking him on board.*

Advertisements often provided precise physical details of a runaway in the hope of having them identified and retrieved. A Brazilian planter (in 1845) described one runaway African as:

> short in stature, thin, well-made body, dark color, face rather long, pale jaw, almost no beard, lips rather full, round head, and is in the habit of going about with long hair, small eyes long eyelashes, good teeth, nose medium large, speaks in a refined, humble, and insincere way.

That same year, a runaway female from Mozambique was described as 'thirty years old, regular height, strong, big breasts, with a mark under her left eye, has one of her fingers defective on her right hand.' An escaped fourteen-year-old was said to be very thin and very talkative. A tall runaway aged eighteen fled, in 1855, 'with manacles on his hands and should have some marks on his feet as a result of wearing irons for some days.' If they had no outstanding physical features, a runaway's clothing might provide a clue: 'a new shirt of Bahia cotton, old pants, and a hat of old leather'; 'cotton shirt, white pants . . . and a hat of rice straw.' Who could fail to notice the forty-five-year-old Camillo (a master carpenter, sailor and 'hydraulic works

* *Cornwall Chronicle*, 26 March 1785, 14 July 1786, in Douglas B. Chambers, *Runaway Slaves in Jamaica (I) Eighteenth Century*, University of Southern Mississippi, February 2013.

machinist') who ran away from a plantation in Sao Paolo in 1872:

> Speaks with a high voice and always looks frightened,
> has some teeth missing in front and lettering on
> his forehead and on the palms of his hand
> which says: 'Slave of Dona Fortunata,' always wearing
> on his head a cap or handkerchief to hide the letters on
> his forehead.*

Such descriptions come as close as possible to a sketch or photograph, and they capture not merely an image of the escaped slave, but the pursuers unwittingly often left us with vivid accounts of the fugitive's misery.

In nineteenth-century Brazil, runaways tended to be younger men, usually with itinerant jobs, with better clothing and rudimentary literary or numerate skills.† The case has been made that slave runaways were *not* typical of their wider slave community. But wherever we look at the enslaved throughout the Americas, their owners were troubled by runaways: constantly trying to staunch the flow of escapes, punishing those who persisted and going to great lengths to retrieve them.

***

In places, runaways came together to form independent communities of freed people, which survived – thrived even, in

* Robert Edgar Conrad, *Children of God's Fire*, pp.362–364.
† Ian Read and Kari Zimmerman, 'Freedom for Too Few', *Journal of Social History*, Vol. 48, No. 2 (Winter 2014), pp.404–426.

some places – despite the general hostility of the local slave-owning regime and their efforts to dislodge and destroy them. Runaway Brazilian slaves joined *quilombos* or *mocambos* – communities which evolved 'in the forests and mountains of the hinterland or near plantation zones and small and large towns.' They evolved in the Amazon forest, in the hills of Minas Gerais, the swamp lands of Mato Grosso and elsewhere. Some, close to Rio, even survived by trading to and from that city, under the cover and protection of the city's resident slaves.

The most durable of Brazilian *quilombos* – Palmares – grew to eleven thousand people and survived for much of the seventeenth century, embracing several villages spread across 370 square miles in the south of Pernambuco. Ruled by powerful monarchs, it was home to a variety of African cultures (some blended with Portuguese) and developed an independent economy which traded with local settlers. The *Palmares* managed to ward off a series of hostile attacks by the authorities until finally defeated – with survivors sold back into slavery – in 1694.*

In the first half of the nineteenth century, *quilombos* thrived close to Recife, Salvador, Rio Grande and Porto Alegre. Though they too were periodically repressed, they nonetheless survived because they offered a refuge to a variety of escapees from slavery (and from the army) and provided supplies for the cities. They also thrived on the country's political instability and external warfare, and were regularly joined by army deserters and yet more slave runaways. For all their success, wherever they existed they were viewed as a threat to slavery itself. Revolts regularly flared from the *quilombos* and they remained a target for the authorities for as long as slavery survived in Brazil.

* Robert Edgar Conrad, *Children of God's Fire*, pp.366–377.

Some astonishing voices – articulate, forceful and persuasive – can occasionally be heard among the ranks of escaped slaves. In 1789 to 1790, fifty rebellious slaves in Bahia fled from their plantation (*engenho*) and established their own independent community (*mocambo*) in nearby forests. After repulsing efforts to defeat them, they issued a precise list of conditions under which they would return. It was, in the words of Stuart Schwartz, 'a vision of the conditions of life and labour on Brazilian sugar plantations at the end of the eighteenth century from the point of view of the slaves.'

Directing their demands to their owner, the slaves declared 'we want peace and we do not want war.' The peace they had in mind involved specific working and living conditions. They wanted to be free on Friday and Saturday 'to work for ourselves' demanding proper equipment for work in the fields, factory and when fishing. They also insisted that other Africans ('your Mina blacks') undertake the search for shellfish. They required specific items of food, clothing and firewood, and laid down the exact number of workers needed to tend the sugar processing. Most important perhaps, they also insisted on the dismissal of their current overseer – and be allowed choose his replacement.* These were practical proposals for an improvement in their daily lives – not a plea for the end of slavery.

What fuelled the persistent escape of Brazilian slaves – which was more widespread and long-lasting than elsewhere in the Americas – was the survival of the Atlantic slave trade. The enormous numbers of Africans which continued to land in

* Stuart Schwartz, 'Resistance and Accommodation in Eighteenth-Century Brazil: The Slaves' View of Slavery,' Document II, *Hispanic American Historical Review*, Vol. 57, No. 1, 1977.

Brazil ensured that African cultural habits persisted in Brazil more powerfully than anywhere else. This African presence, renewed and revitalised, year after year, sparked much of the slave resistance across Brazil, especially the urge to escape and fight back. More than twenty slave revolts erupted in Bahia alone between 1809 and 1835 largely among Africans who had fled, establishing *quilombos* – which became a base for revolt. The most famous of such uprisings was the Male revolt among five hundred Muslim slaves in Bahia in 1835. (Muslim leaders had also been involved in earlier plots and open revolts in Bahia.)

In the Caribbean, runaway communities had initially emerged from the few surviving Taino fighters against Spanish conquest of Hispaniola. Gathered in retreats in the mountains and joined by escaped Africans and Indians from other islands, they became known as *cimarrones* – Maroons. They were in effect guerrillas who waged war on Spanish settlements until a treaty was agreed in 1533. Despite the European conquest of all the Caribbean islands by 1770, Maroon communities had taken root in a number of inaccessible places which were beyond the effective reach and control of hard-stretched colonial military or militias. In Cuba and Puerto Rico such settlements were known as *palenques*, often fortified villages, though sometimes merely temporary villages with residents able to move quickly when threatened. In Jamaica's most inaccessible mountains, Maroon groups became permanent villages, secure in heavily forested and mountainous retreats, and able to wage guerrilla attacks on plantations. They formed a real threat to Jamaican stability, but the British military failed to defeat the two main Maroon communities in two wars against them. The first war, of 1739, ended in a peace treaty which conceded land

and freedom to the Maroons in return for promises of non-belligerence. The French too were dogged by comparable dangers posed by their own various Maroons, notably the runaway slave site of Maniel, in the mountains of St. Domingue. Like the British next door in Jamaica, the French signed a treaty with their Maroons in 1785, but this was just ahead of the convulsion sparked by the revolution in France. In the midst of that global revolution, in 1796, the Maroons in western Jamaica once again found themselves in conflict with the British. Though the fighting was ended by another peace settlement, the island's governor went back on his word and promptly dispatched hundreds of captured Maroons to Nova Scotia. The British adopted the same solution – of wholesale transportation – following their defeat of the 'Black Caribs' revolt in St Vincent in 1797. This time, five thousand people were dispatched to an island off Honduras.*

Solving problems by shipping defeated rebels overseas had long been a preferred policy for the British. In the seventeenth century they had transported criminals, prisoners of war, political rebels and defeated Irish insurgents to their new settlements in North America and the Caribbean. They adopted much the same solution for mounting domestic social problems in the late eighteenth century, especially after American independence closed off North America as a dumping ground for Britain's problems. They now looked further afield. The 'Black Poor' – many from Nova Scotia – were returned to Africa, criminals were removed from the 'hulks' and dispatched, after 1787, to the penal settlement in Australia, and rebellious Maroons were removed from their Caribbean communities to

* B. W. Higman, *Concise History of the Caribbean*, pp.142–143.

other parts of the Americas. Transportation became an important feature of Britain's penal code as well as a central policy in the way it managed the rebellious corners of its slave colonies. Brazil also deported troublesome slaves: in the wake of the Male revolt some two hundred were shipped back to Africa.

Much more dangerous and troublesome for slave owners – more trouble than runaways or their independent communities – were the regular and ubiquitous slave revolts. Though rebellions sometimes flared, as we have seen, from *quilombos*, slave uprisings were a regular feature of Brazilian slavery. Some aimed at the destruction of slavery itself – but most were sparked by individual, specific acts, leaving slaves little choice but to react violently. Many uprisings targeted 'excessive oppression, reducing it to a tolerable level, demanding specific rights, the recovery of lost gains, or punishing especially cruel overseers.' From the late eighteenth century onwards, when the amount of Brazilian land worked by slaves increased substantially, and as ever more Africans were poured in to undertake that work, slave uprisings flared more frequently. What made life more dangerous for slave owners was that many of the newly arrived Africans came from the same ethnic background; young men who understood each other and had a sense of collective identity. Many also came from regions of Africa troubled by warfare, and many had been captured and enslaved as prisoners of war. They arrived in Brazil with military training and combat experience. They proved to be a highly combustible human mix in the slave gangs. In the early nineteenth century, some thirty revolts, largely the work of Hausas and Nagos, erupted in Bahia alone. Not only had they been militarised, but they had been greatly influenced by the spread of Islam in their African homeland. Though efforts were made to curb the activities of those African groups in Bahia, the process was too far gone to prevent slave unrest. It also seems likely that other African rebels 'were inspired by war-like divinities' of their own religions (of Orisa and Candomblé) and everywhere slave owners and authorities suspected the role of 'sorcery', especially.

Brazilian slave owners instinctively pointed to Africa as the root cause of slave rebellions, and though their suspicions were often well founded, there were other important forces at work. After 1791 and the slave insurrection in Haiti, Brazil, like all slave societies in the Americas, could not escape its shadow. Stories of that revolution – some true, some mythical – inspired and influenced slaves everywhere. They also terrified the slave owners. But there were also other forces at work shaking the foundations of Brazilian slavery, notably the complex impact of Christianity.

In places, slaves came to regard a powerful Catholic preacher as a leader able to take them out of slavery: people who could persuade slave owners to grant emancipation. Rebels turned to particular Catholic saints as their guiding light in their rebelliousness. *Our Lady of the Rosary*, for example, was influential in a revolt in Maranhao, while St Anthony was a powerful force in Vassouras, and in a large-scale revolt among Bantu-speaking slaves in the Paraiba Valley. In common with much of Brazilian Catholicism, the beliefs of rebellious slaves were syncretic, blending Christianity with African religious expression and beliefs.*

In the years of massive African arrivals in Brazil, this blend of African and European forces fomented widespread slave

* João José Reis, 'Slavery in Nineteenth Century Brazil', *The Cambridge World History of Slavery*, vol. 4, David Eltis et al., eds., Ch.6.

rebelliousness. Though some regions involved were sorely taxed, the local authorities and the nation's military were ultimately able to curb the slaves' uprisings. It had long been clear to many Brazilian officials (and indeed to officialdom across the enslaved Americas) that the rebellious instinct among the enslaved could never be totally eradicated. It might be crushed or curbed – but it would, despite precautions, flare again. Slave defiance was built into the very fabric of slavery itself. The inescapable difficulty facing slave owners was how to contain it. Reporting on a slave conspiracy in Minas Gerais in 1719, the captain general wrote a cautioning letter to King João V about slave rebellions:

> . . . since we cannot prevent the remaining blacks from thinking, and cannot deprive them of their natural desire for freedom; and since we cannot, merely because of this desire, eliminate all of them, they being necessary for our existence here, it must be concluded that this country will always be subjected to this problem.*

Rebelliousness in all its forms was built into slavery itself. It was both an aspect of a much broader slave defiance that could never be totally eradicated, and it formed the harshest expression of the urge for freedom of the enslaved.

The USA

The British were primarily responsible for the establishment of African slavery in North America (though the French and

* Robert Edgar Conrad, *Children of God's Fire*, p.396.

Spanish played their own role in Florida and the Gulf region). The colonial settlements of the 'Old South' turned to slaves primarily for the cultivation of tobacco and rice, though the number of Africans involved did not approach the huge numbers imported into the Caribbean and Brazil. Nor did Africans ever outnumber whites in any North American colony, though, like other slave colonies, the enslaved population of North America initially increased via imports of Africans. From the 1720s, thanks to the natural increase of the local Black population, the importation of Africans from the slave ships became less important.

Africans were first landed in the Chesapeake in 1619, and though numbers only took off after the development of the tobacco industry, as late as 1690, only 3,500 Africans had been landed in Virginia. That had risen to fifteen thousand by the 1720s: by mid-century some sixty thousand slaves lived in Virginia, the Carolinas and Georgia. Slavery also slipped into most corners of North American urban and rural life. About eleven thousand slaves lived in New England by 1750. It was after the establishment of the cotton industry in the South post-1800 that the real expansion of North American slavery took place. In its turn, cotton was fuelled by the forced migrations of slave labour from the old slave states. By then, the USA did not *need* the Atlantic slave trade: its slave economy thrived on its expanding, *local* slave population. By 1810 there were almost one and a half million slaves in the US. This had grown to four million by 1860.

Until the Civil War, slavery flourished because of cotton, though there was also a (much smaller) sugar industry dependent on slave labour in Louisiana. Cotton plantations quickly spread across swathes of the South, and in the process, the whole of the USA – and not solely the South – prospered. Slave-grown cotton was the nation's biggest export, and formed a lucrative industry for banks, manufacture and trade in a number of northern cities. All that was of course thrown into turmoil – and finally destroyed – by the Civil War after 1860. That war hinged on the complex politics of states' rights – but its essence was the question of slavery.

***

The slave population of the US had exploded in the fifty years to 1860. Like their forebears in colonial North America, the enslaved population of the new American Republic wanted freedom, and took every opportunity to secure it. In common with slaves everywhere they tried to make the most of daily life, adapting to its rigours, making the system work for them when they could. But *freedom* was the overriding vision: freedom to enjoy the full, rounded features of normal, everyday life, with family, friends and community. Yet at every turn, the enslaved people of the USA were trapped by slavery. They were moved around as and when it suited their owners: bought and sold away from family, separated from loved ones and always denied that personal and family security which other people took for granted (and which the US Constitution promised).

We now know a great deal about North American slavery, partly because the documentation of slavery in the US is so extensive and well preserved, more so perhaps than for many other societies. Yet despite the enormous importance of North American slavery in the nineteenth century, it was increasingly at political and moral odds with an outside world which was ever more abolitionist. Anti-slavery critics, in the USA and Europe, produced a vast critical literature denouncing slavery. We also know a great deal about US slavery because slaves *themselves* became increasingly vocal and organised, *and* they too wrote persuasively about their lives. Literacy and, above all, Christianity, became prominent features of slave life in the US. The enslaved expressed themselves in print and on an unprecedented scale everywhere in the Americas. Like the wider society to which they belonged, large numbers of American slaves were literate, vocal and devout, and, inevitably, the historical records are filled with slave voices. Those voices tell not only the history of slave experience, but they also speak to a vision of a different world: a world without slavery.

***

The individual demands for freedom, by Black writers of the late eighteenth century, gave way in the nineteenth century to a much more strident, organised and vociferous chorus of demands for freedom. From roughly 1820 onwards, the voice of the enslaved in North America became a political force to be reckoned with, and as the nineteenth century advanced, two main factors transformed its demands. First, the emergence of increasingly powerful and vociferous Black churches and, closely related, the rise of an educated Black leadership. The desire for freedom remained universal, of course: people of all sorts and conditions wanted an end to their bondage and needed no reminder by better educated contemporaries of their main vision. But the churches they joined were critical in providing organised social and political expression. They were places where Black preachers drew support from the congregations, and the demands which germinated in Black churches (and related organisations) were echoed by new generations of free Black people. Their overriding vision was of a world where freedom was the right of *all* Black people. A growing number of charismatic ex-slaves and free Black people began to campaign against slavery, especially in the northern states (and in Europe). They were part of increasingly powerful abolitionist organisations, on both sides of the Atlantic, which brought the power of their growing numbers, and their persuasive political voice, to the task of demanding Black freedom. It was to prove a long, hard struggle, not least because it was pitched against a US slave system, rooted in cotton, of enormous commercial importance. King Cotton had economic ramifications far beyond the South, reaching into the commercial, financial and trading heartlands of the northern US cities, across the Atlantic, and into the massive textile industries of Europe.

The first formal organisations to embrace slaves and free Blacks emerged in the last years of the eighteenth century when a number of pioneering Black churches, notably Baptist, Methodist and Presbyterian, emerged in Philadelphia, and in the Chesapeake region. Their congregations developed a distinctive Christian voice and a style quite unlike anything white Christians were accustomed to. Moreover, from the first, demands from those churches were not simply religious. Their congregations and preachers sang, preached, prayed and spoke about a very different world: a world where freedom, not bondage, would be the lot of all American citizens. The term 'African-American' first emerged from these churches, and they became part of a broader political movement, as their leaders forged political allegiances and federations among their individual churches. It was a pattern which had transformed slave life in the British Caribbean a little earlier.

A key figure was Richard Allen, a former slave who bought his own freedom at the age of seventeen, moved to Philadelphia and led a breakaway group of freed Blacks from the local white St George's Methodist church, organising their own African-American congregation. In 1794, he founded the African Methodist Episcopal Church in Philadelphia. Equally important, he and his wife were active in establishing a number of social and benevolent organisations for distressed Black people and to assist fugitive slaves. They established a way station in what was to become the Underground Railroad: the lifeline for thousands of slaves fleeing north from southern bondage. Like other pioneering Black preachers of the era, Allen was indebted to earlier abolitionists reaching back to the pioneering founders, to Equiano and his contemporaries.* Despite fractious episodes, the rise of articulate and forceful African-American Christianity proved irreversible. A Black voice could now be heard in the USA – and it spoke to a vision of freedom which may have been religious in origin and design but was secular in its consequences.

***

In common with working-class life across the Western world in the nineteenth century, the autodidact became a feature of Black religion and politics in the USA. Working people everywhere prized literacy: it enhanced personal and communal prospects, elevated self-esteem (and attracted the approval of outsiders). Much the same was true of the enslaved and of freed

* Manisha Sinha, *The Slave's Cause: A History of Abolition*, New Haven, 2016, pp.120–121.

slaves. In a world which increasingly revolved around the printed word, to be illiterate was to be seriously disadvantaged. In the US in the early nineteenth century, Black literacy was transformed by the changes in the world of print. These were the years of new technologies of print and publication, cheap mass communication, and by the eventual emergence of telegraphic communication. News travelled fast, along telegraph and railway lines, and it was repeated and reprinted, in cheap and readily available forms, throughout the Western world. The printed word – and the ability of millions to read it – became a potent political and social weapon.

To politically alert, free Blacks it was clear that they needed their own press to represent Black voices and visions, and to speak up on Black issues (when few people elsewhere did so). The first African-American newspaper, *Freedom's Journal*, was published in New York in 1827 by two men, both free Blacks. Samuel Cornish, who became *the* dominant Black journalist for twenty years, and John B. Russwurm. Henceforth Black newspapers became a forceful mouthpiece for black interests, for anti-slavery, and for Black rights on a broad front.

With the launch of *Freedom's Journal*, Black abolitionism took off, quickly establishing itself as 'the voice of black protest.' The founding editors thought that newspapers were *the* most economical way of bringing about the 'moral, religious, civil and literary improvement of our injured race.' They also wanted to provide 'a single voice . . . in defence of *five hundred thousand free people of colour.*' In the same vein, their first editorial proclaimed, 'We wish to plead our own cause. Too long have others spoken for us.' The newspaper tapped into the networks of existing Black organisations and churches throughout the US north and among friends elsewhere – including Canada,

Britain and Haiti. It became the printed voice of Black freedom and was, despite clashes of political ideals and personalities, a launchpad for the subsequent Black abolition movement in the USA. Slaves, and free Black people in the USA, had found their voice. As with Cugoano and Equiano forty years earlier, Africa was now the focus for a drive to rectify the wrongs and injustices of the slave system.*

***

Women were key figures in all the slave economies of the Americas. As workers, as mothers and as partners, their roles were crucial to the way slave society functioned. Their work was essential both to their owners, and to the slave community. They undertook most of the hard physical demands of the plantation economies: planting and harvesting the crops, processing, loading and dispatching local produce. Though many of the artisan skills were reserved for men, women were pressed into service in and around the slave properties in myriad activities, enabling plantations and their wider societies to function properly. When work for their owners was finished, women returned to other tasks in and around their homes: child-rearing and family care, domestic chores, work in the gardens and plots. Theirs were lives of protracted and unremitting toil.

In addition to the universal problems of pregnancy, childbirth and child-rearing, they also had to endure the ubiquitous and often inescapable danger of sexual exploitation and violence. Slavery was a world where the predatory sexuality of

* Manisha Sinha, *The Slave's Cause,* Ch.7.

white males was legendary: where slave women of all ages were vulnerable to sexual attack and maltreatment, whether they worked as field hands or as domestic servants. They developed their own strategies of coping with life's dangers and raised their young with cautionary tales about those dangers. Like their men folk, women found their own means of resisting, and some were driven to open revolt. There were a number of prominent female rebels, both real and mythical, in all corners of the Americas.

Demands for the rights of slave women took on a more formal, more overtly political expression in the US in the early nineteenth century. In part this was shaped by the emergence of the broader political and social demands of slaves in the American South, but it also reflected the emergence of demands for female rights throughout the Western world. This in turn originated in the 'age of revolution' and in the flurry of debates about human rights in the years after 1776. The democratic debate which flowed from the founding of the American Republic and from the revolution in France (the ideals and vocabulary of the rights of man – and woman – of equality and fraternity) had an irresistibly contagious effect. Here were rights which applied to everyone: men and women, Black and white. It was no surprise, then, that the political voice of slave women was quick to find its own distinctive expression. An early example of Black women's political demands, expressed in an American journal of 1827, offers a vision of how life might be for the millions of Black women scattered throughout the Americas. In her speeches and writing, the ambitious and assertive Maria W. Stewart (1803–79) was 'a driving force behind black female abolition and politics up to her death in 1879'. She became one of the most articulate and forceful

African-American female activists of the late slavery period. She urged 'ye daughters of Africa to arise and distinguish yourselves'. Hers was a vision of transformed Black womanhood.*

***

Scanning the broad sweep of the history of slavery across the Americas, from its first days to its death in 1888, the most telling attacks by the enslaved were not to be found in formal political activity, or in print. The most potent of all attacks on slavery were more visceral and threatening. They were often more personal and vengeful. But this changed markedly and quite dramatically, from the late eighteenth century onwards. The impact of a new democratic vocabulary in the Age of Revolution, the seismic impact of the Haitian revolution, and the emergence and spread of Christian churches, all allied to the spread of formal literacy – all this edged ever more slaves to formal political activity. It was not so much that slaves had not agitated previously, but rather that the politics of the enslaved took on new forms. The demands of the enslaved were channelled into formal organisations, expressed through advertised meetings (with invited speakers and audiences) and through the printed word. Most striking of all, it blossomed in, and from, places of worship.

In the early nineteenth century, Black churches, organised by free Blacks in major US cities, offered a platform for anti-slavery sentiment and activity. Here were the descendants of Africans organising themselves in a manner familiar to the broader political culture – and in ways previously denied

* Manisha Sinha, *The Slave's Cause,* Ch.9, pp.267–268.

them. The demands of Black people for social and political freedom and justice constituted a change with major ramifications. Black organisations, Friendly Societies, Benevolent Societies and Masonic Lodges proliferated, notably in Philadelphia. One, 'The Sons of Africa' mirrored the name used by a small band of Africans writing to the press in London twenty years earlier. On the day US abolition of the slave trade came into operation, 1 January 1808, the Rev. Peter Williams spoke in the New York African Church giving thanks for the end of the trade, and denouncing the widespread belief in Black inferiority.* The language was often verbose – but the point was simple:

> May the time commence when Ethiopia shall stretch forth her hands: when the sun of liberty shall beam resplendent on the whole African race.

Freedom was the birthright of everyone. In the words of the Black abolitionist William Hamilton, addressing the New York African Society for Mutual Relief, in 1809:

> Men have exercised authority over our nation as if we was their property, by depriving us of our freedom, as though they had a command from heaven thus to do. But, we ask, if freedom is the right of one nation, why not of all the nations of the earth?†

* Peter Williamson Jnr, *An oration on the Abolition of the Slave Trade delivered in the African Church in the City of New York, January 1st 1808*, New York, 1808.

† William Hamilton, *An Address to the New York African Society for Mutual Relief, January 2nd 1809*, New York, 1809.

This flowering of Black activism in the USA in the early nineteenth century may seem far removed from African writers in London in the 1770s and 1780s. The North American campaigns, by Black and white abolitionists, to bring down US slavery, faced a mountainous task. The most obvious stumbling block was the prosperity which slavery brought to the USA at large. But much the same had been true of the problem facing the earlier African activists. The British slave system continued until 1833 and US slavery only ended with the Civil War after 1860. But the significance of Black voices, on both sides of the Atlantic, and their demands for freedom, goes deeper than their immediate political consequences. They were the voices of oppressed Africans and their American-born offspring and they were recognisable and persuasive. They spoke to an enslaved African experience which no outsider could match or imitate. It was an authentic voice of Africa – and it demanded freedom.

Part Six

A WORLD TRANSFORMED

16

Beauty and the Beast

THE GROWTH OF Western trade and conquest in Asia, Africa and the Americas, from roughly the sixteenth century onwards, created a cornucopia of Western wealth, which gradually benefitted unprecedented numbers of people. The rewards from the slave systems, for example, accrued not only to the well-to-do and most successful but, in a variety of ways, to millions who seemed far removed from, and even untouched by slavery. In the process, the West emerged as an unusually affluent region of the world. It was moreover a prosperity which allowed its most prominent beneficiaries to flaunt their wealth in the most elaborate ways: extravagance in the way they dressed, what they ate, where they lived and how they spent their leisure hours. Equally, the endless search for ever more wealth – and for the foreign land and resources that underpinned much of that wealth – was a major driving force behind the political friction between Europeans in all corners of the globe. Elites in any number of ancient societies (in India and China for example) had done much the same for centuries.

What lies behind the emergence of Western prosperity, however, is a complex story of exploitation, physical domination and violence which has often gone unnoticed. The gilded face of Western sophistication hid a grim story of aggression and domination. The catastrophic collapse of indigenous people (notably in the Caribbean and the Americas), the enforced movement of millions of Africans and the conquest and domination of swathes of the Indian subcontinent – all and more laid the essential foundations for the emergence of a prosperous and sophisticated Western world. Yet these apparently distinct historical elements – global exploitation and cultural refinement – are rarely linked. It is as if the two germinated and thrived in isolation and as separate historical forces. They were, in fact, two sides of the same coin. Not only that, Great Britain came into being in step with the British empire: both were conceived and nurtured together.*

The wealth which flowed from Atlantic slavery was perhaps most striking in the emergence of an urban culture in the Americas, and it survives to this day in myriad physical reminders. Towns and cities emerged not merely as centres of economic and political life, but as focal points for an increasingly varied social and cultural life. In many respects the urban cultural life of the Americas paralleled the patterns in Europe itself. Settlers and local-born sought to complement their growing economic security and strength by replicating what they regarded as the sophisticated habits of Europe. From Boston to Rio, across the Caribbean and throughout Spanish America, towns developed a complex and sophisticated cosmopolitanism. In those rural areas where slavery dominated the economy, the slave-owning class led isolated lives, but even there, many slave owners tried to balance their cultural isolation by creating a sophisticated

* Timothy Snyder, *On Tyranny*, London, 2021, p.122.

life within their plantation homes. They collected and exchanged books and magazines, wrote extensively about the world around them, experimented with agricultural and horticultural innovations and labour management. Yet all this took place in the midst of barbarous exploitation. There were many slave owners who blended the qualities of enlightened self-education with boundless physical and sexual barbarity towards the enslaved. To modern eyes, there seems to be a grotesque contradiction at play: on the one hand, the cultural pretensions of many prosperous slave owners; on the other, the crude brutality they used against the enslaved.

Many slave owners, however, yearned for something else – for *somewhere* else. Having a good library, cultivating experimental crops, maintaining a lively correspondence – all this was simply not enough. They realised that a more rewarding life was to be had elsewhere – but that meant leaving behind the world of plantation slavery and heading to town. Planters – rarely confident about their physical security – tired of life in remote places surrounded by armies of defiant slaves. They longed for the secure company and pleasures to be found in towns and cities. Churches, civic squares, coffee shops, taverns, clubs – even libraries and theatres – all the features of European urban life, quickly emerged in the Americas. By the late eighteenth century, Cap Francais, the port in St. Domingue where most of the colony's Africans first landed – boasted the latest Parisian fashions, public baths and learned societies. Port-au Prince – a much rougher town – also had a theatre which held 750 people, and even a shop selling musical instruments.* Brazil's major cities – Rio,

* David Geggus, *Slavery, War, and Revolution: The British Occupation of St. Domingue, 1793–1798*, Oxford, 1982, p.7.

Recife, Salvador and Sao Paulo – lured isolated planters to their expanding social attractions. By the early nineteenth century, Rio's impressive collection of civic buildings, churches and merchants' private mansions, offered a much richer social life than was available on any distant slave property.* The beauty of Brazilian colonial architecture is confirmed, to this day, by its continuing attraction for modern tourists. Not surprisingly, many children of successful planters chose life in town, turning their back on plantation life, and opting for new urban careers.

Brazil's planters came later than others to domestic comfort and lavish lifestyle. Outsiders to colonial Brazil were struck by the frugality and even the threadbare nature of planters' homes, indeed their interest in domestic comfort 'only began in the second half of the 18th century.' And that coincided with the move into major cities and the rapid development of a new urban culture. From the 1820s onwards a sharp distinction emerged between styles of living in town and country, as Brazilian cities become home to the cultural facilities common in Europe. Many Brazilians adopted a 'bourgeois European way of life' with French styles and artefacts especially popular among the prosperous from 1850 onwards. The curiosity was that many meagre planters' homes proudly boasted imported Chinaware and costly silver items. And it remained generally true in the early nineteenth century, that Brazilian planters were more concerned about their town houses than their plantation homes.† Of course, towns offered much more than the

* Teresa A. Meade, *A Brief History of Brazil*, New York, 2004, pp.82–83.

† Luis Claudio Pereira Symansky, *Slaves and Planters in Western Brazil*. Ph.D. thesis, University of Florida, 2006, Ch.3.

luxuries and pleasures unobtainable in the countryside. They were vital centres for the functioning of the wider slave economy. In towns – especially in ports – planters and merchants conducted their business, bought Africans, sold their slave-grown produce, borrowed money for investment, and negotiated with other like-minded slave owners for the defence and security of their economic interests.

Planters in the US South also gravitated to the nearest urban delights of New Orleans, Mobile, Savannah and Charleston, though many also created domestic and architectural fantasies of their own, building homes – mansions – and Great Houses on their plantations. Again, like their counterparts in Brazil and Europe, they have become major sites for buses filled with tourists. Mansions were approached via sweeping driveways lined by arcades of trees and surrounded by lavish manicured gardens, the house itself stuffed with the most fashionable (and costly) of domestic fittings and furnishings, carpets and paintings. All was designed to impress peers and to establish the owner's reputation as someone of taste and sophistication. This extravagance existed under the shadow of – in sight of – the slaves toiling in the fields close by, and all within earshot of the crack of the bullwhip. It was as if beauty and the beast lived side by side – a pattern to be found clean across the enslaved Americas.

In the Caribbean slave islands, however, local elites yearned to retire not to Bridgetown or Spanish Town, to Kingston or to Cap Francais, but to head back across the Atlantic: to Paris or Bordeaux, to London or to the familiar and much-lamented pleasures of European rural life. We know of people living in Jamaica in the late eighteenth century, who spent decades dreaming of a prosperous return to Scotland, writing endlessly to relatives and friends across the ocean, telling of their plans to put slavery behind them and return home. As often as not, it remained a pipe dream.*

Those who made astounding fortunes from slavery returned home intent on impressing contemporaries. These 'sugar barons', like Indian nabobs of the same era, became a byword for material opulence and extravagance.† They built stately homes, filled with tasteful furnishings, located in landscaped grounds. They became members of fashionable society, and some even ascended to the highest ranks of nobility and social power. Their fame and status was best secured by the magnificent buildings they left behind. In time, the way such sugar barons had acquired their wealth and possessions slipped from public memory and was effectively forgotten. But then, in the early twenty-first century, there was a sudden revival in awareness of slavery, and of the slave origins of such material well-being. Today, it is all too obvious, thanks to the recent political and social friction which convulsed societies on both sides of the Atlantic. Yet the buildings involved – the town houses and the country retreats, in Europe and the Americas – are only the most striking and obvious of much deeper and broader issues. What lurks behind the material reminders of slavery is a much more confusing and disturbing phenomenon: the intimate connection between slavery and fashionable Western taste.

***

* See the letters between Charles Douglas (in Jamaica) and his brother Patrick Douglas (in Scotland) 1784–1813, *Boswell Collection*, Beinecke Library, Yale University, GEN MSS 150.

† Mathew Parker, *The Sugar Barons: Family, Corruption, Empire and War*, London, 2011.

Like the wealthy of earlier eras, people of substance in both Europe and the Americas were keen to show their sophistication and refinement. Those who made their money by trade and by overseas commercial ventures were quick to ape the social habits of their established social superiors by creating a material world of lavish style and expenditure. Nabobs from India, planters home from the Caribbean or Brazil, high-ranking officers fresh from their efforts in various corners of the globe, and merchants grown fat on the rewards of the slave ships – all and more hastened to proclaim their wealth and status to the wider world. They built lavish homes, in Europe's capital cities (in London, Paris, Lisbon), in the growing towns of North and South America, or in peaceful rural retreats, enclosing their mansions with glorious parkland and gardens. After all, had not European royalty and aristocracy, and the great merchant houses and city states of Italy, done much the same for centuries?

This was different, however. This wealth and the new fashions it created were the reward of commercial enterprise and daring, of entrepreneurial imagination and hard work. But it was also the fruit of rapacious exploitation both of distant lands and alien peoples, most notably in India, Africa and the Americas. This émigré wealth was at its most blatantly abusive in the armies of African slaves strewn across the Americas. Though the connection was sometimes hard to spot, wealthy beneficiaries often left brazen clues for all to see: carved African heads and faces on Bordeaux's dockside warehouses and commercial buildings, street names in Glasgow, Nantes and Bordeaux. For all that, the connection between lavish European prosperity and colonial exploitation was generally hidden by geography. There was a tyranny of distance between the

European homelands and the far-flung centres of colonial wealth: a distance which formed a smokescreen which hid and distorted the harsh realities. It was far too easy *not* to notice the people and labour which underpinned Europe's emergent prosperity.

In the colonies themselves, however, the connection was immediate and unavoidable. No one could doubt that the lavish lifestyle of the most successful slave owners in, say, Rio, Charleston or Bridgetown was rooted in the labour of slaves. At their most lavish, plantation Great Houses became a feature of all the major American slave societies. The pattern was visible from the Chesapeake Bay to Rio de Janeiro, as successful planters, in tobacco, rice, sugar, coffee and cotton, transformed themselves from pioneers in a speculative business into lavish and stylish property-owners.

Conspicuous consumption was not limited to slave owners of course. People of ambition throughout the West sought to project a personal image of good taste and refinement: clothing and personal manners and decorum, homes and their domestic fittings, and the ownership (and display) of paintings, books and portraits.* In the world of slavery, two aspects of this transformation stand out. First, major slave owners were swift to adopt the trappings of refinement. Time and again, we find planters proclaiming their civility and sophistication cheek by jowl with a predatory and often violent management of their enslaved Africans. Today, it affords a perplexing confusion. Secondly, many of the objects which defined contemporary refinement were *themselves* products of slave labour or were linked to it in ways we rarely notice. If, however, we look critically at the fabric

* Keith Thomas, *In Pursuit of Civility*, Ch.3.

of fashionable life, from, say, the mid-eighteenth century, the links to slave labour become unambiguous.

***

One indication of the social sophistication that accompanied rising prosperity was the commissioning of personal or family portraits which, in their turn, became statements not only of a person's status and even grandeur, but reflected the refined domestic world they enjoyed. People gazing at such portraits were expected to be impressed by the highly polished furnishings, the extravagant clothing and the family possessions which were as central to the composition as the subject of the painting.

Many of the most lavish of surviving planters' homes, today, are major tourist attractions, with income from tourists making possible the continuing upkeep and preservation of the buildings. Visitors are invariably dazzled by what greets them. The highly polished gloss of many of the beautiful furnishings can easily deflect us from the grim origins of the entire location. It is often hard to see slavery when enjoying an attractive building and its lavish contents. Take, for example, one of the most popular (and invariably the most eye-catching) of eighteenth-century furnishings – items made from mahogany. The British passion for mahogany furniture spread quickly to North America, and wealthy Americans became equally addicted. Yet that timber is alien both to Europe and North America. Mahogany was imported from the rainforests of Cuba, Jamaica and the Mosquito Coast – and had been logged by gangs of slaves.

Polished mahogany furniture also became a feature of contemporary portraiture, and capturing it in a portrait became a 'great test of an artist's skill and talent.'* The tradition of artists striving to represent valuable objects – precious metals, pearls, gems and others – had originated in the Renaissance among patrons keen to have their opulent taste reflected in their paintings. Now, in the eighteenth century, a similar ambition sought to depict valuable objects that had been acquired in the expansion of the slave empire. The portrait needed to mirror the sitter's status through many of the objects on display in the picture – and especially the centrality of highly polished mahogany furniture. Few used mahogany furniture to greater effect that John Singleton Copley (1738–1815).

Copley, perhaps the greatest portrait painter of late colonial North America, was born in Boston, and his maturing fame caught the eye of the colony's rich and politically eminent. Many of them commissioned Copley to paint their portrait, hoping to capture their fame and prosperity. Today some of the best examples hang in the magnificent collection of Boston's Museum of Fine Arts. It was there, while studying another painting, that my own attention was caught both by Copley's paintings and by yet another remarkable collection displayed close by. Time and again, Copley used mahogany furniture as the centrepiece of a portrait, and only yards from his portraits in Boston, the museum displays some of its eighteenth-century mahogany furniture. The connection is obvious to the naked eye. There was something special about the aesthetic and social role of mahogany in late eighteenth century colonial North America.

Mahogany, a hard wood ideally suited to a craftsman's need to create finely turned pieces which could then be highly

* Jennifer Anderson, *Mahogany: The Costs of Luxury in Early America*, Cambridge, MA, 2012, p.54.

polished, soon became the material of choice for the very best furniture makers in North America and Britain. In their turn they trained whole workshops in the art of converting long planks of imported hardwood, shipped from the tropical colonies, into the most exquisite and costly of household furnishings. The rich and famous throughout the English-speaking world commissioned the best craftsmen to fill their homes – especially the dining room – with beautiful (and costly) items. Today, those dining tables and chairs, alongside an array of accessories, stand in stately homes and museums as thousands of tourists shuffle past in admiration.

Copley put those furnishings to a very different purpose. It had become axiomatic that 'a polished environment was as much the essence of gentility as polished manners'* and when New England's rich summoned Copley, they required portraits that were not merely a true likeness, but also affirmed their wealth and refinement. Aware that clothing and furnishings had to represent more than a mere backcloth to the sitter, Copley carefully arranged the setting for his portraits. Among his most famous American portraits, mahogany was centre stage. Gleaming tabletops provided a focal point for a display of the sitter's hands, sometimes holding a book or documents, sometimes handling an object. Paul Revere, for example, is seen holding a teapot (he was a silversmith and the suggestion is that he made the teapot) alongside a luminous tabletop which acted as a mirror to the item portrayed. Copley's portrait of Mrs Humphrey Devereux (1773) also made use of a highly polished mahogany tabletop to capture an older woman in a

* Jennifer Anderson, *Mahogany*, p.54.

deeply reflective mood.* That same year, his portrait of Mrs John Winthrop used the same technique – with a polished tabletop providing a mirrored reflection of a mature woman in a lighter, smiling mood.†

Copley was only the most famous of American painters who used mahogany furnishings as a central feature in his portraits. Charles Wilson Peale (partly taught by Copley) used a mahogany table to similar effect in his portrait of the Cadwalader family (1772). When Jeremiah Platt, a prosperous New York merchant, commissioned John Mare to paint his portrait in 1767, he too asserted his status by posing with his hand placed on the back of a Chippendale mahogany chair.‡

There is a long list of such paintings all serving to confirm a simple artistic point. Yet they also represent a remarkable historical curiosity. Mahogany had only been introduced as a major import into North America and Britain fifty years previously. Yet why should Americans – or the British – require or desire a wood that had to be imported huge distances by sea? More important, how was that timber extracted from the tropical rainforests?

Unlike Britain, North America teemed with a huge variety of timbers (though not all were suitable for fashionable domestic furniture). There seemed no real need to *import* timber from distant tropical locations. Britain on the other hand faced a very different problem. Local forests had been in decline for centuries, and a series of governments and monarchs had

* Jane Kamensky, *A Revolution in Color: The World of John Singleton Copley*, New York, 2016, pp.139–141, 175–178.

† Portraits all in Jules David Prown, *John Singleton Copley: In America, 1738–1724*, Cambridge, MA, 1966, 2 vols.

‡ Jennifer Anderson, *Mahogany*, p.57.

sought different solutions to the problem of declining woodlands. Timber for fuel, for construction – but above all for shipbuilding – was vital, especially from the late seventeenth century onwards with the massive expansion of British merchant shipping and, later, the Royal Navy. In 1670, the Royal Navy had sixty-nine ships of the line; a century later that had grown to 126. The nation's commercial and military well-being was intimately linked to maritime affairs: economic prosperity depended on the thousands of ships that traded in local waters but, increasingly, in long-distance oceanic trade. If the nation's strength lay in its naval and maritime prowess, there too lay its vulnerability and weakness (a fact illustrated in the two great wars of the twentieth century). In the eighteenth century, however, the nation needed timber to maintain its oceanic presence and defence. Increasingly that timber had to be imported in huge volumes from the Baltic and northern Europe. British warships had traditionally been constructed from oak – a fact proclaimed in the marching song of the Royal Navy, 'Heart of Oak', first played in 1760, the words written by the playwright David Garrick. The Admiralty was acutely aware of the problem: oaks, vital for the navy, were in decline and only imported timbers could fill the gap. Another irony lay buried in that song – but went unremarked:

> To honour we call you, not press you like slaves,
> For who are so free as the sons of the waves?

In that very year, British ships carried thousands of Africans across the Atlantic as slaves.

An answer to Britain's pressing naval requirements was found with the discovery of suitable timber in distant slave colonies.

The heavy import duties levied on imported mahogany were a major obstacle, however: duties which raised the price by upwards of 70 per cent. To accommodate the needs of the Royal Navy, the *Naval Stores Act* of 1721 removed the duties on a string of imported naval stores: tar, turpentine, hemp and particular pine trees used for ships' masts. British Caribbean planters – with their own powerful pressure group in London – agitated for the inclusion of mahogany in the Act's provisions. There was an astonishing irony here because Caribbean sugar planters had been responsible for the destruction of huge tracts of the islands' rainforests, especially in Jamaica, in order to clear the land for sugar cultivation. Their policy of 'slash and burn' had been carried out of course by Africans: just one of their many strenuous tasks in bringing that tropical wilderness into profitable cultivation. Though Caribbean hardwoods had been widely used by early settlers – for construction, furniture and even shingles – most of the islands' mahogany had simply been destroyed.

The wild forested island described by early visitors to Barbados for example had, within a single generation, given way to a transformed ecology dominated by cultivable lands for cotton, tobacco and, increasingly, sugar. The deforestation was effectively complete there, and the island transformed into a slave-based sugar colony. Jamaica was the next in line, though local topography – with its mountainous spine and remote forested valleys – posed more challenging difficulties for settlers and planters. Where they could gain access, Jamaican planters felled the massive mahogany trees, leaving them on the ground or, more likely, burning them. There were, however, other sources in Central America. Mahogany had first arrived in Britain from Central America in the late seventeenth century, crossing the Atlantic as ballast or to be used for dye in the textile industry. Sold by auction, this mahogany ballast found a small market in port cities among craftsmen looking for hardwood. But as long as import duties remained high, the commercial importation of mahogany remained impossible. All that changed in 1721.

Planters saw the proposed Naval Act of that year as a commercial opportunity. If they could persuade Parliament to reduce the duty on mahogany, they could export it instead of destroying it. At a stroke, the Act gave birth to a new and important export/import industry: mahogany from the Caribbean to serve both naval interests but also, and increasingly important, to serve domestic demand (in both Britain and North America) for the manufacture of furniture. By the end of the eighteenth century, however, the commercial logging of mahogany had effectively completed what slash and burn had started: the destruction of Jamaica's mahogany. That island's mahogany had once been abundant, along the island's south coast (which was the effective launch pad for settlement of the entire island). Within fifty years, however, it had all but disappeared, apart from remote and often inaccessible regions of the island. When that timber took off commercially in Britain and North America, Jamaica's surviving mahogany was inaccessible and thus non-commercial. The British looked elsewhere, notably to the untamed frontiers of the Mosquito Coast (present-day Belize and Honduras). There, as in Jamaica (and Cuba), the Western world needed slaves to locate, fell, cut and shift the enormous lengths of timber destined for workshops in North America and Britain. As ever more mahogany was delivered to the quaysides of Britain and North America, gangs of slaves trekked into the depths of the rainforests to locate the best trees.

The biggest trees existed in great profusion in Central America and indeed along a vast coastal littoral stretching from Mexico to the Amazon.* Those were regions under Iberian control, and the British had to find supplies of mahogany on the disputed lands of the Mosquito Coast. The slave logging gangs lived the crudest of pioneering, frontier lives, clearing campsites, living off the land, locating the best trees, felling them and dragging then down pathways towards the nearest water, thence gradually to deeper water and ocean-going vessels preparing to return to North America and Britain. Each step of the way – clearing the land, forging routes to the water, locating and felling the trees – was arduous and often very dangerous. Though there were skilled joiners and woodworkers among the white populations of the Americas, the main workers in the mahogany trade were enslaved. The key man was the 'huntsman': the man who climbed trees to spot the towering mahogany trees close by and who acted as the slave owner's eyes in the entire enterprise. The rapid expansion of the mahogany trade after 1721 was only possible because of the rapidly growing African population, notably the huge numbers arriving via Jamaica. The actual numbers logging in the rainforests were small, and nothing like the numbers we find in sugar or any of the other major slave occupations. The logging gangs lived for many months in isolation, far away from white people and often far removed from the very people who owned them. Out of sight, slave loggers left behind little graphic or literary evidence.

The scrappy, surviving glimpses into the enslaved loggers' world tell of a harsh reality that stands comparison with the

* James Walvin, *Slavery in Small Things*, Oxford, 2017, p.93.

worst of other forms of slave labour (except perhaps in mining). Drivers orchestrated the operation: marking suitable trees, clearing the jungle with axes, saws – and fire – to fell the best examples. The number of men in a logging gang ranged from twelve to fifty, and their most protracted task (taking up perhaps two-thirds of the entire time involved) was to clear pathways to the nearest water. Dragging logs was so oppressive that it was often undertaken at night to avoid the daytime heat. Some timbers had to be floated huge distances (trailed by men in canoes) before reaching a sailing ship. Even there, hauling timbers onto a vessel was both dangerous and laborious. By the early nineteenth century, as logging became a more organised system, the slave gangs were larger.

Throughout, slave drivers had to use the whip cautiously. Gangs of men, living beyond the reach of any form of local authority – and most of them equipped with a fearsome array of working tools – were independent in ways plantation slaves could rarely be. It was a lonely – and largely celibate – and independent life, unusual among the enslaved. Their masters (drivers or owners) lived with them, cheek by jowl, in the crude simplicities of camp life in a jungle. Both sides had to make compromises and come to an understanding of how to live and work side by side. Some slave gangs simply vanished, taking off into the inaccessible wilds of the jungle around them, though that was unusual. In the main, the logging gangs lived out their jungle exile as best they could: learning how to get through the strenuous day without too much trouble, moderating the demands made of them as best they could.

Here was yet another – and neglected – branch of the transatlantic slave economy: slave gangs on the very edge of the American frontier, providing a commodity for distant markets and, with the new fashionable industry blossoming in the North American and British heartlands, to cater for an expanding taste for furniture. As demand for mahogany furniture flourished, fashionable society consumed as much of it as they could lay their hands on, but who among them even realised that the industry depended on slave labour thousands of miles away in American rainforests?

***

The initial North American interest in mahogany seems to have begun with settlers migrating to North America from the Caribbean, taking with them a number of cultural features (most notably architectural styles which, to this day, link Bridgetown with Charleston). Jonathan Dickinson, born in Jamaica in 1663 – soon after the British wrested the island from Spain in 1655 – later settled in Philadelphia and traded to and from the Caribbean. He ordered some Jamaican mahogany in 1698 for local carpenters, but there was little local demand. Yet, by the time of his death in 1722, Dickinson had filled his own home with mahogany furniture. Thereafter, the story was utterly transformed by the dramatic impact of the 1721 Act which slashed the cost of mahogany both in Britain and in North America.

The trade to Britain centred on the small English port of Lancaster. Ships from there had traded to the Caribbean long before 1721 and the first mahogany had most likely arrived as ballast. The Act of 1721 coincided with the arrival in Lancaster of a cabinetmaker, Robert Gillow, who soon developed a thriving furniture trade, importing Caribbean produce, and exporting mahogany furniture, made in his Lancaster workshop, back to the islands. Gillow's reputation as a fine craftsman quickly spread and his furnishings were soon to be found across provincial Britain – and in London. Large numbers of his chairs were dispatched to Jamaica, and his export business thrived, with agents in the Caribbean, and eventually, a shop in London. Gillow also branched into the slave trade, his ships returning to Lancaster with a variety of commodities, but notably with mahogany for the workshops he ran with his sons and apprentices. Lancaster thrived on the transatlantic trade. In the century to 1800, 122 Lancaster ships delivered more than twenty thousand Africans to the Americas and many returned with mahogany. In 1768, the *Thomas and John* shipped 132 Africans to Jamaica, bringing back a cargo that included 35 planks of mahogany. After delivering 174 Africans to Kingston, the *Fenton* returned with 541 mahogany planks.*

Gillow's was a diversified trade to and from the slave colonies: he imported dyes and cotton (for the English textile industry) as well as timbers, though above all, it was his furniture that caught the eye, and he cultivated a fashionable clientele through his shop in Oxford Street, London. The most famous craftsman of the period, Thomas Chippendale, was also a provincial craftsman, and he too established a major metropolitan base in his London workshops, in St. Martin's Lane. Born in 1718 in Otley, Yorkshire, to a carpenter father, Thomas trained as a cabinetmaker in London. After he published his book *The Gentleman and Cabinet Maker's Director* in 1754 he established his own style. Today, his work is regarded as the finest of contemporary furniture. It was widely imitated

* 'Fenton' Voyage 81440, *slavevoyages.org*; Melinda Elder, *The Slave Trade and the Economic Development of 18th Century Lancaster*, Halifax, 1992, p.99.

by other commercial rivals, in Britain and North America, but it is his name – Chippendale – which conjures up images of the finest period pieces.

Chippendale was much sought-after among the rich and the prominent and some of his finest work rests in stately homes scattered across Britain, or exhibited in major museums and galleries. Appropriately perhaps, some of the best examples of Chippendale's work are to be found in his native Yorkshire. His biggest commission was to furnish the new home, Harewood House, of the Lascelles family. They had made their fortune by their lucrative trade to and from the Caribbean islands and via their complex involvement in slave plantations in Barbados and Jamaica. Theirs was a family fortune gleaned directly or indirectly from slavery, and invested not only in one of England's great stately homes but in mahogany furniture of outstanding beauty. But who, today, wandering through the splendours of Harewood House, and admiring the dazzling state dining room filled with Chippendale mahogany furnishings, even makes the connection to the people who made it all possible: the slave logging gangs of the Caribbean?

***

The irony behind this story of extreme labour in the most miserable of conditions is that its purpose was to provide the raw material for craftsmen who, in their turn, produced the most handsome of contemporary objects. Chippendale made beautiful furniture; Copley regularly used mahogany to reflect features of his eminent American sitters. The rich and famous, in Britain and North America, scrambled to buy the most costly of pieces from the workshops of the best of contemporary craftsmen. It was a form of beauty fashioned from the belly of the beast.

Mahogany furniture was not the only link between fashionable taste and slavery. Consider the contemporary story of Chinese porcelain. Today, exceptional examples are sold at the world's major auction houses for thousands of pounds/dollars, testimony to their rarity and much sought-after status. By the mid-eighteenth century, a number of companies – their names now legendary – had mastered the art (previously known only to the Chinese) of manufacturing and decorating the finest of porcelain ware. Dresden, Meissen, Sevres, Worcester, Wedgwood and others, poured out ever greater volumes of tableware for eager consumers. At first, however, porcelain was a Chinese monopoly. Some three thousand kilns at Ching-te-Chen near Nanking produced tons of ceramics destined for Europe. Initially it had been shipped as ballast in the company of the huge volumes of imported Chinese tea. An estimated six tons of ceramics accompanied every ton of tea and silks. It was a curious development: the massive consumption of tea – especially in Britain – prompted a parallel increase in demand for Chinaware. At its early eighteenth-century peak, something like five million items of Chinese ceramics were imported into Britain *each year*. In 1718, one twenty-nine-ton lot contained 250,000 items. By the time the East India Company stopped exporting porcelain, an estimated 215 million items had arrived.* What had once been costly and inaccessible was now relatively cheap and even found its way down the social scale: chipped, second-hand and damaged goods passing into poorer homes.

* James Walvin, *Slavery in Small Things*, pp.22–28.

The teapot and coffee pot formed the centrepiece of porcelain sets desired and needed by both rich and poor, but both were joined by the sugar bowl on the long voyage from China. Yet sugar bowls were manufactured by the Chinese mainly for export: the Chinese normally did not take sugar in their tea. Adding sugar to hot drinks – tea, coffee and chocolate – was a European and American habit which derived *entirely* from the slave empires of the Americas. Thus did the Chinese porcelain sugar bowl become an essential presence in kitchens and homes clean across the Western world, in a unique conjunction of ancient Chinese ceramic skills and African slave labour in the sugar fields.

This may seem a bizarre blending of peoples and cultures. Africans shipped across the Atlantic to produce sugar (itself alien to the Americas) for European and American markets, the sugar then stirred into drinks imported from China (tea) and the Horn of Africa, Indonesia and the Caribbean (coffee). Social customs that rapidly became an unquestioned feature of daily life in Europe and the Americas were made possible by a global trading system which shipped commodities thousands of miles before they were blended with other products cultivated by Africans (who had themselves been transported thousands of miles).

The most expensive of porcelain tea and coffee sets were naturally to be found in the homes of the wealthy. Today, those same items survive, normally in display cabinets, in stately homes and museums. But who, among the lines of tourists wandering past, makes the link? Who sees the connection between such eye-catching beauty and the slave labour on the plantations of the Americas? As we have seen, by the late eighteenth century, drinking tea and coffee (sweetened by sugar) were common habits in Europe and the Americas. Cooking and baking were also transformed by the availability of cheap cane sugar: 'sweeten to taste' was a mantra in contemporary cookbooks. Yet at every turn, these utterly domestic cultures – sweet, hot beverages and Western cuisine – were linked to African slave labour. Coffee now came from the mountainous plantations of St. Domingue (Haiti), later from Brazil, sugar from plantations throughout the Caribbean and Brazil, and tea from distant China. But who notices the African slaves when gazing at a mahogany table, a Wedgwood sugar bowl or a simple earthenware coffee pot? Slavery had permeated the domestic fabric of the Western world – but it remained unseen and unnoticed. Out of sight and generally out of mind.

***

It was a matter of concern to a number of the Founding Fathers of the USA that Americans were being born and raised in a society where refinement and sensibility – some of the key elements in what they regarded as European good taste – were being tainted and damaged by the presence of slavery. The fundamental conflict between slavery and the human and political rights enshrined in both the US constitution and Declaration of the Rights of Man, has haunted North American life from that day to this. It is a clash – a contradiction – which continues to puzzle scholars. Much less publicised, however, were the *cultural* frictions at work: how the people of substance across the Americas sought to present themselves to their contemporaries (and hence, via their surviving possessions, to us) as people of sophistication and sensibility. In many respects, as we have seen, they were merely following the patterns established by their European forebears (and contemporaries) who had, for centuries past, flaunted their power and superiority via lavish comforts and luxurious lifestyles. What had changed, roughly from the sixteenth century onwards, was the emergence of new groups – *nouveaux riches* in the minds of their opponents – who had grown fat on the profits of overseas trade and colonial exploitation. Spaniards, Portuguese, Dutchmen, followed by Britons and French (and their offspring born in the Americas) came to revel in the 'embarrassment of riches' afforded by the wealth derived from Asia and the Americas. And there it resides to this day: in their houses, their portraits, furnishings, libraries – indeed almost everything that we now regard as objects of good taste from the period.

Some of the most substantial survivals are the buildings (and sometimes the ruins of those buildings) designed and constructed by slave owners (but made possible by slave labour). Yet at every turn, the sparks generated by the friction with slavery fly in our direction today. Though it is true that the dwellings of rich and poor had *always* been utterly different (and continue to be so), the world of slavery highlighted much more than the material and domestic differences between rich and poor: they provided a moral lesson for those concerned about slavery itself. A number of very fine planters' homes survive to this day and they prompt, in the minds of many tourists (and scholars) an obvious conundrum: how do we reconcile the material splendour of planters' lives with the misery that was slavery? This was the question which taxed the founders of the American Republic and was repeated time and again by the slaves themselves, most notably in slave narratives.

The juxtaposition of wealthy sophistication and the misery of slavery was at its starkest and most visible on the major plantations themselves. A lavish mansion stood close to lines of slave cabins. Though we need to recall that such grand mansions were the exception rather than the rule, the master's Great House was usually close by the slave quarters. Few slave dwellings survive (because of their flimsy and often temporary nature) but we possess abundant written and graphic evidence about them. We can see them in a multitude of plantation drawings and sketches, on property maps and surveyors' papers and, of course, in the accounts of visitors to the plantations. Slave barracks (always unpopular with the slaves), wattle and daub huts, log cabins, later brick dwellings – these and many more were built to house the enslaved labour force. Most were easily destroyed and damaged in bad weather, many were simply removed when the owner needed land for cultivation or wished to relocate the slaves closer to the fields. The quality of slave housing varied greatly (privileged slaves were normally given better housing) and slaves did what they could to improve their homes, acquiring simple furnishings and even decorations by their own efforts. Yet every description we have of such modest improvement is more than counterbalanced by accounts of poorly constructed homes which leaked in the rain, let in the wind, or suffocated in summer. There was little escape from overcrowding, noise and dirt. Sketches sometimes reveal slave cabins in neatly arranged rows, though what lay *inside* each cabin was often best captured by curious and often critical outsiders. More often than not, they were shocked by what they found (though some thought slave dwellings no worse than the homes of the most wretched of European peasantry or rural poor – and no one seemed worse off than the Irish poor). Slave narratives make great play of the universally painful story of the living quarters endured by the enslaved.

They always offered a stark contrast to their master's home but what exacerbated the distinction in the world of slavery was that it was glaringly obvious that the slave owners enjoyed their material well-being by dint of their slave labour force. Moreover, that labour force was kept at its various tasks by brutal regimes which had effectively disappeared elsewhere in the Western world (with the exception of Russia). Successful planters lived an enviable lifestyle that was unashamedly exploitative. By the late eighteenth century, outsiders had begun to query the very nature of slavery and to doubt the morality of slave labour, but such doubts were generally relegated by slavery's obvious benefits and rewards. Why question slave labour when it yielded such comforts and material benefits to slave owners? What made the meanness of slave housing all the more glaring was that it existed – almost literally in many cases – in the shadow of the Great House. Thomas Jefferson's Monticello is an obvious example.

Jefferson's magnificent home sits on a hilltop at Monticello, outside Charlottesville, Virginia, and is perhaps the best known of such places (partly because it appears on billions of US five-cent coins). The wonderful location, the carefully manicured gardens, the remarkable furnishings and sophisticated contents of the home – and close by the slave cabins that line Mulberry Row. In recent years there have been major efforts to restore the story of the slave experience at Monticello and to place slaves and their physical presence centre stage where they belong. Reconstruction of slave buildings, archeological excavations at slave sites, archival research on slave families (not least the story of Jefferson's liaison with his enslaved servant Sally Hemmings), all and more have served to breathe life into the slave community in and around the Jefferson properties. In the process, the material culture of slave life has been shown to be richer and more varied than many might imagine. Even so, it forms a meagre comparison with the lavish comforts and splendours enjoyed by the Jefferson family. Yet these two worlds existed within yards of each other.

The example of Monticello also raises what, today, has become one of the major oddities of the history of slavery. Tens of thousands of people now visit slave-related tourist sites: African slave forts, American plantations, town houses, European stately homes. What they often see on display, however, are the splendours of the slave owners' achievements: their homes and their lavish contents, their libraries, manicured grounds and settings. Visitors are in effect regaled with a panorama of refinement that was made possible by slave labour. (Some of the prettiest US plantations are even popular as venues for weddings.) Too often, the slaves are mere noises off-stage. In some places they have been simply erased and go unmentioned in the chorus of praise heaped on the material splendours which speak to planters' taste and refinement. The irony is obvious. While slaves dominated the physical space of plantation life – even on those properties employing small groups of slaves (tobacco plantations for example) – they are often marginalised or even forgotten in these modern representations.

***

Of all the historic sites of slave memory, few have greater significance and more powerful an impact than the slave forts of West Africa. Alongside the slave ships (to which they were intimately linked of course) the slave forts represent enslavement at its most brutal and callous. We have few physical reminders of those perishable wooden sailing vessels, but a number of the slave forts survive, and visitors flock to them in huge numbers. An estimated half million in Ghana in 2019, prompted in large part by the massive interest in slavery in the West. Many visitors are driven by the ache among people of African descent to see and understand the locations which were perhaps the point of departure for ancestors on their enforced removal from Africa. What tourists encounter is a painful and chilling experience. For all that, there is a certain grandeur about those huge European forts – medieval in style and format and so out of keeping with Africa, and perched in stunning locations, hemmed in by the confused huddle of local fishermen's villages. And all to the thunderous noise of Atlantic rollers crashing onto neighbouring beaches. It takes little imagination for the mind to drift back to those canoes and small vessels riding the rollers as they headed out, with their consignments of terrified Africans, to the sailing ships, lying at anchor in calmer water.

Once inside the slave forts, the visitor is easily swamped by the stark horrors of these places. But they are, at the same time, a confusing mix. There is piety (a chapel built directly above a slave prison cell) and misery in abundance: the dark, chilly despair of the cobbled holding cells, the 'door of no return'. And all set against the dramatic backdrop of the seemingly unending Atlantic. For tens of thousands of visitors, the forts conjure up ancestral misery. On my own visits, tourists simply wept around me, or wandered off to a quiet corner, to be alone, lost in their own painful thoughts. The forts, like plantation Great Houses, have become the engine behind a massive tourist industry which ranges from hordes of vendors, besieging tourists with their trinkets, through to major government departments actively promoting tourism throughout the

African diaspora. In all this, no one seems to worry too much about the inflation and distortions of the historical story on offer. Numbers are broadcast to groups of tourists – of Africans enslaved and shipped – which sometimes owe little resemblance to the historical reality. Yet the terrible truth is clear enough and needs no exaggeration or gloss. The forts are buildings which speak their own truth to the horrors of enslavement and transportation. Though the analogy is flawed, the sense conveyed by visiting the slave forts is not unlike the feeling generated by the death camps of World War II. They exude a human misery that needs no elaboration – but even then, they can still evade our grasp and understanding.

The chronology of the slave forts is also revealing. They originated, in simple, crude form, in the early days of European pioneering trade on the African coast, but they were at their physical peak in the mid and late eighteenth century, when the Atlantic trade was in full flow. At precisely the same time, those who benefitted most from slavery were actively building their own monuments to slavery. On the West African coast, on African riverine locations, and close to the quaysides of major port cities in North and South America, major buildings were constructed for accumulating, holding and then dispatching enslaved Africans. At much the same time, merchants and planters were commissioning and ordering their own citadels, and, like the slave forts, many survive to this day as monuments to Atlantic slavery. It has, however, taken a great deal of persuasion and argument – over a long period – to win over the owners and the visitors to the idea that such domestic palaces, for all their splendours, are like the slave forts of West Africa, important signposts to the slave past.

***

In the years when the British came to dominate the North Atlantic slave trade, Edwin Lascelles, scion of a Yorkshire farming family turned hugely wealthy merchant and plantation owner, was building what became one of England's great stately homes, Harewood House in Yorkshire. He began in 1759 and by the 1830s, when Britain abolished colonial slavery, the Lascelles family (ennobled as the Harewoods), owned 1,277 slaves on their Caribbean possessions (valued at £27,000 for compensation; today's equivalent is roughly £3.3 million). It was, by any standards, an astonishing rise to riches. It is also a prime example of the link between slavery and wealth, between the harsh lives of the enslaved and wealthy European refinement. At much the same time, Thomas Jefferson was busy creating Monticello in colonial Virginia and his fellow planter and slave owner, George Washington – though never in the same financial league as Jefferson (not to mention Harewood) – was equally occupied between 1758 and 1778 with the reconstruction and expansion of his (more modest) plantation home on the banks of the Potomac. Today, Mount Vernon attracts around one million visitors each year (helped by its proximity to Washington DC). Monticello attracts more than a half million people, figures which now run parallel with the numbers visiting the Ghanaian slave forts. Today the slave forts, Mount Vernon and Monticello – all have been designated World Heritage sites.

Though the cultural stamp of approval for slave sites may seem odd, it also confirms my argument: that slavery and Western taste – inhuman bondage and refinement – have become comfortable bedfellows to millions of people. UNESCO accepts that slavery is embedded in the culture of the Western world and some of its most outstanding examples are also items of great and abiding beauty. Stately homes, plantation mansions and African slave forts: all linked. Grand physical structures whose foundations are rooted in the labour of enslaved Africans.

***

Like many of their European contemporaries, prosperous slave owners adorned their homes in the Americas with hundreds of books. Major collectors ordered custom-built libraries which – like most of their other earthly possessions – spoke to their sophistication. Once again, we encounter an apparent confusion: men of learning and even of scholarly inclinations, were at one and the same time men who orchestrated the brutalisation and vicious punishment of legions of Africans. The Virginian planter Landon Carter personified the problem. Politician, indefatigable writer and major landowner in Virginia (at his death owning some 50,000 acres and five hundred slaves), Carter was a man of great culture – and of equal harshness towards his enslaved labour force. When a young pregnant slave, too tired to work, retreated to her cabin, Carter threatened to use a horse and traces to drag her back to the field: she ran away, was caught and after 'a severe whipping [she] has been a good slave ever since.'* When Carter died in 1778, his home at Sabine Hall housed a library containing more than five hundred books (now in the library at the University of Virginia).

Landon Carter was one of the most learned, best-read and sharpest intellects of his generation of Virginians. His books ranged far and wide, embracing all the standard volumes an

* Rhys Isaac, *Landon Carter's Uneasy Kingdom*, Oxford, 2004, p.211.

educated youth was expected to study, and most of the major books published in his lifetime. He acquired books from Philadelphia, New York and London: scriptural studies, geographical volumes, philosophical treatises, scientific and agricultural volumes. Carter read books of a theoretical bent, and others of direct practical application (important for a man who sought to make the most of his physical and human possessions). He annotated volumes about the latest experiments in crop cultivation and processing, and taught himself about contemporary medical practices, important for a man who often tended to the health of his slaves. He was ever alert to new ideas about how best to tend this land and labour.

A decade later, and many miles further south, Charles Johnson in Jamaica wrote to his brother Patrick, in Ayr, Scotland, 'I wish you would send me the Edinburgh Enciclopediae. I hear much of it.' He also wanted other books, 'History I like.' Letter after letter contained requests for printed matter: 'I am so much in want of Books,' 'I wish you would send me a few books; late Magazines or History.'*

Landon Carter was only one of any number of men in the slave colonies for whom collecting, borrowing and lending books and other printed material was part of their social and economic existence. Such men formed complex networks which linked three continents, not merely through the basics of their trade in humanity and commodities, but in the flow of

* See Letters between the Douglas brothers: 4 November 1788, Box 3 Folder 115: 5 July 1791, Box 3 Folder 118; 22 November 1796, Box 3, Folder 125; 19 July 1802, Box 4, Folder 133; 3 July 1804, Box 4, Folder 136. *The Boswell Collection*, Beinecke Library, Yale, MSS 150.

ideas and the interchange of experiments – all in the interests of advancing their economic well-being.

When Landon Carter was building up his own library in Virginia, another slave owner – though living in much more humble physical circumstances – was following a very similar path in Jamaica. Thomas Thistlewood also greatly valued the world of print: books, magazines, essays, newspapers – which he bought, borrowed and exchanged. Though he lived on the fringe of Britain's sprawling empire, on the south-western tip of Jamaica, he was a fully paid-up member of the contemporary Enlightenment. He had been an avid reader from his English childhood, devouring books, buying them, listing them and writing long extracts from them. When he sailed from England to Jamaica he was accompanied by two tea chests packed with seventy-five books – and steadily added to the number until his death in 1786. At his collection's peak, he owned the best part of a thousand volumes, most purchased from dealers in London.*

Throughout his life in Jamaica, he eagerly awaited the arrival of the next vessel from London, bringing his latest box of printed material. His was not the biggest private library on the island – other major politicians and planters owned many more volumes – but for a man of relatively modest means and standing, Thistlewood's books formed an impressive entrée to his world outlook. Like Carter, 2,000 kilometres to the north, Thistlewood was an autodidact, keeping abreast of the latest science and agronomic developments, poring over the most recent political arguments from London (and around the empire). He read Adam Smith's *Wealth of Nations*, and Edward

* Trevor Burnard, *Mastery, Tyranny and Desire*, pp.106–114.

Gibbon's *History of the Decline and Fall of the Roman Empire.* He also shared his learning, his books and essays with neighbours and friends around Jamaica, just as he exchanged seeds, plants and news about the latest agricultural improvements which were channelled through London, to and from the far reaches of world travel and settlement. Thistlewood was an eclectic reader of a wide range of contemporary publications: novels, philosophy, the world of classical antiquity – there seems to have been no limits to his intellectual curiosity. As his collection grew, he was forever shuffling his books into new arrangements, cataloging and rearranging his book collection.

Above all, Thistlewood seems to have loved science and botany, understandably perhaps for a man whose main role in life was to extract the best returns, via his slaves, from the different properties he managed and owned. He was an agriculturalist and was permanently on the lookout for new ideas, crops or ways of managing both land and slave labour to the best economic end. He was interested in science, in horticulture and gardening, developing his own attractive grounds, and regularly experimenting with new items – cuttings, seeds and plants which might yield innovative crops. He was also quick to pass on his experiments (and failures) to like-minded neighbours. Thistlewood clearly flourished on the exchange of ideas and experiments, keeping up to date with news from Britain and even more distant locations.

Today, however, he is not remembered for any of this: not for the enlightened and intellectually cultured side to his life in Jamaica, but for his despotic violence and his predatory sexuality towards female slaves. In this, he was also in good company in Jamaica.

Despite the importance of Thistlewood's circle of friends and associates – his brotherhood of fellow readers – he was an unusual figure in the world of white Jamaicans. Visitors, or new arrivals to the island, regularly complained of the bone-headed ignorance and crudity of the whites around them. On the plantations, life was especially crude and unsophisticated, and planters and their circles made no pretense at formal learning or intellectual aspirations. There was, of course, an important cultural presence on the island and it was perhaps best represented by a number of eminent men recognised for their learning by major scholarly societies in London itself. But the core, the backbone – the *culture* – of the planter class remained largely immune to such intellectual pursuits. They seemed happy to spend their time in earthier and more basic pleasures. Here, their social and sexual lives ran parallel with the other world of Thomas Thistlewood.

***

Francis Price was one of the junior officers in the Cromwell army that seized Jamaica from Spain in 1655. He was rewarded with a parcel of cultivable land in a fertile valley in the heart of the island. There, in 1670, he founded Worthy Park (still functioning to this day as a sugar estate). From those humble beginnings, his family quickly moved on – and upwards. His grandson Charles, born in England, returned to Jamaica in 1730 after education in Oxford. Thereafter he enjoyed a glittering career as planter, local politician and prominent member of the island's elite. The centre of his wealth was Worthy Park (home to upwards of three hundred slaves at the time of Price's death in 1772). Like many others, Price announced his status by building a grand house, The Decoy, in the north of the island. It was a beautiful wooden structure, surrounded by landscaped gardens and affording a view of the ocean. It caught the attention of Edward Long – historian and chronicler of that island's story, and a man with an eye for telling detail. He liked The Decoy and its gardens 'filled with the most beautiful and useful variety which Europe, or this clime, produces.' What had been 'a gloomy wilderness' had become by 1772 a delightful house and landscaped property.* Price's plans for The Decoy had been nurtured in his years in England – and on the Grand European Tour, at a time when landscaped gardens were becoming a fashionable habit among the wealthy. The grounds even included a folly, 'the salon', similar to the innovation established by 'Capability Brown' at various English sites.† Today, the wilderness has taken its revenge: the property has vanished – cast aside by the subsequent historical tides that have swept across the island, a victim of the relentless and rapid surge of the tropical environment.

Price was merely one of untold numbers of successful planters who sought to assert their status and wealth by building stylish and impressive homes, on their plantations, in secluded rural locations, in the nearest town or even far away from the slave colonies, in the metropolitan heartland. London, Glasgow, Amsterdam, Paris, Bordeaux, Lisbon – all and more continue to bear witness to this day, to the wealth, position – and ambitions – of people who made their fortunes on the back of African slaves.

* Edward Long, *The History of Jamaica*, 3 vols, II, London, 1774, pp.76–77.

† Louis P. Nelson, *Architecture and Empire in Jamaica*, New Haven, 2016, pp.136–138.

Such lavish homes seemed out of place in the tropics but the best of them adapted to the locality, creating architectural and functional styles best suited to the environment. Some Caribbean planters in effect constructed a European mansion in the tropics, but most opted for something different – something distinctive and local. The grand homes of cotton planters along the Mississippi Delta are quite different from their Caribbean or Brazilian counterparts. True, many shared common features: impressive driveways, arcades of trees, balconies which afforded splendid views of the property and neighbourhood, and most had imposing interiors boasting the finest of craftsmanship in fittings and furnishings. Many also sought to impress by their shelves of books and walls lined with family portraits and scenic views. The biggest and grandest became centres for rituals of elaborate social life, playing host to visitors and travelling officials or friends to be entertained with the extravagant meals and drinks which characterised the social lives of the people they aspired to be: the rural wealthy in Europe. The drinks on offer (rum punch and the best of imported wines) a formidable variety of local meats, vegetables and fruits, were all served on the most fashionable tableware. The whole scene was rounded off by an abundance of enslaved servants, bearing witness to their owners' wealth, outfitted in the most elaborate of clothes and trained in the carefully defined protocols required of indoor staff (others toiled behind the scenes in the kitchen). Visitors to the Americas regularly commented on the abundance of domestic slaves: the most prosperous of slave owners seemed to require slaves to help with most of their physical needs. Enslaved domestics woke them, dressed them, cooked for them, fed them, cleaned their rooms and clothing, sometimes even carried them, and cared for their children. All too often, they provided them with sexual pleasure.

This story is repeated time and again, in different guises, from one slave society to another. At times the link between slavery and sophistication is direct and inescapable. The Barbados planter Christopher Codrington not only founded Codrington College in that island (to educate a local elite) but bequeathed £6,000 to All Souls College Oxford, for what is now the Codrington Library, and a further £4,000 for books, to add to his own collection (also destined for All Souls). By the time of his death in 1710, his Barbados plantations were worth £30,000 (more than £5 million in today's currency).*

The most striking of all physical memorials to slave labour are the Great Houses, the stately homes and plantation residences of the most successful planters and slave traders. They survive today, scattered around the landscapes of the former slave colonies; architectural reminders of the wealth generated by the local armies of slaves. In Europe, the lavish homes of former slave owners seem deracinated – even untouched – by a slave past because they are located so many thousands of miles distant from the centres of slavery. Even when splendid buildings survive on their original plantations, they sometimes do their best to detach themselves from – pretending not to be linked to – the slaves who made everything possible. In Brazil, the US South, Virginia (and doubtless elsewhere) the sumptuousness of many Great Houses and the lifestyle they continue to generate for their owners, provide a sepia-tinged setting for tourists, for weddings, for garden tours: for anything but an engagement with the harsh reality of the slave labour that underpinned the entire enterprise.

* Simon Gikandi, *Slavery and the Culture of Taste*, pp.119–123.

By the late eighteenth century, lavish wealth founded in slavery had become an inescapable feature of European social life. Of course, the slave colonies were not the only source of wealth flowing back to the mother countries. The wealth from Indian trade and empire carried others back to their homelands (if they survived) to enjoy eye-watering riches which were the envy even of the grandest of traditional aristocrats. Scholars still wrestle with the exact amounts of wealth which drained from India to Britain. If we unite India and the slave colonies, we begin to get some sense of the astonishing colonial wealth created for both Britain and France. What distinguishes the slave-based wealth, however, was its foundations in a system utterly devoid of any semblance of culture or sophistication. It was an unadorned, rapacious system, designed to strip bare its victims to the level of the beasts of the fields. Yet its rewards enabled the most successful of planters and merchants – indeed anyone who invested successfully in the varied aspects of slavery – to adopt personal and social manners which could stand comparison with the highest in the land.

Needless to say, not everyone involved succeeded, nor did they reach the peaks of material extravagance we see in the grandest of stately homes, or the finest of town houses. Many failed, and many simply scraped a modest living from slavery. Yet, however we calibrate the successes and failures, the central issue remains clear: slavery lay at the heart of an important flowering and display of cultural taste. For some, it spawned extravagance and wealth, which, in turn, became the basis for social standing: good taste and aesthetic beauty. Scholars have only recently come to recognise the relationship between slavery and what Simon Gikani terms 'the culture of taste'. But much the same was also true of contemporaries. How many people, in the mid-eighteenth century, say, even *noticed* the connection to slavery as they stirred sugar into their tea and coffee? Or noticed the link between the beautiful domestic artefacts around them and the brutal realities of slave labour? It was as if beauty and the beast had become ideal companions.

17

A World Transformed

SLAVERY WAS AT the heart of a number of important patterns of cultural taste. It was also central to massive inter-related human and environmental changes which affected not only the human geography of the globe, but, at the same time, utterly changed swathes of the globe's physical environment. Those changes are so much a part of the modern world that it is difficult for most people to imagine what the world was like before those changes. Who, for example, can imagine the Americas without people of African descent? And who can begin to understand the natural habitat of much of that hemisphere before the alien invaders imposed new systems of agriculture and human settlement, replacing great areas of the natural habitat with imported flora and fauna? To put the matter simply, the human and physical world first encountered by Columbus and subsequent pioneers was very unlike the world that had been brought into being a mere century later. The most obvious transformation was in the population of the Americas. In the wake of European invasions, native peoples were swept aside, reduced, minimised – and even destroyed. These human convulsions set in train transformations in the physical appearance of large parts of the newly settled Americas. From the first days, settlers, in the Caribbean, Brazil and later North America, set about converting the land to new human and agricultural systems. But they were always in need of labour for those mammoth tasks and always seeking to secure the best returns from the land. For that, they created new labouring systems. In key areas of the Americas, the critical labour they turned to was enslaved Africans, who, in their turn, changed the human face of the world they toiled in. They also altered the physical face of the landscape itself. African gangs hacked down and burned forest and bush – creating, in their place, orderly manicured landscapes of fields, plots and hillsides. On such converted lands, new crops were cultivated in totally new patterns of rural life. As the land and its labouring peoples changed, so too did the relationships between humans and their environment. What emerged was a landscape shaped and dictated by mankind: an environment that was brought forth by and regulated by human hand – for profitable exploitation. Nature no longer yielded its bounty according to its own rhythms and patterns, but now obeyed the dictates of human management and intervention. At the heart of this upheaval lay the experience of native peoples, and the labours of enslaved Africans. The decisions to cultivate certain crops, and to cultivate them *on plantations*, the destruction of indigenous people and their replacement by enslaved Africans, all blended into a brew of profound and irreversible change. The consequences reverberate down to the present day.

It is now widely argued that mankind's continuing assault on the natural habitat constitutes the greatest threat to the planet's well-being. An early step in that direction was the massive impact of plantation slavery. What came to be known as 'ecological imperialism' was initially most effectively pioneered in the Americas, and though it may seem, at first glance, to be a relatively small-scale enterprise, its consequences were global and profound.

Take for example, the process of deforestation. Though by modern standards the process set in train by settlers in colonial America may seem small-scale, it produced major regional transformations. Strenuous physical effort was required to render land cultivable, and settlers used enslaved labour gangs to clear the wilderness. The process is perhaps best seen by looking at small-scale examples: microcosms of a much broader phenomenon. What happened on the small island of Barbados is a good starting point. That previously densely forested island was quickly reduced to an environment where first tobacco and then, most importantly, sugar could be cultivated. There, and elsewhere in the Caribbean, clearing the forests and bush was harsh work – especially with hard timbers (notably mahogany). But what the axe could not finish, fire could, and ancient forests were reduced to ash and stumps. This deforestation destroyed not just the trees, but caused great damage to the soil, via the removal of important nutrients: the run-off from soil in rainy seasons created major problems of erosion. What appears, then, to have been a simple switch from forest to farmland, actually heralded a profound and unsettling ecological change, by greatly reducing the soil's fertility. This process was hastened, initially, by a local shortage of animals and their natural fertiliser. Though the neatly laid-out fields of sugar plantations created sweet riches for successful planters and their backers, they came at enormous ecological cost – in addition to the human suffering inflicted on the enslaved labour force.

The damaging impact of new forms of agriculture was not restricted to the tropical Americas. It could also be seen in the impact which tobacco culture had on the natural habitat around the Chesapeake Bay. There too, deforestation and land clearance for tobacco cultivation wrought great damage to the rich local soil. Tobacco also reduced the fertility of the formerly forested land, though (unlike Barbados) in so vast a land, depleted soil seemed not to matter, and planters simply moved on, to new settlements to begin the process anew – leaving behind greatly degraded land.

The soil exhaustion which first became apparent in North America in the Chesapeake region, re-emerged, more than a century later, in the southern USA. After 1800, the single crop system of US cotton cultivation spread rapidly across huge expanses of the South (where it was worked by slave gangs, not by task labour as in tobacco). It too was a new industry that led to serious soil degradation. A combination of soil toxins, parasites and erosion stripped the cotton fields of their nutrients, and the whole process was greatly exacerbated by the increasingly intensive demands made by planters of the slave labour force. Throughout the Americas, the lure of single crop cultivation (though never to the total exclusion of other crops) proved profitable for settlers, and was ideally suited to the changing demands of consumers worldwide. It was used in the production of sugar, tobacco, rice, cotton and coffee – and to a lesser degree, timber. These crops set in train a transformation in the physical environment that prefigured the more massive upheavals of the twentieth and twenty-first centuries.

In the Chesapeake, the development of tobacco culture heralded a new, intensive labour regime which could not be satisfied by free or indentured labour. The answer – as others had already discovered in Brazil and the Caribbean – lay in Africa. North American colonial officials and settlers were aware that Caribbean islands were booming on the back of

African slaves. George Downing wrote to John Winthrop Junior in 1645, that in Barbados:

> I believe they have bought this year no less than a thousand Negroes, and the more they buie, the better able they are to buye.*

Slave ships thus began their much longer voyages along the eastern coast of North America, to deliver Africans to the tobacco planters dotted around the Chesapeake Bay. The die was cast both for the Africans and for the local environment.

Throughout colonial North America there was widespread destruction of a range of local trees – for shipbuilding, housing and roofing, for barrels and naval stores and for fuel. Timber became a large export trade for the North American colonies (and later for the USA). The forests of New England for instance yielded enormous volumes of wood destined for the sawmills which proliferated along the north-eastern coastline of North America, with the processed timbers loaded onto local ships for transportation to all corners of the Atlantic economy. As hundreds of acres of trees disappeared, their decline affected the local climate and also diminished a range of local wildlife. What happened in the forests of New England provided an early example of the far-reaching consequences of deforestation.†

***

* George Downing to John Winthrop Jnr, 1645, in *Slavery, Abolition and Emancipation*, Michael Craton et al., eds, p.13.

† Carolyn Merchant, *The Columbia Guide to American Environmental History*, New York, 2002, pp.28–31.

The northern colonies were major importers of goods and commodities (an issue which created friction with Britain, because of duties and taxes levied on imports, and eventually created the political separation of 1776). Here too, the influence of slavery was apparent. By the mid-eighteenth century, an estimated 2.7 million gallons of rum emerged from the distilleries of Massachusetts – but all of it originated on Caribbean slave plantations. Rum rapidly established itself as the dominant alcoholic drink of the northern colonies, but it was much more influential – and damaging – in its impact on the native people of the region. Rum was widely used to persuade Indian peoples to strike unfair trading and land agreements. The European demand for pelts and furs, acquired from indigenous peoples, was lubricated by great volumes of rum offered by Europeans. Alcohol which had originated in the slave plantations became a major factor in undermining Indian communities and paving the way for European dominance and economic control. Rum was an essential exchange commodity in the wider economy of New England, playing a corrosive role on the frontiers between Indians and European traders and companies. It was to be just one example of the early use of alcohol in the seduction and undermining of subject peoples when they fell under the spell of powerful invaders and settlers. The process of weakening and demoralising Indian people by violence and disease was rounded off by alcohol.

***

The 'ecological imperialism', initially described by Alfred Crosby, has prompted some far-reaching analyses of humanity's impact on the natural world. One of the most obvious and long-lasting was the introduction of enslaved Africans, and plantations, to the Americas. The slave plantations made possible the production on a massive scale of commodities which, today, are commonplace but which, before slavery, were local or insignificant. Tobacco (and other similar grasses) were smoked or chewed by native people across the Americas, but slave labour transformed tobacco consumption from the habit of Indian peoples into a global addiction. By the mid-eighteenth century the consumption of tobacco – in pipes, cigars and as snuff – had become a major global industry. It was a deep-rooted social habit long before the development of modern cigarettes. Today, tobacco is consumed by tens of millions of people worldwide. In 1990, the USA produced 695 billion cigarettes, China 1,525 billion. China alone has 300 million smokers. It is calculated that the world's tobacco industries generate $97,197 million worth of business.* It hardly needs saying that tobacco is also the cause of worldwide sickness and ill-health. The cost of repairing the damage caused by tobacco greatly offsets the financial benefits reaped by the tobacco industry (and by governments who tax tobacco heavily).

***

The emergence of tobacco as a popular taste was paralleled by the massive expansion of slave-grown sugar, largely, to begin with, as an additive to tea and coffee. At first Europe relied for its tea on the massive importation of the East India Company, via its trade to and from China, with tea re-exported from

* *The Guardian*, 2 June 2015, p.13.

Britain to Europe. The enormous cargoes of Chinese tea, packed into the company's London's warehouses, had arrived along with huge quantities of Chinese ceramic ware. Thus did global consumption of sweet tea – and the Western taste for porcelain – become an essential element in the thriving trade between China and the West. But it was underpinned by slave-grown sugar. The addition of sugar made tea, coffee and chocolate global drinks.

Sweet tea had become a national British drink by the late eighteenth century: it was customary, for example, to allow servants two cups of sweet tea each day. Even the poor expected sweet tea as part of their meagre diet. Sugar flooded into Europe from the slave colonies, sweetening people's hot beverages: tea in Britain, coffee in Europe. By 1809, each person in Britain consumed 18 lbs of sugar annually. Sugar was also blended into the West's culinary habits. Bags of sugar, and sugar bowls, now took centre stage in domestic routines and diet. Sugar was also largely responsible for mankind's dental problems. Their origins lay deep in the history of slavery.

From the mid-nineteenth century onwards, throughout Europe and the Americas, industrial volumes of sugar were added to the confectionaries which had quickly established themselves as a central feature of the Western diet. Chocolates, sweets (candies), jams, biscuits, cakes – all were produced on a highly industrial scale in large modern factories. In Europe and North America some towns were utterly transformed by those industries, and the local labour force was dominated by work in confectionary production – York and Bourneville (UK, chocolate), Nantes and Carlisle (France and UK, biscuits), Hershey (Pennsylvania, chocolate). By 1900, sweetness was everywhere, and sugar had become an essential ingredient in any number of modern food and drink industries. By the early twentieth century, the lessons were clear, and became the blueprint for the eye-watering success of the mega corporations of the late twentieth century: the massive infusion of sweetness into food and drink created a commercial cornucopia. It did so, however, alongside large-scale, global health problems, especially of obesity and tooth decay.*

North America had turned its back on tea drinking at first partly because of the political rejection of Britain (the outrage caused by taxes on tea and the infamous 'Boston Tea Party'). More important, the emergence of an independent USA led to a gradual realignment of North American trade. A growing volume of US trade began to follow new routes between North and South America, especially to Cuba and Brazil. And here, again, slavery proved inescapable. This was nowhere more evident than in the astonishing volumes of Brazilian coffee imported into the USA. Coffee drinking had overtaken tea in the USA by 1830; by 1850, each American was drinking five pounds of coffee annually. Coffee imports into the USA increased ninety-fold over the nineteenth century, and before Brazilian emancipation in 1888, much of that coffee had been cultivated by Brazilian slaves. American coffee drinkers could (before Cuban emancipation in 1882) sweeten their coffee with cheap slave-grown cane sugar, imported from Cuba and refined at a string of massive sugar refineries which dotted the quaysides of major ports from Baltimore to Boston. It was coffee and sugar, cultivated by slave labour, that created the national drink of the USA. From the 1880s, sugar was also arriving at the docks of San Francisco from the sugar plantations of Hawaii

* James Walvin, *Sugar*, pp.283–291.

(where it was cultivated on plantations by imported Japanese labour).

The West's continuing entanglement with slavery is perhaps best illustrated (and remembered) by the rise of King Cotton in the USA. The people in the slave gangs of the cotton fields of the US South provided the raw material for the rise of the new textile industries in Massachusetts, Lancashire and Germany. There were, of course, other major suppliers of cotton (in the British case, notably India and Egypt) but it was primarily US slave-grown cotton which fuelled the rise of modern industrial society. Liverpool – once the HQ of British slave trading – became the main entrepôt for the import of US cotton and the export of finished textiles to the wider world. Slavery thus underpinned the expansion of industrial Britain and North America in the nineteenth century, much as it had formed the labouring infrastructure of economic well-being in the eighteenth century. In the process Britain's dominance as an imperial and colonial power provided a global market for its manufactured goods. Britain's ascendant colonial role made possible a global standing – but it was one rooted in a tradition which reached back to the world of Atlantic slavery.

***

Slave owners made the most of enslaved labour by harnessing that labour to the plantation system. Plantations became the test bed for the conquest of the natural habitat and its conversion to profitable agriculture, though they had a long history before their introduction into the Americas. They had been used in Palestine, in North Africa and in various Atlantic islands long before the European encroachment into the

Americas. Plantations had also been used as means of transplanting people into new settlements, in Ireland and North America. But plantations populated with enslaved Africans and their children, cultivating major export crops, were very different. It was this combination of enslaved Africans working on plantations which became the foundation of so much American and European well-being. The plantation quickly proved itself the perfect tool for imposing a new, man-made order on a landscape that had remained untouched by human hand. It was as if the plantation had helped to bring nature to heel. (The process of 'slash and burn' was the necessary origin of most plantation economies.) Plantations not only changed the way the environment *looked*, but they also created a model of what could be achieved elsewhere. Slave-based plantations were followed by plantations using other forms of cheap or unfree labour, and much of that labour was often shipped great distances, mainly for the development of a wide range of single-crop economies.

Today such plantation-based economies are most vividly on display (and at their most spectacularly disastrous) in the vast palm oil plantations of Malaysia and Indonesia, in East and West Africa, and South America. Malaysia (as colonial Malaya) had served its plantation apprenticeship to the rubber industry. Similarly, huge tracts of land in India, Sri Lanka and East Africa were turned over to tea plantations. In South Africa, huge plantations cultivate sugar. Elsewhere, notably in Mozambique and Swaziland, even greater areas of land were converted to timber production. Modern Hawaii developed on the back of first sugar then pineapple plantations (courtesy again of the importation of large numbers of labourers – this time, from Japan). Brazil's coffee plantations cover more than 10,000 square miles of that immense land. Meanwhile, Brazilian loggers continue to tear down, or slash and burn, huge areas of Amazonia – just as their forebears did in the early years of European settlement. Timber logged for export, and timber removed to clear land for other uses, continues to burn immense holes into Amazonia on a scale which is hard to comprehend and with consequences which are both dire and possibly irreversible.

Plantations devoted to sugar cultivation continue to boom, despite the rise of beet sugar and, more recently, despite competition from chemical sweeteners. Though the slaves have gone and, on bigger plantations, the large labour gangs have also gone (replaced by enormous machines), plantations live on. In Brazil and Australia sugar plantations have grown to an immense size that would have amazed even the most successful of colonial planters. Florida's sugar plantations continue to use grossly exploited labour, much of it shipped in from neighbouring poor countries. Like their colonial forebears, Florida's sugar plantations continue to damage the ecosystems of the unique Florida Everglades (by encroachment, soil erosion but especially via chemical pollution).

Plantations were also developed for the cultivation of cocoa in West Africa – the source of so many of the enslaved people bound for the Americas. Chocolate manufacturers (their sugar-laden products selling the world over) relied on West African plantations for their supplies of cocoa. The region became mired in controversy in the early twentieth century, when it emerged that the Portuguese continued to use slave labour on plantations, notably on their colonial possessions of São Tomé and Principe. Those tiny islands, so important in the emergence of sugar and slave plantations in the sixteenth century, and later as way stations for Atlantic slave ships, were revived in the early twentieth century by cocoa cultivation. Some of Europe's major chocolate manufacturers bought their cocoa in West Africa (and the Caribbean). Though not on the scale of the Belgian atrocities in the Congo (in pursuit of rubber), those reminders of an enslaved past (which had ended only a half-century earlier) were more than enough to cause outrage.

***

In studying the massive recent damage to the world's ecosystem little attention has been paid to the role of slavery, and it is rarely noticed that plantation slavery had been the *springboard* for mankind's changing relations with the tropical and semi-tropical environment. There was a direct line of descent from colonial experiments with slave labour on plantations, to bringing that luxuriant environment to heel and converting it to profitable export crops for global consumption. Plantations were, obviously, not the only means by which humans set their mark on enormous swathes of the natural world, but they were pivotal. Here was a system that confirmed what could be achieved – if suitable labour could be found to work them. And, for four centuries, that labour was enslaved, and it was found in Africa. After the decline of slavery, other non-servile forms of labour were drafted in: indentured labour from India, Malaysia, from China and Japan, from South Pacific islands (to Australia), all were scattered across the face of the globe to satisfy the labour needs of a new generation of plantations. Throughout their modern history, plantations were generous with the lives of others – enslaved and bonded.*

* Christer Petley, *Plantations in the Atlantic World*, Oxford Bibliographies, https://www.oxfordbibliographies.com

The widespread use of servile labour had, as we have seen, ancient and worldwide roots. But it is hard to think of earlier slave systems that yielded the lavish prosperity and material well-being produced by slavery in the Americas. The longevity of the American slave systems and the tenacity with which slave owners clung to slavery in the face of mounting opposition, confirm slavery's commercial viability. When slavery ended or collapsed, it rarely did so because slave owners had had enough of it. Slave resistance, the universal refusal of the enslaved to accept their enslavement (and news of the terrible fate they endured when they struck out against it) all served to compound the rising sense, across the Western world, that slavery was morally rotten and indefensible. For all that, it lived on, often in slightly different forms and for different purposes. The fact that slavery survives to this day is itself proof of one of slavery's remarkable characteristics: its astonishing adaptability – and durability.

***

If we are looking for less obvious transformations wrought by slavery, the culture of anti-slavery stands out as an unsurpassed historical irony. Here again, the British were pre-eminent. The people who had dominated slavery in the North Atlantic, and who had, more than any other, populated the Caribbean and North America with enslaved Africans – the British – became the pioneering crusader of abolition in the nineteenth century. The British were not alone of course, but they were effectively the first and – courtesy of their new-found naval power and diplomatic clout – the most important. They led the charge first against the slave trade, then against slavery worldwide, using their considerable military and political power to prevent others doing what they had done for centuries: profiting hugely from enslaved African labour.

The pursuit of abolition – at sea and on land – became a major British obsession as the nineteenth century advanced, directed first at those Europeans who continued to ship enslaved Africans, then against nations in the Americas where slavery remained a major institution. Yet at the same time, Britain continued to derive great benefit from its trade with, and investments in, slaving nations (especially with the USA and Brazil). The British attacked slavery wherever they encountered it, notably in Africa and in India, bringing subject rulers and people to heel with military muscle and imposing abolitionist agreements and treaties. At the same time, they led a diplomatic campaign to win over the world's most powerful nations to ban slavery in all its forms. (For years, anti-slavery was the largest department in the British Foreign Office.) No less curious, the British people at large took on the culture of anti-slavery. Their politicians, churches, newspapers, trade unions and other cultural expressions rallied to the vocal outrage about slavery. The British united behind the belief that they were an abolitionist people and took great pride in their continuing struggles to extinguish slavery in all corners of the globe.* In the process, they lost sight of their own slaving history, which did not fully resurface until the late twentieth century. When it did, it emerged in large part because of the migration of people from the Caribbean and Africa to settle in Britain itself. The British past looked very different through the eyes of the descendants of the enslaved and the colonised.

* James Walvin, *Freedom: The Overthrow of the Slave Empires*, London, 2019, Ch.11.

The rise of anti-slavery as a central principle of international diplomacy, especially post-World War II, through the United Nations, has seen slavery cast into outer darkness. It continues of course, with millions still driven into various forms of bondage, largely because of poverty. Nonetheless, today slavery is illegal, morally repugnant and universally deplored.

Here then, is *the* most profound transformation brought about by slavery. The institution which brought untold material benefits to the Western world, while playing havoc with swathes of Africa, and which imposed years of immeasurable suffering on its victims throughout the Americas, now occupies a pariah status. Only a fool or a lunatic would publicly support slavery (even though many continue, illegally, to benefit from it). The world has been utterly transformed.

18

Slavery Matters

The furore which swept round the globe in the wake of the killing of George Floyd in May 2020 brought slavery back into widespread public debate. Not since the days of slavery itself had it been so widely scrutinised, and so heated a topic of public outrage. That brutal police killing of a single African-American on top of so many others sparked a bushfire of protest, first across the USA then, quite rapidly, around the globe. It was as if the world was poised for an outpouring of outrage about the racism that sustained such a violent injustice. Critics everywhere were swift to point out that the origins of that injustice lay deep in the history of relations between Black and white. And that, inevitably, took the argument back to the history of slavery. It was even argued that it is impossible to write a page of Brazilian history without the question of slavery becoming an aspect of the debate. By mid-summer of 2020, and in the subsequent swirl of demonstration and argument, slavery had slipped its moorings in Africa and the Americas and was now everywhere.

The immediate cause of this astonishing upsurge of anger was the killing of one man. But that killing was only the latest of a seemingly endless list of ugly outrages against African-Americans by US law officers. Police violence, and the mass incarceration of African-Americans across the USA, had long been at the heart of a furious debate about racism in the USA, and about the scant regard shown for Black lives. The Black Lives Matter (BLM) movement (founded some years before George Floyd's killing) promptly became the epicentre of the campaign. The events of 2020, however, gave it immediate and massive support, and not only among African-Americans. Protests and demonstrations attracted enormous crowds – Black and white, male and female, young and old – in a huge number of the world's major cities. It was as if BLM had tapped into a deep reservoir of anger about the state of racial issues around the globe. Arguments that swirled around the BLM movement involved not only matters of immediate political concern but gained authority from the centuries of troubled relations between Black and white, especially, but not only, in the USA. The arguments ranged back and forth about each and every phase of Black–white relations: the legacy of Civil Rights in the 1960s, the earlier history of US segregation and the post-Civil War Jim Crow legislation. Above all, it was the painful history of slavery itself that suddenly found itself centre stage. In the summer and autumn of 2020, slavery had, literally, become front-page news. Serious British newspapers commissioned special pieces dealing with slavery.*

The intrepid *New York Times* had, unwittingly, prefaced the entire discussion a year earlier by the publication of an important (though much contested) campaign – The 1619 Project

* David Olusoga, 'A Black British history lesson', *The Times*, 3 October 2020.

– which had given front-page coverage to the history of US slavery. Launched in August 2019 to mark the four hundredth anniversary of the first enslaved Africans landing in Virginia in 1619, it intended 'to reframe the country's history by placing the consequences of slavery and the contributions of Black Americans at the very centre' of US history. It was a bold and imaginative enterprise which prompted a major, and often angry debate among all sorts and conditions of people, ranging from politicians who were anxious to let sleeping dogs lie, through to eminent academic historians (some keen to spot the smallest of factual errors or contest a nuance of interpretation). For all the divisiveness involved, the protracted debate around The 1619 Project extended far beyond the events of 1619 itself, developing into a valuable discussion about the making of the USA. Even those critics of the project who felt that the role of slavery had been greatly overstressed, did not deny the importance of slavery in the history of the USA. The central point at issue, the stumbling block, was just *how* important, how central and seminal, was slavery in shaping the nation's historical (and therefore its current) identity. From August 2019 arguments about slavery raged in the press, on televised and social media, on political and educational platforms – inevitably reaching Trump's White House.* Then, in late May 2020, George Floyd was killed.

What followed was an unprecedented explosion of public anger, first across the USA, then around the world. It was as if the world was primed for outrage. Everywhere, protesters looked not simply at the immediate, current complaints (of police violence and racism) but they pointed the finger of

* 'The 1619 Project', *The New York Times*, 14 August 2019.

blame for our present discontents at the historical past. Naturally enough, slavery became a topic of universal discussion in ways not seen since the days of slavery itself. In 2020, it became abundantly clear that slavery mattered.

On countless occasions in 2020, political and social events returned to questions of slavery, and to the question of how far current problems arose from slavery. The political convulsions of 2020 were part of a massive engagement with the slave past in all its forms, with the consequences of slavery for the way we live today, and with the need to confront, and perhaps purge, Western societies of many of the blatant reminders of slavery in the world around us. Statues of men linked to slavery were toppled, distinguished universities (with slave endowments) were humbled, august commercial companies (beneficiaries of slavery) were shamed, wealthy institutions (banks, insurance, the law) were called to account, churches, cities and whole nations were dishonoured by demands for apologies – and compensation – for their historic role in slavery. Museums, galleries – even anatomy departments – were urged to return their treasures (or their body parts). Stately homes scurried to explain and offer redress for their slaving past. Families hastened to distance themselves from their slaving forebears. The broadcasting media was alive with daily debate about slave-related matters, and the streets of major cities filled with massive crowds of protesters demanding not only justice for a host of contemporary ills, but for a recognition of the historical foundations on which all this seemed to rest.

At the heart of this upsurge, one major problem stood out: how to detect where responsibility for the slave past started – and where it ended. In *all* slaving nations (i.e. most of maritime Europe and the nations which evolved from their American settlements) slavery had so permeated their history that it is hard to distinguish those who were *not* involved, in some capacity, with slavery. There were, for example, tens of thousands of poor working men who worked on board the slave ships. Similar numbers serviced those vessels in ports and cities all round the Atlantic. Similarly, armies of people earned a living in industries which filled the slave ships with essential cargoes. And what about the consumers of slave-grown produce? What role should we assign to the millions of smokers of slave-grown tobacco, or the even greater numbers of consumers of slave-cultivated sugar and coffee? The basic fact of the slave economy is that, for centuries, the *Western world at large* was inextricably entangled with slavery. Some made vast fortunes from it, but most merely enjoyed the pleasures and benefits of slave labour. At this level, it becomes impossible to disentangle slavery from the everyday social experience of millions of people across the Western world. Slavery was part of the warp and weft of Western life.

***

In the angry outbursts of 2020, it mattered little that slavery had ended in the nineteenth century. What mattered was the global insistence that the West confront its past and take steps to redress the sins of the fathers. Time and again, aspects of the history of slavery were excavated and paraded in order to rectify a number of current problems. It proved a heady, intoxicating period, rendered all the more combustible by the devastating arrival of a global pandemic. Needless to say, the BLM movement had its enemies and was met by a coalition of opposition which ranged from some who simply denied the facts or the strength of the historical arguments, through to political extremists whose own political leanings shared the intolerance and racism of the world of slavery.

For people who had spent years writing and teaching about slavery, it was both exciting and yet perplexing, not least because the public arguments, broached on an almost daily basis, so often hinged on a simple assertion: *why were we not told*? In truth, the *evidence* about slavery has never been hidden, and is available in abundance. It lies all around us. Though it is undoubtedly true that a variety of obstacles have traditionally been raised to a more open discussion about slavery, the availability of readily and easily accessible information is quite stunning. (A simple search on Google will more than satisfy anyone keen to learn about the role of slavery in Western history.) Nonetheless, it was clear enough that much of what came to light in 2020 struck many thousands of people as startlingly new. For many people, 2020 proved a revelation: that slavery was deeply rooted in Western history, had generated a great deal of material well-being (for its beneficiaries) and even more misery (for its enslaved victims). Whatever disputes arose (and continue), however contentious the politics involved, one simple fact emerged as an indisputable reality: slavery matters. It matters about the way we were, and it matters about who we are.

***

Although the BLM movement originated in the USA and was driven by anger about the long and persistent police violence towards African-Americans, it quickly took off the world over. Associated campaigns sprouted in all corners of the globe, from New Zealand to Europe. Everywhere, there were specific, local complaints about the treatment of Black people (and other minorities), but the recurring theme around the world was the problem of policing and Black people. The demonstrations and arguments opened up much wider discussions about the question of racism – and how racism came about. Again and again, the arguments returned to underlying, historical causes, and throughout, slavery loomed large as a major explanation.

It was an explanation which had greater force in the Atlantic world – in the old imperial heartlands, and in those nations in the Americas which had formerly been their slave-based colonies. In Britain, France, Spain, Portugal, Belgium and the Netherlands, the slaving past was, undeniably, a major aspect of the nation's history (and well-being). Each of those nation's was beset by a range of problems which derived directly from their own particular imperial past, and each had their own social and political response. Although all had been major players in the world of Atlantic slavery, in addition, all had become major imperial powers in the years *after* slavery – notably in Africa. All had retreated from their imperial engagements – some less willingly than others – and all had faced complex post-colonial problems at home. The most obvious and visible consequences of Europe's post-colonial experiences were the migrations of people from former colonies to the European heartlands. From the 1950s, the movement of people to Europe from the Indian subcontinent, from Africa, the Caribbean and from South East Asia created new urban communities whose identities had been shaped by very different historical pasts from the host society.

This was strikingly obvious in the world of education. Children born to immigrant parents found that traditional historical explanations did not apply – or make sense – in their own experience. The historical past looked (indeed *was*) very different from the world outlined in conventional historical accounts. There was then, a dissatisfaction with history as taught across Europe to the offspring of immigrants from former colonies. Not surprisingly, people of Caribbean and African descent wanted historical explanations that viewed the imperial past differently. Much the same was true for people of South East Asian descent. At first, the demand was for education that took account of the role played by those groups in the domestic shaping of the country they now lived in. But that quickly morphed into a much broader reappraisal of history itself, and the need to discuss national history not as a triumph of major imperial prowess, but one which addressed a harsher, bleaker story. It was *this* story that was missing from conventional accounts. The call was for a *different* kind of history: a move away from what seemed a triumphalist Western interpretation, to one which incorporated the experience of the subjects – the victims – of the imperial story. Needless to say, this created as many political as educational questions. What should be taught (and how) became matters of political as well as educational argument. As the discussion widened, people of African and Caribbean descent began to ask one simple question: how could we discuss Europe's history without looking at the story of slavery? What gave the matter greater complexity – and relevance – was that the academic discipline of history had itself shifted quite radically.

***

In the course of the recent past – roughly from the 1960s – the study of slavery shifted from being a marginal interest to a topic of mainstream academic concern. When I began my own work on slavery, it was of limited interest among British historians. Few of them had undertaken scholarly research on slavery, and it was taught only in a few, specialist locations. Inevitably, the historical literature was also sparse. Of course, the story was totally different in the USA where slavery had always been basic to the national experience. Yet even there, until quite recently, slavery was viewed, researched and taught largely as a Southern phenomenon: it was a regional concern that forced itself onto the national scene mainly via the Civil War. There were of course, exceptions to this, but the main point is clear: slavery was interesting – but largely regional. In Britain (and throughout most of western Europe) it was insignificant. Today, that is no longer true, and slavery occupies a central position in the intellectual and educational life of the West, though it also continues to attract resistance and stubborn distrust in many quarters. Hence The 1619 Project by the *New York Times* and the confused reaction to it.

The academic study of slavery has slowly evolved into a subject of growing interest throughout the educational system of different European nations. It attracts specialist attention in research centres and higher education but has also generated growing importance in European schooling systems (though not without dogged resistance in many quarters). This shift from the margins resulted from a number of factors, the first being the rapid and widespread decolonisation and the collapse of Europe's great colonial empires, especially in Africa in the 1950s and 1960s. Calls for freedom from colonial control were as old as imperialism itself, but they gained strength in the twentieth century, and gathered pace during and immediately after World War II. The ideals of that war – of freeing people from the oppressive yoke of foreign invaders – did not apply solely to Nazi Germany or imperial Japan. The USA, for example, was unwilling to pay such a heavy price in men and material, merely to help the restoration or strengthening of the British, French or Dutch empires in Africa and Asia. Demands for self-determination applied not only to France or Poland. What about Africa, India – or the Caribbean islands?

A number of prominent Allied war leaders – Churchill most significantly – were resistant to the idea of colonial independence (not least because they had been nurtured in a powerful imperial tradition and had, in some cases, fought as young men for the empire). There were many others, however, who could see, even in the midst of World War II, that the old empires were doomed. Britain's imperial status had been dealt a shattering blow by the Japanese army (which was itself an imperial army). During the war, the British began to plan to leave India when the time was ripe – if only they could secure agreement among Indian politicians. At the same time, voices for African independence – again with precedents going back many years – began to make themselves heard. Such voices were greatly strengthened by the massive contribution of the empire to the war itself: manpower, raw materials, food and distant bases – all served to sustain Allied war efforts. The empire helped to support Britain – especially before the US entered the conflict. Political leaders in those widely scattered places used the political credit earned in wartime to push for independence. Indians, Africans and West Indians had not made such enormous sacrifices merely to be returned to the pre-war status of imperial subjects. They wanted freedom from Britain. Similar stories unfolded in France (in North Africa and Indo-China) and the Netherlands (and Indonesia).

In the space of two decades, Europeans withdrew from empire returning home via complex processes of withdrawals: a mixture of violent defeat, prolonged and bloody warfare, peaceful and negotiated withdrawal – and precipitous departure. From the wreckage of their empires there emerged a proliferation of new nation states. Moreover, many of the citizens of those new nations had a legal right of entry to the countries of their former colonial masters, and many had served in those nations' militaries; many had even lived there. These were the seeds for the subsequent post-war migrations from former colonies to the imperial heartlands. And therein lay the subsequent debate about the history of relations between subject peoples and imperial nations.

The migrant generation – some of whom, in the British case, became known as the 'Windrush generation' – endured hard struggles to make their way. But leaders emerged, mainly at local and industrial levels, who argued their corner against the deeply entrenched racist problems they faced – from housing to employment. Their children, however, born and raised mainly in Europe's major cities, developed a new critique. Taught in local schools, they were confronted by a historic past that owed little if anything to their own family and personal experience. In addition, the issues of national pride and achievement which tended to be lauded and emphasised in schools were, for them, often painful matters. Tales of imperial conquest and of glorious deeds in distant colonies rang hollow to the children of parents from the Caribbean, Africa or Asia.

At much the same time, a major transformation was taking place in education in those same former colonies. National independence had been followed by a rapid extension of local schooling, often from an extremely low base, courtesy of colonial neglect. (As late as 1968, I visited a classroom in a poor rural school in Jamaica where the only pictures on the walls were of the Queen, the Duke of Edinburgh – and Admiral of the Fleet, Sir Andrew Cunningham.) There was also a rapid expansion of local institutions of higher education. Initially, they too inherited curriculums that followed the habits of their former governors. But European history looked very different when viewed from, say, Ghana or Senegal, from Bridgetown, New Delhi or Singapore. The development of a local curriculum which addressed important local issues inevitably challenged many of the accepted wisdoms of older interpretations. History itself began to look different.

The educational needs of newly independent states, though often modelled on the prototypes of their former colonial governors, clearly differed from the European versions. This was especially true in the arts and social sciences. And it was there that the challenge to existing educational interpretations took place. New voices made themselves heard from all corners of former colonial societies: voices that also caught the attention of the diasporic communities scattered in Europe (and North America). Critical influences emerged from within diasporic communities and from the independent nations that had once formed the colonies of European empires.

Through all this, attention returned, with increasing regularity, to the question of the historic past. The very nature of imperial peoples – especially those scattered by the economic tides of imperial adventure and exploitation – demanded explanation. Growing numbers of people wanted to know about *their* history. How was it that so many people of African descent were living in the Americas? What had enabled a group of relatively small nations in northern Europe to conquer and control great swathes of the globe? How had Europeans become the Lords of Human Kind? How were they able to conquer enormous regions of the globe, then promptly fill them with millions of people shipped great distances across the ocean? What had enabled the West to scoop up so many people from India and scatter them around the world: to the Caribbean, to East and South Africa and to islands in the Pacific? And what, more pressingly, had been the *benefit* of all this to those imperial heartlands? What was the connection between the astonishing material well-being of Europe (and North America) and the imperial systems they had created, by destroying native peoples, seizing their land, and tapping its potential by the labour of transplanted people? And how could we explain the contrast between Western prosperity and the poverty left in the wake of retreating empires? The questions were legion, and the answers – at least persuasive answers – were hard to come by. Until, that is, a different kind of historical research became available. And that began, again at a glacial pace, in the post-war years.

***

World War II inevitably obstructed intellectual debate but two books in particular, one published in 1938 the other in 1944, were to have a revolutionary impact on the study of slavery: C. L. R. James' *The Black Jacobins* (1938) and *Capitalism and Slavery* (1944) by Eric Williams. Both men were Trinidadians, they knew each other, and James' original work clearly influenced Williams' doctoral work which culminated in *Capitalism and Slavery*. Although those books seem unrelated, both had the effect of placing slavery in the mainstream of European history in ways that had not been attempted before. James' elevation of the Haitian slave uprising as a seminal role in *Western*, not merely slave, history, was to have a profound impact – though it took years for its importance to register fully. Similarly, Williams' analysis of the relationship between slavery and capitalism launched an utterly new appraisal and understanding of slavery. It prompted some of the most important subsequent research into the history of slavery. Of course, both books received more than their fair share of criticism. *But* the study of slavery has never been the same since their publication. Whatever their flaws, those two books serve to anchor slavery as a major determinant in the shaping of Western history.

In recent years, scholars have picked up the Williams' theme to analyse the history of North American slavery and its role in the rise of modern US capitalism.* Though a number of other books were also important, the outcome has been an astonishing cascade of scholarship about slavery. Where slavery was once marginal or ignored, it now occupies centre stage. Nor has this simply been the preserve of specialised academic work. The influence of slave scholarship has percolated (unevenly) throughout different educational systems, on both sides of the Atlantic. Though it has faced some rugged resistance and denial, the teaching of slavery has been widely diffused in ways few could have expected a mere generation ago. There are complaints that slavery continues to be marginalised and even threatened. But the importance of slavery as a major element in the making of our past – and our present – is now hard to deny.

The recognition of the importance of slavery has also been enhanced by fundamental changes in the nature of historical

* Richard Follett, Sven Beckert, Peter A. Coclanis, Barbara Hahn, *Plantation Kingdom: The American South and Its Global Commodities*, Baltimore, 2016.

study. The rapid growth of social history, roughly from the 1960s onwards (but with earlier roots in French scholarship – notably sociology and anthropology) transformed the practice of academic history. In the process, some areas of historical research and teaching which once dominated, have been elbowed aside (not always with beneficial results). As ever more historians turned to new fields of study, the passion for 'history from below', which began with a concern for plebeian life, soon turned to the lives of oppressed people the world over. In addition, scholars in recently independent countries needed to excavate their own people's past from underneath the historical rubble of old colonial interests. New historical studies emerged of the peoples of Africa, India and of the Caribbean. In the process, and among many other issues, there emerged the history of slavery. Again, it was a process of historical discovery which developed on both sides of the Atlantic and although it seemed to offer an increasingly fragmented history (with histories emerging of all the constituent parts of the post-imperial story) it was now possible to think of a much broader historical account. Slavery emerged not merely as an important aspect of the history of the West and its dealings with the wider world, but it came to be viewed as the elemental fusion which brought together people and places into a historically coherent whole.

Our understanding of slavery has also been totally transformed by it becoming a focus for a wide range of disciplines, in addition to history. Indeed, our understanding of the importance of slavery has been greatly enhanced by disciplines which have brought new techniques and new data to the reconstruction of the slave past. Linguistics, for example, analysing African languages and their survival and transformation in the Americas, has greatly changed our view of the way

Africans adapted to the Americas; and how that maintained and created new social and personal networks and how their beliefs – reflected in their language – became part of African-American life – notably in Brazil and Spanish America. Archaeologists too have turned to slavery, their forensic excavations at various American sites helping, for example, to reconstruct the material culture of the enslaved. We have learned about African origins from the examination of skeletal and dental remains: teeth filed in a particular fashion for instance, found in slave graves in Mexico City.* Such work, however, inevitably raises sensitive matters of respect for the dead and what are seen to be unwarranted violations by modern intruders. Most significantly perhaps, scientists led by geneticists, working on fragments from the Taino period, have substantially changed the estimates of the number of native peoples in the Caribbean before and after the arrival of Europeans and Africans.† Marine archaeologists, working on the wrecks of slave ships (of which there are hundreds) have qualified what we know about those vessels.

The most profound impact on the study of slavery, however (though this is shared by perhaps every aspect of life), has been the impact of computers and digital learning. The retrieval, analysis and sharing of data – in this case of historical evidence – has not only transformed our knowledge of slavery but has rendered it accessible to millions of people. Perhaps the most notable databases which illustrate this are the slave trade database, the leader and pioneer in the field, the slave legacy website, and the gathering of information about lost family members in

* Nicholas St. Fleur, *The New York Times*, 1 May 2020.

† Carl Zimmer, *The New York Times*, 21 February 2021.

the USA. The astonishing growth of evidence, the global sharing of that evidence and the swift transfer of scholarly finding into the public domain have added incalculably to the global debate about the history of slavery and about its significance today. Moreover, non-specialists can now add their own findings – local, familial, archival – to the accumulation and analysis of slave evidence.

***

In the USA, the reconstruction of the Black past lifted slavery out of its essentially regional setting. Here too, the impact of social history, as in Europe, turned historical attention to slavery. There had, of course, been a rich earlier scholarship, notably in the South, but the 1960s saw not only a major revision of Southern history – with its soothing bromides about slavery and the world of plantations – but also a concerted effort, along a broad front, to analyse the social history of slavery: slave family, communities, voices and labour. This US historical exploration also ran parallel with trends in European scholarship (and indeed was sustained by the same intellectual forces). In its turn, this new US slave scholarship had a galvanising influence, notably on British and Caribbean historical research. The outcome, again, was a massive upsurge in slave scholarship to the extent that, today, the major annual listing of scholarly publications now cites thousands of new items – books and articles – published each year. The current volume of slave scholarship is astonishing: it is also rich and varied, available in all major languages and directed at every conceivable aspect of the slave past. Quite simply, we know more about slavery than ever before – to the point that it is difficult for any single scholar to master the annual scholarly output. And yet, the cry still goes out . . . 'Why weren't we told?'

***

The major transformative force in promoting the concern with slavery, however, was not scholarly, not historical – but social and political. The interest in the history of slavery was nurtured by a rising chorus of demands which emerged from the US Civil Rights movement. The protracted campaign against segregation, and for social and political equality in the USA, but especially against the continuing and blatant discrimination of people of African descent, inevitably focused attention on historical roots – and on slavery. There had been periodic violent outbursts throughout the twentieth century: outbursts of violence against Black communities ('race riots' and lynchings) and persistent discrimination in most walks of US life. In response, throughout the same period, a number of political movements had developed, among them some of the nation's most radical – and some of the nation's most outstanding Black leaders – but all demanding Black equality – Civil Rights. Wherever the arguments flared, and whatever route the participants took towards equality, the shadow of slavery was never far behind. It was clear enough that the racism which nurtured US segregation and discrimination did not suddenly emerge in the post-slavery world, but rather that it found its social and political roots in slavery itself. Moreover, this was true of course across the Western world – not solely in the USA.

Critics, however, tended to dismiss the links to slavery. After all, slavery had ended in the mid-nineteenth century and what was its relevance to the world, say, of the mid-twentieth century

– or today? One answer would be to turn such questions on their head. Is it conceivable – even imaginable – that a slave system which had forged an exploitative relationship between Black and white, and which held Black people as *things* – as mere *chattel* – had little or no influence on the way the Western world viewed Black humanity? Racism – notably the variety that flourished in the nineteenth and twentieth centuries – clearly drew its inspiration from a variety of sources. Its deep foundations, however, lay in a widely accepted belief that Black humanity was unalterably inferior. That, after all, had been the essential philosophy which underpinned slavery for four centuries. Is it conceivable that this outlook – which inspired the West's dealings with Africa and African people for centuries – simply vanished when slavery was abolished?

***

One major consequence of World War II was its influence on the question of reparations. The punitive reparations imposed on Germany after 1918 (for their role in starting that conflict) had disastrous consequences for the origins of the next global conflict. After 1945, however, arguments about reparations embraced a much wider challenge. The development of the legal concept of 'crimes against humanity' (developed by the Cambridge Professor of Law, Hersch Lauterpacht) had profound consequences, and not only for the prosecution of leading Nazis at Nuremburg.* In the years after 1945, a variety of courts and tribunals accepted that compensation was due to the victims of Nazi crimes. The compensation paid to wartime victims – most notably Germany's

* Phillipe Sands, *East West Street*, London, 2016.

compensation paid to Israel, and to the millions of people used as slave labour throughout the conquered lands of the Third Reich – became critical precedents. They were taken up in international courts and conventions, especially when adopted through the various agencies of the United Nations. Other nations also paid compensation for a range of historical crimes: the Nazis, of course, Japan to Korea, the British to various colonies for property expropriation, and the USA paid reparations for the wartime damage inflicted on interned Japanese-American citizens. These cases, however, involved problems from the *recent* past. How far back in time could a case for reparations be pressed? The legal argument which evolved – argued most notably by the British barrister Lord Gifford – was that there was no legal obstacle against pursuing a case for damages done to *ancestors*. And that led, inexorably, to slavery – and to the question of reparations for slavery.*

By the late twentieth century, demands for reparations for slavery had become an inescapable issue in the USA, the Caribbean and some African nations (notably South Africa), all of whom argued for reparations inside the UN and its various ancillary bodies. Today (2021), demands for 'reparative justice' have established themselves as a major theme in the wider debates about racism, and in discussions about the history of slavery. At international diplomatic gatherings, inside regional political organisations – in Africa and the Americas – and within the UN

* Lord Anthony Gifford, 'Formulating the case for reparations', in *Colonialism, Slavery, Reparations and Trade: Remedying the 'Past'?*, Fernne Brennan and John Packer, eds., London, 2011. The best analysis of the history of reparations is Ana Lucia Araujo, *Reparations for Slavery and the Slave Trade: A Transnational and Comparative History*, London, 2017.

itself – calls for reparations for slavery are, now, more widespread and vociferous than ever. But how did wrongdoings from such distant historical epochs become the stuff of contemporary diplomacy, politics, and popular street demonstrations?

One important factor in the rising chorus of demands for reparations has been the recent awareness that compensation played an important role in the history of slavery. It was, however, the compensation paid to slave owners, *not* to the enslaved. It is true that promises of compensation had been dangled before freed slaves in the USA (the famous order of 1865 by General Sherman offering 40 acres and a mule to the families of freed US slaves). And France and the Netherlands compensated their slave owners for the emancipation of their slaves, but Venezuela was the only state in the Americas to compensate its slave owners. The most lavishly rewarded people at emancipation were the British owners of slaves. Historians have long known that British emancipation in the 1830s was achieved by distributing a staggering £20 million compensation to British slave owners (thought to be the largest capital sum set aside, up to that point, by the British Parliament for any project apart from warfare; today's value would be in the region of two and a half trillion pounds). British slavery was ended by the largest slave transaction of all time. A complex bureaucracy handled claims from slave owners, and British officials assessed and adjudicated those claims, allocating payment on a per capita calculation of the number of slaves involved.

The voluminous paperwork of that scheme has long been available in the British National Archives, but it took pioneering doctoral work by Nicholas Draper, and his subsequent book, followed by the creation of a website by his colleagues at

University College London, to give slave compensation its full significance – and public attention.* The work of Draper and his colleagues – all now easily available online – has had a profound impact on our understanding of the relationship between the British people and slavery. It revealed, in precise detail, that slave ownership permeated British society. Thousands of people scattered across Britain owned slaves in the Caribbean. Indeed, one half of all the slave compensation was paid to people living, not in the slave colonies, but in Britain itself. Slave ownership ranged from former planters who owned hundreds of slaves and thousands of acres in the Caribbean, through to individuals who had never stepped foot in the colonies, but who acquired one or two slaves, usually via an inheritance from a slave-owning relative. The money received by Britain's former slave owners had a remarkably diverse and widespread impact on British, and British imperial life. It was invested in a huge range of activities and properties: in commerce, industry, housing, land, educational and imperial institutions. Equally important, this information – complex and far-reaching – is now readily and freely available online. The subsequent media attention paid to this single research project inevitably led to a widespread public awareness of, and discussion about, the pervasiveness of slavery in British life. Thanks to television and social media coverage, British slavery was again front-page news.

As *public* knowledge of British slave compensation spread, it appears to have come as a surprise – a shock even – to many

* Nicholas Draper, *The Price of Emancipation: Slave-Ownership, Compensation and British Society at the End of Slavery*, Cambridge, 2010; *Legacies of British Slavery – UCL:* https://www.ucl.ac.uk/lbs

people. It also prompted one simple question – repeated time and again in print and public. If slave owners could be compensated for slave emancipation – why not their enslaved victims? Not surprisingly, demands for reparations were quickly adopted by a number of campaigns, and were demanded most volubly by the Black Lives Matter campaign. Picked up by most media outlets, the demands for reparations moved from what had been the concern of largely Black campaigns, to centre stage in public debates both in Europe and the USA. It also sparked a scrutiny of links to the slave past. In the USA and Europe, institutions of all kinds, from corporations to universities, were exposed for their links to slave-based money. There was a flurry of reports commissioned in all corners of the Atlantic world, and they revealed what historians had long known: that links to slavery were *ubiquitous*. The material well-being that flowed from slavery and the slave trade could be found hiding in plain sight throughout the Western world. It was no surprise that major international organisations, from the UN downwards, renewed their demands for compensation – reparations – for the sins of the fathers.

This rising tide of scrutiny into the slave past inevitably drew on existing slave scholarship. But in the early years of the twenty-first century, it was closely linked to a number of immediate political concerns. It was, at this point, that the killing of George Floyd brought anger and outrage to a totally new level. In the process, the all-too obvious public reminders of the slave past were scrutinised as never before. Nowhere was this more potent – more toxic – than in the USA. There, reminders of slavery were not only ubiquitous, but they were, in places, glorified – hence the drive to topple statues, remove names, break windows and boycott those institutions which exalted people and events associated with the slave South. The friends of the Confederacy hit back of course. But by 2021 the genie was out of the bottle. The campaign to expose the slave past was not about to rest until the nation had not only come to terms with slavery but had purged itself of any glorification and admiration of the slave South. Slavery was no longer the scholarly preserve of historians: it was a topic of immediate, and angry political debate.*

Comparable outbursts erupted across the Western world, and where they flared, people learned about local links to the slave past. The most obvious connections were of course the human ties: the diasporic communities of people whose ancestors had been enslaved. These were the very same people who had long demanded a different kind of history, and who had, for years, sought to rectify the imbalance in the way the past was discussed and taught. Now, hard evidence about the slave past permeated public awareness and political debate. It was indisputable that the material well-being generated by slavery not only flowed back to the West but was on display to this day. Thus it was that demands swelled for the removal of those traces of the slave past that affronted and hurt. The culture wars had finally brought the focus of political attention to the question of slavery. Who could now deny that slavery matters?

* Ana Lucia Araujo, *Reparations for Slavery and the Slave Trade*, London, 2017.

Acknowledgements

I BEGAN TO WRITE this book in September 2019 in the ideal surroundings of the Huntington Library in California, where I had the good fortune to be visiting fellow for 2019 to 2020. For that, and much else besides, I am greatly indebted to the Director of Research, Dr Steve Hindle, whose enthusiastic support for, and leadership of researchers was impeccable. Steve and Louise Hindle also made us welcome in their home on high days and holidays. Catherine Wehrey-Miller and Natalie Serrano steered us through the complexities of taking up the fellowship and were always helpful and timely in all practical issues.

I was one of a group of scholars whose congenial company hugely revitalised my work. I owe all of them a generalised thanks, but I am especially grateful to Stephen Cushman, Ed Russell and Elizabeth Dillon for a multitude of fruitful conversations. Emily Bergquist Soule proved to be a generous and invaluable guide to the history of early Spanish America. John Styles conducted a masterclass on the history of textiles and persuaded me to rethink one section of this book. Two other fellows deserve special mention, partly for their intellectual companionship but above all for their friendship. First, my neighbour, the eminent US historian Chris Clark, and one door along, Dympna Callaghan, the distinguished Shakespeare scholar and brilliant companion. Their friendship alone made the fellowship worthwhile.

I had written a rough draft of this book when the pandemic struck, forcing all of us to scatter to our respective homes. It was months before I could return to the task, back in York. What follows is, then, a book that came to fruition under the shadow of the 2020 pandemic. Its origins, however, go back much further.

This book has been shaped by work in a host of archives and libraries, beginning in 1967 when I worked on plantation papers kept in rural Jamaica. That was the start of a paperchase that was to lead me to archives and libraries on both sides of the Atlantic and even to Australia. Not all these places and collections appear in my footnotes and bibliography, but all have served to shape my thinking and my writing about the history of slavery. They also stand as widely dispersed signposts to the story of slavery itself. Like the millions of people scattered by Atlantic slavery, the paperwork which followed their story became a global phenomenon.

I owe a general debt to many (anonymous) people who, responding to my lectures on slavery, provided a public education in the difficult and often fraught history of slavery. More specifically, I owe specific debts to several colleagues and friends. To the outstanding David Blight, I am indebted for his support and friendship. For years, James Horn enabled me to work in Virginia. Steve Fenton, a friend from our time together as graduate students at McMaster University, produced a detailed and perceptive review of my first draft, and what follows has been immeasurably improved by his meticulous and thoughtful critique.

In recent years I have made extensive use of the following libraries: the Rockefeller Library at Colonial Williamsburg, the Beinecke Library at Yale, the Yale Center for British Art, the Huntington Library at San Marino and the J. B. Morrell Library of the University of York. Visits to these and other libraries were made possible by the hospitality of various friends, especially by Marlene Davis and by Tolly and Ann Taylor in Williamsburg. Over many years Selma Holo and Fred Croton have made me welcome to their home in Los Angeles. More recently, they made us part of their social and family life in and around Los Angeles. Closer to home, Rachel and Martin Pick, and my late friend, Byron Criddle, were always generous hosts in London. Once again, I am greatly indebted to my agent Charles Walker for his efforts on my behalf. In Duncan Proudfoot at Little, Brown I had an editor who was both enthusiastic and supportive. I am also hugely indebted to Una McGovern for her exemplary copy-editing of my initial text.

I would never have weathered the hazards of 2020 to 2021 without the wonderful NHS medical staff in York. Finally, and above all else, the support and care of my wife, Jenny Walvin, restored me and enabled me to complete this book – which is dedicated to her.

James Walvin, April 2021.

Guide to Further Reading

THIS GUIDE IS designed to help the general reader to follow up the major issues discussed in each chapter. Specialist readers need no help in finding the best sources and reading matter. I have selected items which are generally accessible. But for the most recent publications, readers might consult the annual scholarly bibliography, the most recent being Thomas Thurston, 'Slavery: annual bibliographical supplement (2019)', *Slavery and Abolition*, 2020, vol. 41, No. 4.

General

Ira Berlin, *Many Thousands Gone: The First Two Centuries of Slavery in North America*, Cambridge, MA, 1998.

Robin Blackburn, *The Making of New World Slavery*, London, 1997.

The Cambridge World History of Slavery, vol. 3, AD 1420–AD 1804, edited by David Eltis and Stanley L. Engerman, Cambridge, 2011.

The Cambridge World History of Slavery, vol. 4, AD 1804–AD 2016, edited by David Eltis, Stanley L. Engerman, Seymour Drescher and David Richardson, Cambridge, 2017.

P. D. Curtin, *The Rise and Fall of the Plantation Complex*, Cambridge, 1998.

Seymour Drescher, *Abolition: A History of Slavery and Antislavery*, Cambridge, 2009.
David Eltis, *The Rise of African Slavery in the Americas*, Cambridge, 2000.
Padraic X. Scanlan, *Slave Empire: How Slavery Built Modern Britain*, London, 2020.
James Walvin, *Freedom: The Overthrow of the Slave Empires*, London, 2019.

Chapter 1. The Scattering of People

T. F. Earle and K. J. O. Lowe, eds., *Black Africans in Renaissance Europe*, Cambridge, 2005.
Miranda Kaufman, *Black Tudor: The Untold Story*, London, 2017.
David Olusoga, *Black and British: A Forgotten History*, London, 2016.
Olivette Otele, *African Europeans: An Untold Story*, London, 2020.
Gustav Ungerer, *The Mediterranean Apprenticeship of British Slavery*, Madrid, 2008.

Chapter 2. Spanish Origins

J. H. Elliot, *Empires of the Atlantic World: Britain and Spain in America, 1492–1830*, New Haven, 2006.
Toby Green, *The Rise of the Trans-Atlantic Slave Trade in West Africa*, Cambridge, 2011.
B. W. Higman, *A Concise History of the Caribbean*, Cambridge, 2011.
Andres Resendez, *The Other Slavery: The Uncovered Story of Indian Enslavement in America*, New York, 2017.
Emily Burquist Soule, 'From Africa to the Ocean Sea: Atlantic Slavery in the Origins of the Spanish Empire', *Atlantic Studies*, vol. 15, No. 1, 2018, p.21.
Hugh Thomas, *The Slave Trade: The History of the Atlantic Slave Trade, 1440–1870*, London, 1997.

Chapter 3. Spain and the Other Slavery

Alex Borucki, David Eltis and David Wheat, 'Atlantic History and the Slave Trade to Spanish America', *American Historical Review*, April 2015.

J. H. Elliot, *Empires of the Atlantic World: Britain and Spain in America 1492–1830*, New Haven, 2006.

B. W. Higman, *A Concise History of the Caribbean*, Cambridge, 2011.

Kris Lane, *Potosi: The Silver City that Changed the World*, Berkeley, 2019.

Andres Resendez, *The Other Slavery: The Uncovered Story of Indian Enslavement in America,* New York, 2017.

Chapter 4. Slavery, Sugar and Power

Robin Blackburn, *The Making of New World Slavery,* London, 1997.

Vincent Brown, *Tacky's Revolt: The Story of an Atlantic Slave War,* Cambridge, MA, 2020.

Linda Colley, *Britons: Forging a Nation,* New Haven, 1997.

David Eltis and David Richardson, *Atlas of the Atlantic Slave Trade,* New Haven, 2010.

Robert Harms, *The Diligent: A Voyage Through the World of the Slave Trade,* Oxford, 2002.

Sidney Mintz, *Sweetness and Power: The Place of Sugar in Modern History,* New York, 1986.

William Pettigrew, *Freedom's Debt: The Royal African Company and the Politics of the Atlantic Slave Trade, 1672–1752*, Chapel Hill, 2013

James Walvin, *Sugar: The World Corrupted, from Slavery to Obesity,* London, 2017.

Chapter 5. Bound for Africa: Cargoes

William Dalrymple, *The Anarchy: The Relentless Rise of the East India Company*, 2020.

Jordan Goodman, *Tobacco in History: The Cultures of Dependence,* London, 1993.

Toby Green, *A Fistful of Shells: West Africa from the Rise of the Slave Trade to the Age of Revolution,* London, 2019.

Joseph E. Inikori, *Africans and the Industrial Revolution in England,* Cambridge, 2002.

Linda A. Newson and Susie A. Minchin. *From Capture to Sale: The Portuguese Slave Trade to Spanish South America in the Early Seventeenth Century*, Leiden, 2007.

Marcus Rediker, *The Slave Ship*, London, 2007.

Chapter 6. The Dead

Manuel Barcia, *The Yellow Demon of Fever: Fighting Disease in the Nineteenth Century Transatlantic Slave Trade,* New Haven, 2020.

Marcus Rediker, *The Slave Ship: A Human Story,* New York, 2007.

Stephanie Smallwood, *Saltwater Slavery: A Middle Passage from Africa to American Diaspora*, Cambridge, MA, 2007.

E. R. Taylor, *If We Must Die: Shipboard Insurrections in the Era of the Atlantic Slave Trade*, Baton Rouge, 2006.

James Walvin, *The Zong: A Massacre, the Law and the End of Slavery,* London, 2011.

Chapter 7. Upheavals

Robert H. Gudmestad, *A Troublesome Commerce: The Transformation of the Interstate Slave Trade*, Baton Rouge, 2003.

Walter Johnson, ed., *The Chattel Principle: Internal Slave Trades in the Americas,* New Haven, 2004.

Gregory E. O'Malley, *Final Passages: The Intercolonial Slave Trade of British America, 1619–1807*, Chapel Hill, 2014.

Michael Tadman, *Speculators and Slaves: Masters, Traders, and Slaves in the Old South*, Madison, 1996.

Chapter 8. Brazil's Internal Slave Trade

Robert Edgar Conrad, *Children of God's Fire: A Documentary History of Black Slavery in Brazil*, University Park, Pennsylvania, 1994.

Walter Johnson, ed., *The Chattel Principle: Internal Slave Trades in the Americas,* New Haven, 2004.

João José Reis, 'Slavery in Nineteenth Century Brazil', in *The Cambridge World History of Slavery*, vol. 4, AD 1804–AD 2016, edited by David Eltis, Stanley L. Engerman, Seymour Drescher and David Richardson, Cambridge, 2017.

Christopher Schmidt-Nowara, *Slavery, Freedom and Abolition in Latin America and the Atlantic World*, Albuquerque, 2007.

Chapter 9. The Domestic US Slave Trade

Ira Berlin and Ronald Hoffman, eds., *Slavery and Freedom in the Age of the American Revolution*, Charlottesville, 1983.

Walter Johnson, ed., *The Chattel Principle: Internal Slave Trades in the Americas*, New Haven, 2004.

Jennifer L. Morgan, *Laboring Women: Reproduction and Gender in New World Slavery*, Philadelphia, 2011.

Michael Tadman, *Speculators and Slaves: Masters, Traders, and Slaves in the Old South*, Madison, 1996.

Heather Andrea Williams, *Help Me to Find My People: The African American Search for Family Lost in Slavery*, Chapel Hill, 2012.

Chapter 10. A World of Paper: Accounting for Slavery

B. W. Higman, *Plantation Jamaica, 1750–1850: Capital and Control in a Colonial Economy*, Kingston, 2005.

Kenneth Morgan, *Slavery, Atlantic Trade and the British Economy, 1660–1800*, Cambridge, 2000.

Justin Roberts, *Slavery and the Enlightenment in the British Atlantic, 1750–1807*, Cambridge, 2013.

Caitlin Rosenthal, *Accounting for Slavery: Masters and Management*, Cambridge, MA, 2018.

Chapter 11. Managing Slavery

Trevor Burnard, *Mastery, Tyranny and Desire: Thomas Thistlewood and his Slaves in the Anglo-Jamaican World*, Chapel Hill, 2004.

B. W. Higman, *Jamaica Surveyed, Plantation Maps and Plans of the Eighteenth and Nineteenth Centuries*, Kingston, 1988.

Peter Kolchin, *American Slavery, 1619–1877*, New York, 1993.

S. D. Smith, *Slavery, Family and Gentry Capitalism in the British Atlantic: The World of the Lascelles, 1648–1834*, Cambridge, 2006.

E. P. Thompson, 'Time, Work-Discipline and Industrial Capitalism', *Past and Present*, No. 38, 1967.

Chapter 12. Brute Force

Trevor Burnard, *Mastery, Tyranny and Desire: Thomas Thistlewood and his Slaves in the Anglo-Jamaican World*, Chapel Hill, 2004.

The Cambridge World History of Slavery, vol. 4, AD 1804–AD 2016, edited by David Eltis, Stanley L. Engerman, Seymour Drescher and David Richardson, Cambridge, 2017.

David Brion Davis, *Inhuman Bondage: The Rise and Fall of Slavery in the New World*, New York, 2008.

Andrew Delbanco, *The War Before the War*, New York, 2019.

Richard Follett, *The Sugar Masters: Planters and Slaves in Louisiana's Cane World, 1820–1860*, Baton Rouge, 2007.

Christer Petley, *White Fury: A Jamaican Slaveholder and the Age of Revolution*, Oxford, 2018.

Padraic X. Scanlan, *Slave Empire: How Slavery Built Modern Britain*, London, 2020.

Chapter 13. Working

Sven Beckert, *Empire of Cotton: A New History of Global Capitalism*, London, 2014.

Stephen Innes, ed., *Work and Labor in Early America*, Chapel Hill, 1988.

Walter Johnson, *River of Dark Dreams: Slavery and Empire in the Cotton Kingdom*, Cambridge, MA, 2013.
David Beck Ryden, *West Indian Slavery and British Abolition, 1783–1807*, Cambridge, 2009.

Chapter 14. Finding a Voice

G. J. Barker-Benfield, *Phillis Wheatley Chooses Freedom*, New York, 2018.
Vincent Carretta, ed., *Unchained Voices: An Anthology of Black Authors in the English-Speaking World of the Eighteenth Century*, Lexington, Kentucky, 1996.
Vincent Carretta, *Equiano, the African: Biography of a Self-Made Man*, Athens, Georgia, 2005.
Henry Louis Gates Jnr and Nellie Y. McKay, eds., *The Norton Anthology of African American Literature*, New York, 1997.

Chapter 15. Demanding Freedom

David Brion Davis, *Slavery and Human Progress*, New York, 1984.
Manisha Sinha, *The Slave's Cause: A History of Abolition*, New Haven, 2016.
James Walvin, *Freedom: The Overthrow of the Slave Empires*, London, 2019.

Chapter 16. Beauty and the Beast

Jennifer Anderson, *Mahogany: The Costs of Luxury in Early America*, Cambridge, MA, 2012.
Simon Gikandi, *Slavery and the Culture of Taste*, Princeton, 2011.
Teresa A. Meade, *A Brief History of Brazil*, New York, 2004.
Matthew Parker, *The Sugar Barons: Family, Corruption, Empire and War*, London, 2011.
James Walvin, *Slavery in Small Things*, Oxford, 2017.

Chapter 17. A World Transformed

Carolyn Merchant, *The Columbia Guide to American Environmental History*, New York, 2002.
Geoffrey Parker, *Global Crisis, War, Climate Change and Catastrophe in the 17th Century*, New Haven, 2017.
David Watts, *The West Indies: Patterns of Development, Culture and Environmental Change Since 1492*, Cambridge, 1987.

Chapter 18. Slavery Matters

Ana Lucia Aranjo, *Reparations for Slavery and the Slave Trade: A Transnational and Comparative History*, London, 2017.
Nicholas Draper, *The Price of Emancipation: Slave-Ownership, Compensation and British Society at the End of Slavery*, Cambridge, 2010.

Websites

There is a proliferating number of websites devoted to the history of slavery and the Atlantic slave trade. The following are among the more useful.

Slave voyages: https://www.slavevoyages.org
Legacies of British Slavery (UCL): https://www.ucl.ac.uk/lbs
Last seen: Finding family after slavery: https://informationwanted.org
Runaway slaves in Britain: https://www.runaways.gla.ac.uk
Freedom on the move: https//www.freedomonthemove.org

Index